MONEY, FINANCE AND EMPIRE

MONEY, FINANCE AND EMPIRE

1790–1960

Edited by

A.N. PORTER AND R.F. HOLLAND

LONDON AND NEW YORK

First published in 1985

Published 2006 by Routledge
2 Park Square, Milton Park, Abingdon, Oxon OX14 4RN
605 Third Avenue, New York, NY 10017

Routledge is an imprint of the Taylor & Francis Group, an informa business

First issued in paperback 2013

British Library Cataloguing in Publication Data
A CIP catalogue record for this book
is available from the British Library

Money, Finance and Empire

ISBN 13: 978-0-415-38214-4 (hardback)
ISBN 13: 978-0-415-84899-2 (paperback)

Routledge Library Editions: Economic History

THE JOURNAL OF IMPERIAL AND COMMONWEALTH HISTORY

Volume XIII   May 1985   Number 3

Published by
FRANK CASS & CO. LTD.
GAINSBOROUGH HOUSE, GAINSBOROUGH ROAD
LONDON E11 1RS

Money, Finance and Empire
1790 to 1960

Scholars have recently begun to pay renewed attention to the economics of empire, focusing in particular on the requirements of metropolitan Britain's economy and on the activities of imperial businesses. Within this broad field, financial questions, not least the subject of investment overseas or the 'export of capital', have long had a prominent place and have also been affected by the development of new approaches. The consensus of opinion as to the volume and direction of Britain's overseas investments is being vigorously challenged. Technological advances have encouraged on a greatly enlarged scale the compilation and analysis of information about British shareholding and investment abroad. The gradual easing of restrictions on many business records has opened up facilities for the study especially of imperial and colonial banking. Work on the financial policies of central government is revealing much of interest to students of twentieth-century colonial rule and decolonization. This collection of essays brings together a selection of the latest research on these and other related themes, and for comparative purposes includes a summary of some recent French work.

A. N. Porter
R. F. Holland

J. A. Hobson, Financial Capitalism and Imperialism in Late Victorian and Edwardian England*

by

Peter Cain

I

As is well known, J.A. Hobson's theory of economic imperialism was formed by the fusion of two important ideas: first, there was the attack on the conventional view that full employment of resources was the norm in capitalist society; secondly, there was the claim that the driving force behind British imperialism in the late nineteenth and early twentieth centuries was financial need, centred on the export of surplus capital. When these two ideas were brought together for the first time in 1898, the argument ran thus:[1] starting from the evidence of a great inequality in the distribution of property in Britain, Hobson went on to infer a maldistribution of income which resulted in under-consumption by the many, over-saving by the few, and a chronic tendency to domestic over-investment. To avoid the consequences of this, those who controlled surplus savings tried to find outlets for them overseas. The search for profitable opportunities abroad and the need to protect them when found was the primary motive force behind imperialism.

Generally speaking, the received view of Hobson's theory is still that it was an attempt to explain British, and other European, interest in the Scramble for Africa in the late nineteenth century; and, since it can easily be shown that the bulk of overseas capital flows went elsewhere rather than to Africa, it has become commonplace among imperial historians to believe that Hobson was simply wrong and that the Scramble – which is usually taken to be the most important example of imperialist activity between 1880 and 1914 – must have been undertaken for other, probably non-economic reasons.[2] Recently, however, a number of specialist critics of Hobson's work have claimed that Hobson was fully aware that British foreign investment largely bypassed Africa. According to this view, Hobson's interest was in trying to find out how it was that the marginal amounts of British capital involved in Africa could lead on to massive extensions of British political authority there; and, more specifically, how it was that a small group of financiers in Britain, whom Hobson identified as the key agents of imperialism, could wield such a large influence over governments and public opinion. As Dr Allett has recently expressed it, Hobson's famous book *Imperialism. A Study* (1902) was an attempt to identify a small group of people – a 'military-industrial' complex –

organized and directed by those who owned surplus financial wealth and who, he believed, had managed to hijack British foreign policy for their own purpose.[3] One interesting extension of this line of reasoning is Trevor Lloyd's claim that, as regards tropical Africa, Hobson's thesis may be relevant to the establishment of, for example, the chartered companies. If they absorbed only a tiny fraction of Britain's overseas capital they were nevertheless vital to the establishment of British control in West and East Africa and Rhodesia.[4]

Despite the radicalism of this attack on the conventional views of Hobson, most of the revisionists still believe that Hobson was principally concerned to explain the African partition. But the most recent contributor to the debate, Dr Norman Etherington, is convinced that Hobson was not interested in the Scramble, except in the case of South Africa, and that in so far as he referred to it in *Imperialism* he did not use it to illustrate his theory of surplus capital. Etherington argues that when Hobson mentioned acquisitions of territory in tropical Africa he explained them in terms of the influence of colonial bureaucrats, military men, armaments dealers, local traders on the make and other pressures, all of which would have been familiar to Cobden writing 50 years earlier. He goes on to claim that Hobson's concern, like that of many of his contemporaries in Europe and America, was with what he saw as the very recent emergence of a problem of surplus capital, related to the rise of big business and the spread of industrialization, and leading to pressure on governments to adopt a much more aggressive and protectionist policy in the search for overseas outlets. Hobson thought that the South African crisis, beginning with the Jameson Raid of 1895 and the subsequent struggle for control of the Boer Republics, marked the beginnings of this new imperialism of finance;[5] and he was far less interested in peripheral matters such as African partition than in the apparently imminent absorption and development of China by the major industrial powers, and the transformation in the economic and political structure of the whole world which he felt must follow.[6]

Hobson was aware that far more British capital went to newly settled countries than to backward parts of the world such as tropical Africa.[7] Nonetheless, despite Etherington's argument to the contrary, he appears to have assumed that surplus capital, even in marginal amounts, did influence partition. In his 1898 article, Hobson looked back on a colonial policy where we had spent 'all our energy and superfluous cash in wrangling with other nations for markets in Africa and Asia', and it was in this context that he explained how British investors benefited by providing loans which then led to the export of goods.[8] In *Imperialism*, directly after a discussion on the extension of Britain's empire over the previous 20 years, Hobson went on to say that

> the policy by which the investing classes used the influence of the State for private business purposes is most richly illustrated in the history of her wars and annexations.[9]

Lloyd's argument is thus warranted by the evidence of Hobson's own writings[10] although it cannot be extended to the South African case where British investment was very substantial. On the other hand, neither Lloyd nor any other of Hobson's recent critics, including Etherington, have considered the significance of Hobson's belief that the occupation of Egypt in 1882 was a prime example of financial imperialism. Though he refers to Egypt only in passing in *Imperialism*,[11] in later writings Hobson gave the occupation of Egypt the same sort of status which he accorded to the South African war[12] and once explicitly argued that

> in our own recent history, the efficient causation of the Boer War and the Occupation of Egypt are perhaps the most instructive instances of the utilization of national forces by private business.[13]

At the time of occupation Egypt could hardly be described as marginal to British investors.[14] Etherington's emphasis on Hobson's interest in South Africa and China rather than tropical Africa is very salutary but, as the example of Egypt demonstrates, the events which Hobson was describing and analysing in 1902 were not seen by him as entirely novel but as the culmination of trends going well back into the nineteenth century when viewed in a British perspective.

It was the Egyptian crisis in the 1880s which led to the first clear formulation of the radical view that imperialism was the result of the overweening power of British financial interests;[15] and it is hardly surprising that Hobson, as heir to this radical tradition, should have found theories of imperialism based on financial conspiracy appealing. Conspiratorial explanations of imperialism are pervasive in Hobson's work, as most of his critics have stressed, and his interest in them was reinforced by the war in South Africa which directed his attention to a small group of financial capitalists, predominantly Jewish and European rather than British, whose main interest was in 'the promotion and financial manipulation of companies' or 'dealing in shares in these companies' and who directed the savings of a mass of smaller investors.[16] This is the basis for the arguments in *Imperialism* where Hobson speaks of 'the financier, the general dealer in investments' who controls 'great businesses – banking, bill discounting, loan floating, company promoting'. These groups form the 'central ganglion of international capitalism'. The conspiratorial strain in the argument in clearly revealed in his claim that the mass of investment funds are 'controlled by men of single and peculiar race' who are 'in a unique position to manipulate the policy of nations'. And it is encapsulated in the rhetorical flourish:

> Does one seriously suppose that a great war could be undertaken by any European state, or a great state loan subscribed if the house of Rothschild and its connexions set its face against it?[17]

It needs to be emphasized that this rather naive reference to financial power is not the sum of Hobson's theory. What he argues for, often with great subtlety, is that finance plays the central part in the orchestration of a vast array of interests which make for imperialism. This is what lies behind Hobson's famous statements that, while other interests provide the 'motor power' of imperialism, 'finance is rather the governor of the imperial engine' and 'finance manipulates the patriotic forces which politicians, soldiers, philanthropists and traders generate'.[18] Hobson first offers a list of those who benefit from imperialism – the military, professional administrators, missionaries, armaments manufacturers, certain traders and industrialists with overseas interests.[19] Besides these there are those who profit from the fact that imperialism helps to maintain the *status quo* by providing economic stability and taking the public mind away from the thought of internal reform.[20] They rally instinctively to the cause. Much of the support, as Hobson stresses, comes from groups with a genuine desire to spread civilization, Christianity, liberty and good government. But their support could, like that emanating from the jingoistic and the super-patriotic, be harnessed and manipulated, largely via the press which Hobson was convinced was controlled by those with a clear interest in encouraging overseas adventure. All these forces were important ingredients in encouraging imperialism but 'final determination rests with the financial power' because 'the financial interest has those qualities of concentration and clear sighted calculation which are needed to set Imperialism to work'.[21]

Although conspiracy plays a very prominent rôle in Hobson's work in 1902 and in later writings[22] it does not provide his only answer to questions about the springs of imperial activity. The conspiratorial element is missing from the original 1898 article which offers an explanation of imperialism entirely in terms of structural maladjustments in the British economy. With this in mind it has been suggested that Hobson was interested in working out a theory of financial capitalism which would provide a systematic link between the structure of the British economy and imperial policy, and that his experiences as a journalist in South Africa were not helpful to the cause. The second Boer War inevitably focused his attention upon the machinations of a few financiers such as Rhodes and tempted him to overlay his emerging analysis of British financial capitalism with a conspiracy theory which was not easy to reconcile with it.[23]

Dr Peter Clarke has attacked this view vigorously. It is evident that he believes it saddles Hobson with ideas which more properly belong to Hilferding and Lenin. In his view

> Hobson's theory does not depend upon a concept of finance capital in this sense; all it needs is an understanding of financial capitalism as the investment function of the economy .... Large surplus revenues in the pockets of one class provided the funds for speculative investments abroad. In the hands of financiers like Rhodes the funds become the governors of imperialism. Under-consumption thus permitted imperialism. In South Africa, Hobson thought he

could demonstrate their malign influence at work. In this respect his is a conspiracy theory.[24]

According to Clarke, here following Porter's line of argument,[25] the distinction between the creation of surplus capital in general and financiers interested in imperialism in particular was essential for Hobson. Only by making this distinction was he able to demonstrate that imperialism was unnecessary and in the interests only of the few.

Clarke's criticism was met at the time by denying that it was necessary to the logic of Hobson's position that he should identify a small group of financial conspirators, and by claiming that

> it is surely wrong to assume that, because Hobson offers a structural explanation of imperialism, this involves him in asserting that imperialism was inevitable. What it actually means is that attempts to eliminate imperialism could be brought about only by fundamental economic, social and political reforms – reforms which Hobson evidently considered possible.[26]

Hobson's work on the burgeoning Western penetration of China at the end of *Imperialism*, cast in terms of an economic imperialism which would lead to the transformation of whole civilizations in both the industrial and underdeveloped worlds, is also an example of Hobson's ability to develop a consistent argument without recourse to an approach which Clarke holds to be essential.[27] Subsequently Etherington has also pointed out that a theory of imperialism can be constructed from Hobson's famous book without the need to invoke conspirators at all and that the conspiratorial element serves only to obscure the thread of that argument.[28]

Etherington, however, also argues that the major influence on Hobson as a systematic thinker was not his South African experience or any episodes in Britain's imperial past, but his reading of long forgotten American theorists of surplus capital, particularly the socialist Gaylord Wilshire.[29] He claims that Hobson's 'Free Trade and Foreign Policy' article of 1898 only 'vaguely' suggests his developed theory of 1902 since it 'ignores trusts and cartels and mentions foreign investment only as an incidental by-product of the struggle for foreign markets'.[30] What galvanised Hobson was reading an article written in 1901 by Wilshire, himself instructed by a close study of the American financial press, which provided him, according to Etherington, with the crucial link between big business, cartelization, the generation of surplus capital and aggressive imperialism. This theme then appeared in Hobson's work for the first time in a *Contemporary Review* article of 1902 entitled 'The Economic Taproot of Imperialism' which used Wilshire's work extensively. The article later appeared, with only minor alterations, as Chapter VI of *Imperialism*, where it is the centrepiece of the economic analysis in Part I of the book. This argument not only stresses Hobson's indebtedness to sources in the United States but also places him alongside Hilferding,

Schumpeter and Lenin as one who linked together the development of monopoly capitalism and imperialism.

This interpretation of Hobson's development is open to serious criticism.[31] Hobson's under-consumptionism is a product of the 1890s and it was a perfectly natural extension of this theory to say in 'Free Trade and Foreign Policy' that foreign investment was a form taken by oversaving. The drift of the argument in 1898 was not that foreign investment was a 'by-product' of the search for foreign markets, but that the need for markets was a consequence of overseas investments made necessary by surplus capital accumulated in a corrupt capitalist system. Again, Hobson's failure to mention trustification in the 1898 article was not a failure of perception: it reflects the fact that he was talking about Britain where big business, on the American or German scale – the conjuncture of cartelized industry and a few big banks – did not exist. In 1902 he was engaged on a task different from that of 1898, a global analysis of economic imperialism and Wilshire's work was valuable to him as an insight into the American case. Britain's economy is hardly mentioned in the chapter: but although Hobson avoids actually saying that the economic structures of Britain and the United States were similar, the way the chapter is written does leave that unfortunate impression. There are other instances, too, where in trying to analyse imperialism as a worldwide phenomenon, he succeeds in evoking a picture of financial capitalism, based on big business, which was inapplicable to Britain. This may also be another example of the way in which the South African case coloured Hobson's vision, since something akin to monopoly capitalism existed in the mining industry there, even though South African industry was untypical of the structures found in Britain and its empire.[32]

Hobson's references to the Egyptian crisis which had occurred before big business had become typical anywhere are examples of his belief that financial imperialism was not necessarily the direct result of modern business capitalism. What I should like to argue is that, despite the confusion introduced by his occasional attempts to subsume many different industrial structures under one 'finance capitalist' theory, Hobson did occasionally offer suggestions about a British form of financial capitalism and the imperialism to which this gave rise. These insights were never put together in any convenient form and are scattered in writings over many years, but they are well worth examining.[33]

II

As early as 1891, long before he became really interested in imperialism, Hobson was forecasting the possible de-industrialization of Britain and other advanced industrial nations. Western capitalists would soon find it in their interests to harness the skill and cheap labour of Asia which would then become the industrial centre of the world, destroying, on the one hand, industrial society and democracy in the advanced countries but ministering, on the other, to the development of a European rentier capitalist class. Since labour was much less responsive than capital to new economic opportunities, Britain would develop as a semi-feudal service economy, so that

> another century may see England the retreat for the old age of small aristocracy of millionaires who will have made their money where labour is cheapest and return to spend it where life is pleasantest. No productive work will be possible in England, but such labour as is required for personal service will be procurable at a cheap rate, owing to the reluctance of labour to keep pace with the migration of capital. Thus, without any wild stretch of the imagination, we may look forward to a revived feudalism in which the industrial barons will rule, with that absolute sway which wealth must exercise over poverty, the more sentimental or less adventurous menials who shall cling to their old country, in preference to following into India, China or Heaven Knows Where, the march of emancipated capital.[34]

What is chiefly remarkable in this early piece is the explicit antagonism which Hobson saw between the aims of industry and its workforce and those of the controllers of financial wealth. At the time Hobson was even willing to suggest protection and the prohibition of capital export as possible remedies.[35] There is also present the germ of the idea that, as a result of these wholesale changes in its economic structure, Britain might be moving towards a civilization in which financial wealth and traditional aristocratic culture were merged.

This line of thinking re-appears in *Imperialism*, though with some significant refinements, during Hobson's discussion of the impending development of China by European and American capital. Again he warned of

> the gigantic peril of a Western parasitism, a group of advanced industrial nations, whose upper classes draw vast tribute from Asia and Africa, with which they supported great tame masses of retainers, no longer engaged in the staple industries of agriculture and manufacture, but kept in the performance of personal or minor industrial services under the control of a new financial aristocracy. Let those who would scout such a theory as undeserving of consideration, examine the economic and social condition of districts in Southern England today which are already reduced to this condition, and reflect upon the vast extension of such a system which might be rendered feasible by the subjection of China to the economic control of similar groups of financiers, investors, and political and business officials .... [36]

Earlier he had claimed that China's economic prospects seemed

> so enormous and so expansible as to raise the possibility of raising whole white populations of the West to the position of 'independent

gentlemen' living, as do the small white settlements in India or
South Africa, upon the manual toil of these laborious inferiors.[37]

Imperialism in the past had already created a whole class of these
businessmen and officials who now populated the south of England.

> Could the incomes expended in the Home Counties and other large
> districts of Southern Britain be traced to their sources, it would be
> found that they were in large measure wrung from the enforced toil
> of vast multitudes of black, brown or yellow natives .... [38]

If the predictions about the industrialization of the East and its consequences have proved misleading up until the present, the description of
the south of England as an economy dominated by a rentier capitalism
which lived off imperialism is one worth taking further.

Hobson's persistence with this particular argument is also apparent in
an article written in 1910 in which he tried to analyse the relationship
between voting behaviour and economic structure as exemplified in the
recent general election. In the largely Liberal and Labour stronghold of
the north of England – 'Producer's England' – industry set the tone of life.
In the Tory south – 'Consumer's England' – the leisured class played the
dominant role in confirming attitudes and expectations.[39] This leisured
class, and the service economy of which it was the centre, was clearly
intertwined with rentier capitalism.

> The Home Counties, the numerous seaside and other residential
> towns, the cathedral and University towns, and in general terms,
> the South are full of well-to-do and leisured families, whose
> incomes, dissociated from any present exertion of their recipients,
> are derived from industries conducted in the North or in some
> over-sea country. A very large share, probably the major part, of
> the income spent by these well-to-do residential classes in the
> South, is drawn from investments of this nature. The expenditure of
> these incomes calls into existence and maintains large classes of
> professional men, producers and purveyors of luxuries, tradesmen,
> servants and retainers, who are more or less conscious of their
> dependence upon the goodwill and patronage of persons 'living on
> their means'. This class of 'ostentatious leisure' and 'conspicuous
> waste' is subordinated in the North to earnest industry: in the South
> it directs a large proportion of the occupations, sets the social tone,
> imposes valuations and opinions. This England is primarily
> regarded by the dominant class as a place of residence and play-
> ground in which the socially reputable sports and functions (among
> which church-going, the theatre, art, and certain mild forms of
> literary culture are included) may be conducted with dignity and
> comfort. Most persons living in the South certainly have to work for
> a living, but much of their work is closely and even consciously
> directed by the will and the demands of the moneyed class .... [40]

Hobson was, therefore, in no doubt that the principal owners of surplus capital in Britain were the rentier class of the south of England who were linked with the traditional landed class and the gentlemanly professions. It was this class which, via the Conservative Party, Hobson believed to be promoting overseas expansions.[41] Surplus capital, and the interest in imperialism which it fostered, was not confined to the south, of course, since anyone in possession of some inherited privilege or monopoly, in industry or otherwise, might gain from imperialism. Hobson's attitude to the possible benefits to industry from imperialism was complex. He obviously did not believe that the new territories Britain had acquired in Africa in the later part of the nineteenth century had brought many new markets for industry and trade as a whole.[42] On the other hand, he could see the direct interest in imperialism that the armament manufacturers had, and he believed that 'with them stood the great manufacturers for export trade' since

> The public debts which ripen in our colonies, or in foreign countries that come under our protectorate or influence, are largely loaned in the shape of rails, engines, guns and other materials of civilization sent out by British firms. The making of railways, canals and other public works, the establishment of factories, the development of mines, the improvement of agriculture in new countries, stimulated a definite interest in important manufacturing industries which feeds a firm imperialist faith in their owners.[43]

If some export industries had a vested interest in imperialism at that time, Hobson was still convinced that in the long term the interests of industry and English rentier capitalism were incompatible. Ever since 1891, Hobson had stood by a theory in which industrial capitalism and financial capitalism were separated, regionally and structurally, and in which, unless present trends were reversed, the antagonisms between them would lead to the destruction of Britain's industrial core and the distinctive life style of both manufacturer and artisan. Imperialism was vital to the Home Counties but fatal to Lancashire and Yorkshire. Radical social reform would, however, lead to a different outcome. The abolition of surplus would end imperialism and rentier capitalism which were two parts of the same phenomenon, for social reform would remove inequalities in income distribution and the foreign investments and extended foreign trade which went with it. But the reform process would also create, via the redistribution of income and widening equality of opportunity, a greatly extended home market. If the large export manufacturers went down with rentier capitalism, then the remaining, small-scale enterprise of the industrial provinces would be reborn.[44] Industry in general, if not the 'shareholders of a Lancashire mill',[45] the rentier element, had a vested interest in the ending of an overseas policy directed by the finance capital whose chief home was the south of England.

Hobson did put an exaggerated emphasis on the financier as controller of imperial activity; but he also tried to show, at various times, how the power and influence exercised by financiers was the result of the existence of a service economy with a powerful rentier component. This strand in Hobson's thinking was, in many ways, a further development of a set of ideas handed down from the English radical tradition;[46] and Hobson's diagnosis also found an echo in the writings of some of the famous contemporary theorists of imperialism who recognised a few of the features peculiar to British capitalism. Rudolf Hilferding, for example, although apparently unaware of Hobson's work, was well aware of the need to point up the differences between Britain's economic evolution and that of the United States and Germany. The latter were at the forefront of technological advance and their institutional structure had developed accordingly. They were the begetters of finance or monopoly capitalism in its truest sense; that is, their economies were dominated by interlocking, oligopolistic industrial and banking corporations. Britain, by contrast, was still the country of the small industrial firm with an efficient traditional method of raising capital for industry which largely bypassed the banking structure and the City of London. Because Britain's growth rate was slow (a consequence of the slow pace of change in manufacturing industry), it had an abundance of savings for overseas ventures which helped to maintain its position as an international trader and as an imperial power and to put off the inevitable day when it would be superseded as the world's foremost international economic power. The nature of Britain's overseas presence was, therefore, intimately related by Hilferding to its relative industrial decline and the special prominence in Britain of an abundance of rentier capital.[47]

Lenin took the same sort of analysis rather further. Unlike Hilferding, who was clearly open to the view that European and American industrial capitalism had many possibilities for dynamic development, Lenin had read *Imperialism*, and was strongly influenced both by Hobson's underconsumptionist theories and by the argument, based mainly on Hobson's interpretation of the British case, that Western industrialism was in decline. Lenin believed that monopoly capitalism stifled competition, inhibited technological change and inevitably forced capital to find outlets abroad. He noted that the growth of overseas investment had already led in the advanced capitalist countries to the

> extraordinary growth of a stratum of rentiers, i.e. people who live off 'clipping coupons', who take no part in any enterprise whatever, whose profession is idleness .... The export of capital ... sets the seal of parasitism on the whole country that lives by exploiting the labour of several overseas countries and colonies.[48]

Lenin supported his views on the inevitable decay of Western industrialism with a long quotation from Hobson on the future of China to which he added the approving comment: 'The author is quite right. If the forces of imperialism had not been counteracted they would lead precisely to what he has described'. Lenin undoubtedly believed that Britain had gone further down this path than most other industrial nations and had degenerated into a rich man's sporting and tourist centre. He even tried to prove, using very dubious statistics, that the number of persons employed in British manufacturing industry was falling.[49] Warren has recently attacked Lenin for his belief in the decay and parasitism of industrial capitalism, a decay which, looked at from the standpoint of the whole Western economic system, has clearly not been in evidence up to the present time.[50] But, as we shall see, it has some relevance to the British case which Lenin, relying on material provided by Hobson, used to generalize about the future of Europe and the United States as well.

Although chiefly concerned with American and German imperialism, Thorstein Veblen did occasionally notice some of Britain's distinguishing features. In one of his later works, he described the ruling elite in Britain as 'gentlemen investors'[51] whose support 'comes to them in the way of income from investments at home or in foreign parts or from equivalent sources of accumulated wealth or official emolument'.[52] Much of it came from investment in 'commercially backward countries abroad' or from the 'creation of colonial offices', and, Veblen went on,

> the advancement of commercial and other business enterprise beyond the national frontiers ... is so bound up with national ideals, under any gentlemanly government, that any invasion or erosion of the rights of investors in foreign parts, or of any business involved in dealing with foreign parts, immediately involves not only the national interest but the national honour as well.[53]

Veblen's attempt here to merge a financial and a 'feudal' motive for imperialism does tend to confirm the view that the notion of Britain as dominated by a rentier capitalism which had emerged from a gentlemanly, landed culture was, in varying degrees, fairly pervasive among theorists of imperialism.

III

What evidence is there to support this Hobsonian diagnosis of Britain's economic structure and its implications? Recent research does suggest that, although industrialization obviously made great changes in British life, its importance as a creator of wealth may have been over-rated. Landed wealth did not cease to be predominant until well after mid-century; and it was superseded thereafter not just by industrially-derived wealth but also by that earned in commerce and finance. Studies of large fortunes and of the fragmentary income tax returns which have survived also suggests that the number with middle-class (i.e. tax-paying) incomes and above rose faster in the service sector, centred on London and its environs, than elsewhere.[54]

The data on which some of these conclusions are based are fragmentary and some of the inferences drawn from them may be exaggerated; but the new work has established the importance of service, as well as landed and industrial, income and wealth in the nineteenth century. The rising importance of services in the latter half of the century is also emphasised in Lee's work on the changing occupational structure of Britain. Lee has shown that, as early as the 1840s, the service sector was growing faster, in terms of employment, than the others. Service industries developed most rapidly in the south-east of England – London and the Home Counties – and created a demand for a wide range of consumer goods industries which took root in the region at this time. By 1914, the south-east probably already had the highest average per capita income of any British region. At its centre was London, not only the seat of government but the home of the City.[55] It was no coincidence that the growth in the importance of the south-east and the corresponding relative decline of the heavy industrial provinces, should take place at the same time as Britain's position in the world economy was becoming more dependent upon invisible trade and services.

London's banking and financial institutions and the service economy of the south-east were certainly not dependent upon the emergence of a continental-style finance capitalism, any welding together of the joint-stock banks, or the money market and Stock Exchange, with manufacturing industry. Banks with a primary interest in long-term industrial investment did appear in the 1860s and 1870s but their lives were brief.[56] As Kennedy puts it,

> a point had been reached when the entire system had to be re-organised to withstand the greater risk of steadily enlarging industrial requirements or the system had to withdraw from long-term industrial involvement. The system withdrew.[57]

Kennedy interprets the withdrawal as a failure on the part of the major British financial institutions to adapt to new conditions, but is it correct to speak generally of 'steadily enlarging industrial requirements'? The financial needs of provincial industry had been met over the years, not by London but by a complex of methods including provincial stock exchanges and a host of private, local contracts so widespread and so informal that contemporaries found it hard even to guess at the level of investment in domestic industry before 1914.[58] No great changes, either geographical or technical, occurred among traditional industries after 1870 sufficient to disturb these financial relationships seriously or to render them obsolete. Indeed the ease and cheapness with which capital could be raised for established industrial concerns was probably one of the chief reasons for the maintenance of a high degree of competition in British industry and the persistence of the small firm.[59] The joint-stock banks were given no great incentive to offer anything other than their time-honoured services to industry – principally overdraft facilities and short-term credit[60] – and the City remained similarly remote from industrial investment. The merchant banks and the Stock Exchange were clearly best fitted to handling the large loans floated by national and municipal governments or large corporations rather than the small sums required by the typical British firm; and they usually came into contact with home industry only on those relatively rare occasions when a substantial loan was floated as part of a company's conversion from partnership to joint-stock status.[61] The City was geared to the transfer into rentier home and foreign stocks of the vast and swelling savings of the rapidly developing service sector after 1850, and this flow of savings abroad helped to increase Britain's export earnings and to maintain the profitability of the great staples, thus strengthening barriers to institutional and technological change. As a result, it was not only savings generated in the south of England which went into government and railway stocks abroad: provincial funds which for one reason or another had no ready channel into local industrial investment also began to be routed through the London market.

Although the timing, the intensity and the geographical spread of foreign investment were heavily influenced by the pull of foreign demands for capital, there was also a general tendency for the weight of British savings to push down interest rates and drive investors to look for more profitable opportunities abroad as the economy, after 1870, adjusted to a permanently lower rate of growth.[62] Investors, including banks and insurance companies were all beset by difficulties which more or less forced them to look abroad to maintain income, especially in the 20 years before the First World War.

Agricultural mortgages were a losing game after the decline in arable agriculture under the stress of foreign competition; Gladstonian finance limited severely the amount of new government paper on the market and helped push down the rate of interest on government stock;[63] and new issues by those traditional favourites, domestic railway companies, were not only in short supply after 1870 but the profitability of the companies was also under severe pressure.[64] The obvious response, in the absence of any growing industrial demand at home, was to find similar profitable alternatives abroad. The shift towards investment in overseas government stocks and railway companies is very marked, for example, in the records of the leading insurance companies whose foreign holdings often increased from under 10 per cent of a firm's total assets in 1870 to 40 per cent or more by 1913.[65] The joint-stock banks, too, became considerably more adventurous in their investment policies, especially in the 1890s when the rate of return on traditionally secure investment at home began to fall, and by 1913 'bonds of all kind came to be grist to the banker's mills'.[66]

The extension of foreign investment often involved an increase in risk-taking as the emphasis shifted over time from government-backed loans to investment in foreign, private railway companies in an ever-widening range of countries.[67] But it would be wrong to overemphasise the risks associated with most of the new foreign investments of Britain which were often carefully tailored to suit the needs of the growing body of rentier investors looking for safe, fixed interest securities,[68] whose income might have fallen to alarmingly low levels without a marked movement into foreign stocks after 1870.[69] John Vincent once pointed out the extent to which, in mid-nineteenth-century England, wealth-holding was concentrated, 'not in the hands of entrepreneurs and captains of industry, but in the hands of widows, spinsters, rich farmers, clergymen, academics, squires and rentiers claiming gentility'.[70] There was a shift of wealth-holding away from rural sources towards the industrial and service sectors after 1860 but, as Rubenstein's figures indicate and as the fore-going analysis suggests, there was still an enormous supply of wealth cut off from direct industrial employment. Safe overseas investment was one way of employing it usefully in 1900, just as home railways and the national debt had been fifty years before. What is of particular interest here is the extent to which wealth initially made in manufacturing also began to move in the direction of overseas too in the late nineteenth century.[71] Considering that there was a direct link between the export of capital and industrial goods, it is clear that there was a growth of a more important common economic interest between the industrial provinces and the rentier class in this period than was evident before.

The bias in London financial markets was natural in the circumstances and reflected, in a very real sense, the configuration of the economy, but this does not necessarily mean, of course, that heavy overseas investment was without long-run deleterious effects. The very ease with which capital could be sent abroad and the virtual certainty of the returns probably had an influence in tempering entrepreneurial drive.[72] More specifically, the most recent statistical work indicates that a high level of foreign invest-ment was inimical to domestic growth. Before 1870, home and foreign investment fluctuated more or less in unison and in conformity with the familiar seven-to-nine year trade cycle. After 1870, the paths of home and foreign investment diverged, each settling into a pattern of swings ap-proximately 20 years in length which were inverse to each other.[73] When foreign investment was high, exports, and the export-producing regions,[74] boomed but both domestic output as a whole and,it appears, manufactur-ing output grew more slowly. The growth of manufacturing output (and investment) was far more dependent upon changes in domestic activity than on changes in exports.[75] The sharp fall in foreign demand in the downswing after 1873 affected manufacturing growth only slightly: low levels of foreign investment and the miserably slow growth of exports in the 1890s were accompanied by a considerable revival in industrial growth; and the dichotomy between buoyant foreign investments and poor manufacturing performance is clearly marked in the statistics for the 1880s and after 1900. (See Appendix.) If foreign investment had directly beneficial effects on exports it appears to have acted as a barrier to change elsewhere in the industrial economy. Had foreign investment been, for whatever reason, considerably less, then the staple exports would have been forced to adapt themselves more quickly and interest in domestic opportunities would have been wider, with inevitable effects on the struc-ture of capital markets and financial institutions. Foreign investments, like formal empire, may have proved a considerable force in favour of conservatism in industry.[76]

Professor Platt has recently argued that the extent of British overseas investment in the nineteenth century has been exaggerated and that the conventional figure of around £4000 million for all British assets abroad in 1913 may have to be written down by about one third.[77] Some contemporaries also suggested that London was 'acting as a funnel through which other people's money was poured rather than as a stirrup pump spraying domestically generated savings over the rest of the world.'[78] Against this there is the evidence that an increasingly large percentage of the money raised in London after 1870 was for British-owned companies rather than the portfolio investment – investment in foreign owned companies – upon which Platt concentrates, and this may have meant a greater British involvement in overseas lending than he allows for.[79] What is clear is that, even if Platt's downward revision of Britain's overseas assets is realistic, the growth of these assets in the late nineteenth century would still have been one of the most remarkable features of British economic life at the time, and Platt's work also helps to concentrate attention, not just on London as a channel for capital export but as an international service centre. As the focus of a vast network of international banks, holder of the reserve assets of an array of colonial banks, strongbox for spare international funds and provider of vast quantities of short-term credits, Britain was the world's great middleman, distributor and financier. London institutions managed a vast flow of short-term funds and the fact that, when temporarily unemployed, these funds could be placed in easily saleable stocks offering a steady rate of return was a way of retaining them. As Michie put the matter recently:

> In international terms, Britain was becoming a service economy utilizing a portfolio of liquid and safe securities in order to attract temporarily funds from abroad, as a basis on which to transact a profitable business in the finance of world trade.[80]

The growth of the London-based service sector represented, among other things, a further phase in the long relationship between financial wealth and land. Finance had long been a high-status occupation,[81] and its links with the peerage and the gentry were made yet stronger in this period by intermarriage, shared public school and Oxbridge education and subsequent employment in the civil service and government (as the interaction between Earls Grey and Wantage and their City friends and relations amply illustrates).[82] In this phase, the balance of power tipped heavily in favour of finance since arable agriculture suffered so badly from foreign competition after 1870. The shifting balance is perhaps most graphically illustrated in the case of the Devonshires who moved their assets out of agriculture and industry to such effect that, by the 1920s, the family were dependent for two-thirds of their income on investments overseas.[83]

As early as the 1880s, T.H.S. Escott, an editor of the influential

Fortnightly Review, was arguing for a convergence of landed with commercial and financial wealth, claiming that, 'There is in fact but one
standard of "social position", in England and it is that which is formed by
the blending of the plutocratic and the aristocratic elements'.[84] It is
certainly true that if the social tone in Britain was set by 'Society', high
finance was an integral part of this while industry figured within it hardly
at all.[85] The fusion of these two main elements – aristocratic values and
financial acumen – helped to forge a key component in a complex,
gentlemanly culture which was the dominant force in Britain then and, in
subtly modified forms, later.[86] The links between City 'interests' and the
socially and politically influential were already strong in 1870 and they
grew much closer thereafter.[87] It is hardly surprising, given those strong
social and ideological bonds, that when governments wanted economic
advice they went instinctively to the City rather than to Manchester or
Birmingham.[88] The chief source of advice was, of course, the Bank of
England, whose directors came from the merchant banking fraternity and
the acceptance houses in the money market rather than from the much
larger, but indelibly provincial, joint-stock banks.[89]

The ability of what Nairn has recently labelled 'patrician' culture[90] to
maintain itself was greatly helped by a correspondence at crucial points
between the interests of the service sector and some parts of the heavy
industrial core. A significant section of the wealthy in the provinces were,
like their southern cousins, Anglican in religion and, especially after
1880, Tory in politics.[91] And, whereas finance had a high enough status to
allow successful families to continue in that line for generations, industrialists often betrayed a strong sense of the inferiority of their own
position by the rapidity with which they abandoned industry for the
gentlemanly life.[92] More important, perhaps, was the fact that many
industrialists shared a common economic interest with the City. Many
great manufacturing industries, including cotton textiles and shipbuilding, had no need of a German-type finance capitalism and their interest
was served both by free trade and foreign investment especially since the
latter often led to an increase in demand for their goods abroad.[93] They
also shared in the orthodox view that government expenditure should be
severely limited both to keep down taxation and to maintain the external
value of the currency. This free trade cosmopolitanism did not suit either
the iron trades of the Midlands or, to a lesser extent, the wool trades,
which were worried by foreign competition and demanded protection.
Nor did it necessarily meet all the needs of the new industries, vital to
Britain's future industrial growth. But the parallellism between the
interest of the City and a large phalanx of industry was sufficient to ensure
that the dominant ideology was subject to no overwhelming threat before
1914.

IV

It remains only to investigate briefly whether or not this Hobson-inspired
distinction between a south-east dominated by a professional and gentle-

manly service class and with a peculiarly British form of finance capitalism, and provincial industrial capitalism has anything to offer in interpreting the nature of British expansion overseas and imperialism after 1880.

Hobson was aware of the possibilities of an informal Empire[94] and much of his discussion of future European policy in China is cast in terms of influence rather than direct control. But he completely ignored the imperialist implications of the fact that so much British capital went to the newly settled world, especially Latin America and the white colonies. It was in the newly settled, emergent-capitalist states that a London-based banking system was dominant and where a dependence upon British loan capital produced conditions altogether more profitable to the metropole than anything which might result from pushing back the frontier among the un-Westernized; and it was in these area' that the link between British capital exports, British trade services and the export of staple commodities was at its strongest.[95] As Charles Jones has recently argued, it was precisely because of the success of this kind of development in settler societies that Hobsonian imperialism in many 'backward' areas proved unnecessary. At the same time, this development had within it an imperialist strain. The rise of foreign investment in Argentina, for example, took the British from the position of influential traders on the coast to controllers of the banking system and owners of crucial public utilities with considerable market power; British investors became the prime determinants of the patterns of Argentine development, and, in so doing, explicitly attacked 'the right of the State to determine the pattern of development of the national economy by control of supply and direction of investments and determination of the exchange rate'.[96]

This ushered in a new phase in the relationship between Britain and Argentina within which the need for economic orthodoxy, as defined in London, and the influence of British 'cultural imperialism'[97] did battle with a growing resentment of British economic power and consequent chauvinist reaction. The existence of informal empire within a network of worldwide commitments based on free trade and foreign investment were more solid and enduring features of British overseas strategy than Hobson was willing to allow.

Even if one argues, as some historians do, that the British presence in newly settled countries cannot be described as imperialism,[98] it is still obvious that this extension of the arm of British financial capitalism was far more significant in economic terms than was the Scramble for tropical Africa where, if anywhere, industrial-provincial lobbies made their biggest impact upon imperial policy.[99] But if, on the Gold Coast and in Uganda, the British were 'scraping the bottom of the barrel',[100] the occupation of Egypt and the Transvaal, where the British financial and industrial presence was considerable, presents more complex and interesting issues. An approach to these crises based on the kind of Hobsonian analysis described would have to work on the following lines: irrespective of the strategic or political importance of Suez and the Cape, one can still only understand the reasons for occupation and war by recognising that the stability and security for which Britain was looking could only be achieved, in the eyes of the official class who took the decisions, when local elites were seen to be both able and willing to play the economic game by London rules. In other words, in explaining the working-out of these crises, it is important to avoid the bogus distinction so often made in the literature between 'political' or 'strategic' motives for activity and 'economic' ones. The distinction was not made, and could not have been made, by the men who took the decisions. If historians are to find more satisfying explanations of British imperialism in Egypt and South Africa (and many other places where British control was extended) then an economic content must be put into concepts such as 'collaboration' and the 'official mind'.[101] There is a strong tendency, for example, to see the latter as a kind of objective umpire in disputes whereas, in fact, the decision-makers were largely recruited from the public school-educated sons of the professional classes of southern England,[102] and shared a number of economic assumptions which could influence policy. These included: a strong emphasis on the benefits of an unhindered market system and a policy of free trade; an adherence to Gladstonian attitudes on public finance and taxation; a lack of knowledge of, and distrust of. industrialism and industrial capital which contrasted remarkably with their general tolerance of the activities of the City of London. It was these men and these ideas which dominated British policy in India, spread to the newly acquired African empire, and had a significant impact upon crisis politics in Egypt and South Africa.[103]

Britain forged elaborate economic links with Egypt and South Africa which involved not only London finance but numerous industrial interests, thus forming the basis for that loose alliance of City and provincial interests which Hobson had drawn attention to. The security of this complex capitalist structure was seen as a prerequisite for the safeguarding of national interests; without it no other objective, either economic or non-economic, could be safely realized. Neither Arabi in 1882 nor Kruger in the late 1890s appeared to be willing or able to offer the necessary guarantees, and this is one reason why they had to be either removed or rendered harmless. It is therefore reasonable to argue that the Egyptian occupation was undertaken by Gladstone not on behalf of aggrieved bondholders but in order to ensure a stable economy, run on British monetary and financial principles, which would safeguard Britain's political and economic interests in the Middle East and the Mediterranean and in which, as a matter of course, foreign creditors would be paid in full and on time. Similarly, the Boer regime in the Transvaal had to be controlled or defeated not just because the mineowners found their profits injured by local policies but because Boer intransigence seemed to impede the development of a capitalism which was the surest means not only of bringing peace and prosperity to South Africa but of promoting both Britain's economic and strategic needs in the area.[104]

A clear view of some of the differences between London-based financial capitalism and industrial capitalism may also help to illuminate some of the issues involved in the Tariff Reform campaign so strongly associated with Joseph Chamberlain. Chamberlain was one of Hobson's villains, the man at the forefront of the new imperialism. In giving Chamberlain's political philosophy such centrality within the framework of his ideas in *Imperialism*, Hobson misrepresented their importance. He assumed that the programme of protection for British industry – tariff walls around the empire and state-directed development of newly acquired colonies – was in the interests of all the groups he had identified as the owners of surplus capital. In part this was because he recognised that a protectionist policy provided a general source of revenue to support a steadily growing militaristic policy abroad and rising public debts without the need to resort to increases in the income tax which hurt those who owned the surplus.[105] More important than that, though, was Hobson's perception of a symbiotic relationship between imperialist force and protectionist finance: imperialism extended markets abroad, protection consolidated them and kept them free of competition.

> Imperialism represents a more or less conscious and organized effort of a nation to expand its old political boundaries and to take in by annexations other outside countries where its citizens have acquired strong industrial interests. Protection represents the converse tendency, an effort to prevent industrial interests from wandering outside the political limits of the nation, to keep capital and labour employed within the political arena, confining extra-national relations to commerce within the narrower limits of that term.[106]

This analysis did not come to grips with the deep split between the financial interests and their industrial allies who favoured free trade, and those like Chamberlain and the Tariff Reformers who saw it as disastrous for Britain's economic growth prospects and position as a great power. Chamberlain represented the uncompetitive area of British industry which objected both to free trade and what was seen as the diversion of British capital from domestic use to the direct or indirect support of foreign rivals. It was those fearful of de-industrialization and the loss of great power status, rather than the City or the cotton and shipbuilding industries, who were strong for protection and the economic unification of the empire and most impressed with the need to develop the backward parts of it with state funds if necessary.[107] After 1898, Hobson failed to appreciate that protectionism was a sectional industrial interest and one which repeated much of his own critique of the dominant economic ideology. Protectionists, too, forecast the de-industrialization of Britain and looked forward, gloomily, to the time when

> while London and a few other great towns will become ever larger agglomerations of labouring populations, the rest of England will remain an agreeable place of residence for *rentiers* big and little, and

will flourish on the 'tourist industry' and – though with some new features – the history of Holland will have been repeated.[108]

It is true that the Unionist party with which City opinion was in sympathy, when faced with Lloyd George's income tax socialism in 1909, opted for protection as a means of defending their order;[109] and even cotton capitalists were beginning to wonder, just before the war, whether Free Trade would have to be sacrificed in order to avoid economic radicalism.[110] But this was a political expedient in a crisis which involved no real commitment to the defence of domestic manufacturing industry or any concessions of importance to Chamberlain's dream of a protected British empire less dependent economically upon the outside world.[111] The defeat of the Tariff Reform movement at this time was also a defeat for a strategy which would have put domestic industry, rather than overseas economic interests, at the forefront of policy.[112] Hobson practically wrote a manifesto for protectionism in 1891 with this aim in mind.[113] His inability, later, to recognise the affinities between his own diagnosis of Britain's crises and that of the protectionists arose from his distaste, developed in the late 1890s, for the imperialism of the movement. He stood for social reform, a revived domestic market, a movement away from dependence on foreign trade and a Cobdenite foreign policy. The protectionists stood for social reform in the context of prosperity and strength given by a united, industrially strong, defence-minded empire. One of the enduring ironies of Hobson's position was that the City was much closer to his views than he seemed to have realized. City men, too, were worried by heavy military spending and by alarm of war because these were likely to upset the cosmopolitan world economy and the position of sterling on which their prosperity and power depended.[114]

V

Hobson did develop a picture of a finance capitalist Britain. His division between a rentier south of England and industrial provinces has some meaning even though he never explicitly said why the south was the dominant partner in the relationship; he underestimated the dynamism of the south-east with its growing industrial base, and probably overestimated the extent to which the upper and middle classes relied on overseas property income.[115] But he did recognize the common interests at that time of overseas finance and some parts of British industry, an interest which included imperialism. Hobson failed to make full use of his theory in explaining policy abroad. More important than this, though, is the fact that he provided a conceptual analysis which modern historians can use, in attempting to understand both the dynamics of the British economy in the late nineteenth and twentieth centuries and its expansion overseas, which is more subtle and penetrating than those which have generally been employed in the past.

University of Birmingham

APPENDIX

RATES OF GROWTH OF GROSS DOMESTIC PRODUCTION AND MANUFACTURING
EXPORTS AND CHANGES IN FOREIGN INVESTMENT, 1873-1913 (ANNUAL
PERCENTAGE GROWTH RATES)

	1 GDP	2 Manufacturing Output	3 Exports (Current Values)	4 Overseas Investment* (£million)
1873-82	1.9	2.3	-0.7	+ 2.4
1882-89	2.2	1.9	0.4	+31.9
1889-99	2.2	2.3	0.7	- 8.0
1899-1907	1.2	1.6	6.1	+12.9
1907-13	1.6	1.0	3.6	+80.8

*Figures in col. 4 indicate increases and decreases in the average level of foreign investment in each period compared with the previous period. For example, the average level of foreign investment in 1865-73 was £46.1 million and in 1873-82 £48.5 million and was therefore £2.4 million higher on average in the latter period.

Sources: Cols. 1 and 2: C.H. Feinstein, R.C.O. Matthews and J.C. Odling-Smee, 'The Timing of the Climacteric and its Sectoral Incidence in the United Kingdom, 1873-1913' in C.P. Kindleberger and G. di Tella (eds.) *Economics in the Long View. Essays in Honour of W.W. Rostow* (1982), Vol. II, Pt. I, pp.175, 178.

Col. 3: Derived from data in B.R. Mitchell and P. Deane, *Abstract of British Historical Statistics* (Cambridge, 1962).

Col. 4: Calls on British Portfolio Investments as compiled by M. Simon, 'The Pattern of New British Portfolio Foreign Investment, 1865-1914' in J.H. Adler (ed.), *Capital Movements and Economic Development* (1967), and reprinted in A.R. Hall (ed.), *The Export of Capital from Britain 1870-1914* (1968).

NOTES

*This article is a part of a much wider study, undertaken with Professor A.G. Hopkins, on the economic background to imperialism. Work on it, and the project as a whole, has been greatly helped by a SSRC Personal Research Grant during 1983. I should like to thank Professor Hopkins for his great help over the years in getting me to think out my views on economic imperialism. The editors' comments on the original draft have also had a salutary effect. Versions of this paper were also read at Portsmouth Polytechnic and Wolverhampton Polytechnic, in Oxford at the Commonwealth History Seminar, and at Worcester College of Higher Education, and I should like to thank the audiences there for their stimulating criticisms.

1. J.A. Hobson, 'Free Trade and Foreign Policy', *Contemporary Review* LXXIV (1898). The importance of this article was first recognised by B. Porter, *Critics of Empire: British Radical Attitudes to Colonialism in Africa, 1895-1914* (London, 1968).
2. Two prominent examples of the use of this kind of reasoning are D.K. Fieldhouse, *Economics and Empire 1830-1914* (London, 1974) Ch. III and W. Baumgart, *Imperialism. The Idea and Reality of British and French Colonial Expansion, 1880-1914* (Oxford, 1982), Ch. IV. I took a similar line in my original article on Hobson: P.J. Cain, 'J.A.Hobson, Cobdenism and the Radical Theory of Economic Imperialism, 1898-1914', *Economic History Review* 2nd Ser. 31 (1978), 568.
3. J. Allett, *New Liberalism. The Political Economy of J.A. Hobson* (Toronto, 1981), pp.149-53. An approach to Hobson also sympathetic to this view is P.F. Clarke's

Liberals and Social Democrats (Cambridge, 1978), pp.90–99.

4. T. Lloyd, 'Africa and Hobson's Imperialism', *Past and Present* 55 (1972).

5. N. Etherington, 'Theories of Imperialism in Southern Africa Revisited', *African Affairs* 81 (July 1982). 389.

6. The preceding paragraph is based on the *African Affairs* article cited above and N. Etherington, *Theories of Imperialism. War, Conquest and Capital* (London, 1984), esp. Chs. 3 and 4.

7. J.A. Hobson, 'Capitalism and Imperialism in South Africa', *Contemporary Review* 77 (1900), 2.

8. 'Free Trade and Foreign Policy,' 177.

9. J.A. Hobson, *Imperialism. A Study* (London, 1968 ed.), p.54.

10. Whether the argument is historically accurate is a different question. See p.99 *infra* and fn.17.

11. Hobson, *Imperialism*, pp.54, 108, 199.

12. See for example, the discussion in his book *Democracy After the War* (1919 ed.), pp.89–90.

13. J.A. Hobson, *Free Thought in the Social Sciences* (London, 1925), p.192, fn. 1.

14. On the growth and extent of the Egyptian debt, see R. Owen, *The Middle East and the World Economy* (London, 1981). p.122–8.

15. See, for example, H. Richard, *Mr Chamberlain's Defence of the War* (London, 1882).

16. 'Capitalism and Imperialism in South Africa', *Contemp. Rev.* 77 (1900), 3–5.

17. Hobson, *Imperialism*, pp.56–7.

18. Ibid., 59.

19. Ibid., 46f.

20. This theme is elaborated upon in ibid., Pt. II, Chs. I and III. It also appears in many other works such as the *Psychology of Jingoism* (London, 1901).

21. Hobson, *Imperialism*, p.59. For another statement on the same theme see ibid., p.212. See also Allett, *New Liberalism*, p.163.

22. For example, in Hobson, *Democracy After the War*, esp. pp.84–101.

23. Cain, 'J.A. Hobson, Cobdenism and the Radical Theory of Economic Imperialism', 568.

24. P.F. Clarke, 'Hobson, Free Trade and Imperialism', *Economic History Review*, 2nd Ser. 34 (1981), 310–11.

25. B. Porter, *Critics of Empire*, pp.216–19.

26. P.J. Cain, 'Hobson's Developing Theory of Imperialism', *Economic History Review*, 2nd Ser. 34 (1981), 315.

27. For Hobson's discussion of the future of China and its relations with Europe, the United States and Japan see *Imperialism*, pp.304–318; P.J. Cain, 'International Trade and Economic Development in the Work of J.A. Hobson before 1914', *History of Political Economy* 11 (1979), 412–19; and Etherington, *Theories of Imperialism*, pp.76–80.

28. Etherington, *Theories of Imperialism*, p.70.

29. Ibid., Ch. 1 and pp.40–4. See also N. Etherington, 'The Capitalist Theory of Capitalist Imperialism,' *History of Political Economy* 15 (1983).

30. Etherington, *Theories of Imperialism*, p.45.

31. For a criticism of Etherington's argument as it stood in his 1983 *History of Political Economy* article, see P.J. Cain, 'Hobson, Wilshire and the Capitalist Theory of Capitalist Imperialism', *History of Political Economy* (forthcoming).

32. Cain, 'J.A. Hobson, Cobdenism and the Radical Theory of Economic Imperialism', 569. For the South African influence on Hobson's views on finance capitalism see *The Evolution of Modern Capitalism* (London, 1906 and subsequent eds.), Ch. X, sec. XI.

33. My interest in this question was spurred on by a reading of Tom Nairn's *Break Up of Britain* (London, 1st ed. 1977), Ch. I. Nairn has recently extended this interesting analysis, based on Hobson's work, in the second edition of his book (1981: pp.385–87) which appeared while the present work was in progress.

34. 'Can England Keep her Trade?' *National Review* 18 (1891), 11.

35. Ibid., 10.

36. Hobson, *Imperialism*, pp.384–5; cf. p.314.
37. Ibid., p.313.
38. Ibid., p.151.
39. J.A. Hobson, 'The General Election: A Sociological Interpretation', *Sociological Review* 3 (1910), 112–13.
40. Ibid., 113. See also his article 'The Two Englands' in his *A Modern Outlook* (London, 1910), pp.302–10.
41. It was the party 'which still retains the title Conservative', which was the home of 'Imperialism, Militarism, Protection, Oligarchy'. 'The General Election', 114.
42. Hobson, *Imperialism*, Pt. I, Ch. II.
43. Ibid., p.49; cf. pp.107, 142.
44. For Hobson's arguments about the relationship between social reform, the decline of foreign trade and the rise of the home market see my articles, 'J.A. Hobson, Cobdenism and the Radical Theory of Economic Imperialism', 571–73, and 'International Trade and Economic Development in the work of J.A. Hobson before 1914', 415–20. His thinking about foreign trade after 1906 contained a more optimistic assessment of the gains to be made by the population as a whole. It is not strictly compatible with his earlier thought and contradicted his theory of imperialism to some degree. See my 'J.A. Hobson, Cobdenism and the Radical Theory of Economic Imperialism', and the controversy between myself and Clarke cited above.
45. H.N. Brailsford, *The War of Steel and Gold. A Study of the Armed Peace*, (Shannon, 1971 ed.), p.80.
46. For a brief discussion of this see my 'Hobson, Wilshire and the Capitalist Theory of Capitalism Imperialism'.
47. R. Hilferding, *Finance Capital. A Study of the Latest Phase of Capitalist Development* (London, 1981), pp.305–7, 323–5, 332, 334–5.
48. V.I. Lenin, 'Imperialism. The Highest Stage of Capitalism' in *Collected Works*, Vol. 22 (Moscow, 1964), p.277.
49. Ibid., pp.289–92.
50. B. Warren, *Imperialism: Pioneer of Capitalism* (London, 1980), esp. Ch. III.
51. T. Veblen, *An Inquiry into the Nature of Peace and the Terms of its Perpetuation* (New York, 1919), p.249.
52. Ibid., p.288.
53. Ibid., p.290.
54. W.D. Rubinstein, *Men of Property. The Very Wealthy in Britain since the Industrial Revolution* (London, 1981), esp. pp.56–73: also the same author's 'The Victorian Middle Classes: Wealth, Occupation and Geography', *Economic History Review*, 2nd Ser. 20 (1977), and also his 'Wealth, Elites and the Class Structure of Modern Britain', *Past and Present* 76 (1977), esp. 99–112.
55. C.H. Lee, 'Regional Growth and Structural Change in Victorian Britain', *Economic History Review*, 2nd Ser. 34 (1981).
56. P.L. Cottrell, 'The Financial Sector and Economic Growth: England in the Nineteenth Century', *Revue Internationale d'Histoire de la Banque* 4 (1971).
57. W.P. Kennedy, 'Institutional Response to Economic Growth: Capital Markets in Britain to 1914', in L. Hannah (ed.), *Management Strategy and Business Development. An Historical and Comparative Study* (London, 1976), p.160.
58. J.M. Keynes, 'Great Britain's Foreign Investments', *New Quarterly* (1910), reprinted in *Collected Works of John Maynard Keynes* XV (Cambridge 1971), p.58.
59. L. Davis, 'The Capital Market and Industrial Concentration: The U.S. and the U.K., a Comparative Study', *Economic History Review* 19 (1966), 255–72.
60. P.L. Cottrell, *Industrial Finance 1830–1914. The Finance and Organization of English Manufacturing Industry* (London, 1980), pp.210–44.
61. Keynes, 'Great Britain's Foreign Investments', 58: A.R. Hall, *The London Capital Market and Australia 1870–1914* (Canberra, 1963), esp. Ch. I: R.C. Michie, *Money, Mania and Markets. Investment, Company Formation and the Stock Exchange in Nineteenth Century Scotland* (Edinburgh, 1981), esp. Pt. V: M. Edelstein, *Overseas Investment in the Age of High Imperialism. The United Kingdom 1850–1914* (London,

1982), Ch. III.

62. Edelstein, *Overseas Investment, passim.* There is a convenient summary of his findings on pp.288–311.

63. Thus allowing the conversion of Consols in the late 1880s. C.K. Harley, 'Goschen's Conversion of the National Debt and the Yield on Consols', *Economic History Review,* 2nd Ser. 29 (1976.)

64. For reasons for this see P.J. Cain, 'Private Investment or Public Utility? Output, Pricing and Investment on English and Welsh Railways 1870–1914', *Journal of Transport History,* 3rd Ser. (1980).

65. B. Supple, *The Royal Exchange Assurance* (Cambridge, 1970), pp.330–48; B.L. Anderson, 'Institutional Investment before the First World War. The Union Marine Insurance Company, 1897–1915' in S. Marriner (ed.), *Business and Businessmen, Studies in Business, Economic and Accounting History'* (Liverpool, 1978); J.H. Treble, The Pattern of Investment of the Standard Life Assurance Company 1875–1914', *Business History* 22 (1980), 170–88. See also Hall, *The London Capital Market,* pp.47–55.

66. C.A.E. Goodhart, *The Business of Banking, 1891–1914* (London, 1972), pp.127–41. The flurry of interest in overseas investment after 1909 may have some connection with the fears of swingeing increases in taxation by the Liberal Chancellor of the Exchequer, Lloyd George. See H. Withers, *Stocks and Shares,* (London, 2nd ed. 1917), pp.295–9.

67. R.C. Michie, 'Options, Concessions, Syndicates and the Provision of Venture Capital, 1880–1913', *Business History* 23 (1981), 149–50.

68. On the rentier character of British overseas investment after 1870 see Hall, *The London Capital Market,* p.45: W.P Kennedy, 'Foreign Investment, Trade and Growth in the United Kingdom, 1870–1913', *Explorations in Economic History* 11 (1974), pp.425–39: D.R. Adler, *British Investment in American Railways 1834–98* (Charlottesville, 1970), pp.197–98.

69. Supple, *Royal Exchange Assurance,* p.335.

70. J. Vincent, *Pollbooks. How Victorians Voted* (Cambridge, 1967), p.41.

71. The holding of fixed interest overseas stocks became a feature of wealth holders in general in the latter part of the century. Rubinstein, *Men of Property,* pp.187f. For the shift of capital out of industry into overseas investment in one particular area, Scotland, which was in many ways the most advanced industrial region of Britain after 1870, see T. Dickson (ed.), *Scottish Capitalism. Class State and Nation From before the Union to the Present* (London, 1980), esp. pp.248–55.

72. R.C.O. Matthews, C.H. Feinstein and J.C. Odling-Smee, *British Economic Growth, 1856–73* (Oxford, 1983), p.355.

73. The best explanation of this emergence of the 20–year cycle is given by H.J. Habakkuk, 'Fluctuations in House-building in Britain and the United States in the Nineteenth Century', *Journal of Economic History* 22, (1962), reprinted in A.R. Hall, *The Export of Capital from Britain, 1870–1914* (London, 1968). There is a vast literature on this subject to which the best introduction is P.L. Cottrell, *British Overseas Investment in the Nineteenth Century* (London, 1975), pp.35f.

74. There is a detailed examination of the relationship between long swings in investment and exports in A.G. Ford, 'The Transfer of British Foreign Lending 1870–1913', *Economic History Review* 2nd ser., 11 (1958–59) and in the same author's 'Overseas Lending and Internal Fluctuations, 1870–1914', *Yorkshire Bulletin of Economic and Social Research* 17 (1965). On the alternation in the level of activity between export regions and other parts of the economy see J. Parry Lewis, *Building Cycles and Britain's Growth* (New York, 1965), esp. Chs. 5–7.

75. Matthews, Feinstein and Odling-Smee, *Britain's Economic Growth,* Table 9:10, and p.282.

76. Ibid., pp.254–6. It has been argued, with considerable force, that one consequence of the bias of the London market towards safe home and overseas stocks was a neglect of opportunities in the new industries. See esp. Kennedy, 'Institutional Responses to Economic Growth', *passim.*

77. D.C.M. Platt, 'British Portfolio Investment Before 1870: Some Doubts', *Economic History Review* 2nd ser., 3 (1980), 15–16.
78. B.R. Tomlinson, 'The Contraction of England: National Decline and Loss of Empire', *Journal of Imperial and Commonwealth History*, 11 (1982), 63–4.
79. P. Svedberg, 'The Portfolio-Direct Composition of Private Foreign Investment in 1914 Revisited', *Economic Journal* 88 (1978).
80. R.C. Michie, 'Options, Concessions, Syndicates,' 160.
81. M. Weiner, *English Culture and the Decline of the Industrial Spirit 1850–1980* (Cambridge, 1981), p.128.
82. R.C. Michie, 'The Social Web of Investment in the Nineteenth Century', *Revue Internationale d'Histoire de la Banque* 18 (1979), esp. 164–68.
83. D. Cannadine, 'Landowner as Millionaire: The Finances of the Duke of Devonshire, c. 1800–c. 1926, *Agricultural History Review* 25 (1977), 77–91.
84. T.H.S. Escott, *England: Its People, Polity and Pursuits* (London, 1886), p.315.
85. T.H.S. Escott, *Society in London, By A Foreign Resident* (London, 5th ed. 1885). Society's constituents are listed as royalty, the aristocracy, diplomats, the representatives of high finance, 'Turf and Stock Exchange', judges, lawyers, eminent medical men and soldiers, leading politicians, literary figures, prominent journalists, entertainers and artists. The only figure who had any direct contact with industry mentioned in the course of the book is Joseph Chamberlain. Escott noted the importance of financial wealth and the links between City figures such as Rothschild and senior politicians (pp.86–7, 90). He also pointed to the pervasiveness of the gambling spirit in society: 'when it is not the Turf, it is the Stock Exchange, and perhaps this is the reason that the City plays so large a part in the arrangements of the West End'. This provided him with an explanation why 'Duchesses and other Ladies of rank' were 'so demonstrative in their affections for the wirepullers of the London money market, to say nothing of a crowd of stockjobbers and stockbrokers' (pp.117–18).
86. Max Weber argued, on the basis of mainly German experience, that status was the largely exclusive pursuit of those who could exist without labour and that the holders of status were consciously opposed not to 'common physical labour' but often to 'every rational economic pursuit'. H. Gerth and C.W. Mills (eds.), *From Max Weber* (London, 1948), pp.180–93. High finance and the upper reaches of professional life such as the law and the civil service, of which London was the centre, are important as examples of occupations which, if not as socially acceptable as landownership, offered a chance of participating fully in Britain's most successful economic sector while retaining caste.
87. For a revealing insight into the various blendings of City money and aristocratic and gentlemanly life styles see R. Palin, *Rothschild Relish* (London, 1970). Palin joined the firm in the 1920s but his early contacts were with people whose links with the firm went back well into Victorian times. The financial interest of members of Parliament on both sides of the House of Commons was also very marked as is clear from the work of J.A. Thomas in *The House of Commons, 1832–1901. A Study of its Economic and Functional Character*, (Cardiff, 1939) and his *The House of Commons 1906–1911. An Analysis of Its Economic and Social Character* (Cardiff, 1958).
88. S.G. Checkland, 'The Mind of the City, 1870–1914', *Oxford Economic Papers* NS 9 (1957), 261–263.
89. On the social distinctions between joint stock bankers and City financiers see M. de Cecco, 'The Last of the Romans', in R. Skidelsky (ed.), *The End of the Keynesian Era* (1977), p.20.
90. Nairn, *Break Up of Britain*, 2nd ed., p.26.
91. See, for example, the religious affiliations of the great cotton barons in Rubinstein, *Men of Property*, pp.82–6. On the Toryism of the most wealthy, including many manufacturers, see ibid., pp.145–63.
92. Ibid., pp. 134–7.
93. Kennedy, 'Institutional Responses to Economic Growth', 176–7.
94. Allett, *New Liberalism*. pp.176–7.
95. On the white colonies see M.W. Doyle, 'An Essay on the Structure of Britain's

Extended Economy in the Nineteenth Century', *Revue Internationale d'Histoire de la Banque* 19 (1979), 101ff; and on the relationship between British investment and British export trades see D.C.M. Platt, *Latin American and British Trade, 1806–1914* (London, 1972), esp. Chs, VI, X, XI.

96. C. Jones, ' "Business Imperialism" and Argentina, 1875–1900: A Theoretical Note', *Journal of Latin American Studies* 12 (1980), esp. 441; see also the same author's 'Great Capitalists and the Direction of British Overseas Investment in the Late Nineteenth Century: The Case of Argentina', *Business History* 22 (1980).

97. The concept of 'cultural imperialism', and its implications is discussed in R. Graham, 'Robinson and Gallagher in Latin America. The Meaning of Informal Imperialism' in W.R. Louis (ed.), *Imperialism. The Robinson and Gallagher Controversy* (London, 1976).

98. For arguments to this effect see H.S. Ferns, *Britain and Argentina in the Nineteenth Century* (Oxford, 1960), pp.487–91; and D.C.M. Platt, 'Economic Imperialism and the Businessman: Britain and Latin America before 1914', in R. Owen and B. Sutcliffe (eds.), *Studies in the Theory of Imperialism* (Oxford, 1972).

99. For an introduction to the literature on the partition of tropical Africa in this context see P.J. Cain, *Economic Foundations of British Expansion Overseas, 1815–1914* (London, 1980), pp.53–5; W.G. Hynes, *The Economics of Empire. Britain, Africa and the New Imperialism, 1870–1895* (London, 1979); and B.M. Ratcliffe, 'Commerce and Empire: Manchester Merchants and West Africa, 1873–95', *Journal of Imperial and Commonwealth History* 6 (1979).

100. R.E. Robinson and J. Gallagher, 'The Partition of Africa', *Cambridge Modern History* 11 (1962), 593.

101. The concept of the 'official mind' comes, of course, from R.E. Robinson and J. Gallagher with A. Denny, *Africa and the Victorians.* (London, 1962) For collaboration see R. Robinson, 'Non-European Foundations of European Imperialism. Sketch for a Theory of Collaboration' in Owen and Sutcliffe, *Studies in the Theory of Imperialism.*

102. For the domination of imperial employment by the sons of the public-school educated, professional classes of Southern England, see L.H. Gann and P. Duignan, *The Rulers of British Africa 1870–1914* (1978), Ch. 2, 3, 5 and 6.

103. There are some suggestive comments on British officials overseas as a 'service class' in R.C. Bridges, 'Europeans and East Africans in the Age of Exploration, '*Geographical Journal* 129 (1973), esp. 227–9.

104. For an introduction to the recent literature on economic imperialism in Egypt and in South Africa, see Cain, *Economic Foundations*, pp.52–3, 55–7. Two recent important studies are B.R. Johns, 'Business Investment and Imperialism. The Relationship between Economic Interest and the Growth of British Intervention in Egypt 1838–82' (unpub, Ph.D. thesis, Exeter Univ., 1981); and S. Marks and S. Trapido, 'Lord Milner and the South African State', *History Workshop* 8 (1979).

105. *Imperialism*, Pt. I, Ch. VIII.

106. 'The Inner Meaning of Protectionism', *Contemporary Review*, 84 (1903), 366–7.

107. Dr A.J. Marrison has recently warned historians against an economic determinist approach to the tariff question, pointing out that some individuals and firms had reason to support both free trade and protection depending upon which of their complex interests was at stake. He also points out that protection might be supported for political reasons even when it brought little economic benefit. Nonetheless his list of the main supporters and critics of Tariff Reform does not appear to disturb the broad judgements made in this article. A.J. Marrison, 'Businessmen, Industries and Tariff Reform in Britain, 1903–30', *Business History* 25 (July 1983), 148–64, especially 162.

108. W.J. Ashley, *The Tariff Problem* (London, 1903) pp.267–68. There is a very cogent defence of orthodoxy in W.S. Churchill, *The People's Rights* (London, 1909; reprinted London, 1970), Ch. III.

109. H.V. Emy, 'The Impact of Financial Policy on English Party Politics before 1914', *Historical Journal* 15 (1972).

110. P.F. Clarke, 'The End of Laissez-Faire and the Politics of Cotton', *Historical Journal* 15 (1972).
111. For a discussion of the Tariff Reform movement in the context of Britain's relative industrial decline see P.J. Cain, 'Political Economy in Edwardian England: The Tariff Reform Controversy', in A. O'Day (ed.), *The Edwardian Age. Conflict and Stability 1900–1914* (1979), pp.35–59. For Chamberlain's largely unsuccessful battle with the Treasury for empire development funds see R. Kesner, *Economic Control and Colonial Development. Crown Colony Financial Management in the Age of Joseph Chamberlain* (Oxford, 1981).
112. Edelstein believes that a tariff would have protected those industries most open to German and United States competition and these were, relatively speaking, highly capital-intensive – iron and steel, metal manufacture and machinery. A tariff would, therefore, have boosted domestic manufacturing investment. Persistence with a policy of free trade 'probably meant a less favourable environment for domestic manufacturing investment' and, given the unresponsiveness of savings to interest rate changes, stimulated foreign investment (*Overseas Investment*, p.222).
113. On Hobson's early protectionist and imperialist sympathies see Cain, 'International Trade and Economic Development in the work of J.A. Hobson before 1914', 406–10.
114. See esp. P.M. Kennedy, 'Strategy versus Finance in Twentieth Century Great Britain', *International History Review* 3 (1981), esp.45–52.
115. The South East derived a smaller share of its income from other regions of Britain or from abroad than did the areas dependent upon heavy industry. For further insight into this apparent paradox, see Lee, 'Regional Growth', 450.

The Export of British Finance, 1865–1914

by

Lance Davis and Robert A. Huttenback

I

Introduction

In the late nineteenth century a tourist might view the size of the Crystal Palace or the height of Tower Bridge as evidence of Britain's development. If that tourist was a businessman from the American Midwest or the German Ruhr he was likely to equate power and development with sparks from the forges of Cleveland or the sound of riveting from the shipyards of the Clyde. It was, however, the City that drew the attention of the foreign 'men of money', be they J.P. Morgan, the American financier, or Gustav von Meuissen, the president of the Darmstadt Bank. Christened by contemporaries the Eighth Wonder of the modern world, the City provided the link that bound the vast accumulations of Victorian savings to investments in locations as disparate as the Midlands, the Midwest, and the Mid-Pacific. It was to the City that Andrew Carnegie had turned to finance his first steel enterprise and it was there, too, that the Nizam of Hyderabad had gone for funds to finance his railway in the hills of South Central India. Nor was the market limited to overseas investment; it also continued to fuel the engines of domestic industrial growth. Vickers, for example, drew extensively on the City to finance its growth from a small special steel producer on the River Don to the armament giant of the early twentieth century.

Perhaps even more important, the interest and profits generated by these investments flowed back into London, and were a major source of prosperity that characterized the British economy. Schumpeter, in discussing the 'third Kondratieff' – a cycle caused in most of the world by the innovation of electricity and electrical equipment – noted that 'the English case presents a striking contrast'. So striking were its features, that he labelled the period the 'neomercantilist' Kondratieff.[1]

> The strong increase in capital exports … complements this. Foreign and particularly colonial enterprise and lending was the dominant feature of the period. Rubber, oil, South African gold and diamonds, Egyptian cotton, sugar, irrigation, South American (Argentinian) land developments, the financing of Japan and colonial communities (municipalities, particularly Canadian) afford examples of the way in which England, more than through domestic development, took part in the industrial process which carried the

Kondratieff prosperity. The London money market concerned itself mainly with foreign and colonial issues to an extent never equalled in England or in any other country. The great issuing houses in particular, almost exclusively cultivated this business, managing, sometimes rigging, the market for it.[2]

Schumpeter wrote just before the outbreak of the Second World War, but the importance of the London market was well understood by contemporaries as well. Among the classical economists both Mill and Marx had worried about the effects of overseas capital transfers. To the former the flow provided a means to increase the supply of cheap food, establish markets for British manufacturers and arrest the decline in the rate of profit in England:

> Thus the exportation of capital is an agent of great efficiency in extending the field for that which remains and it may be said truly that up to a certain point the more capital that we send away the more we shall possess and be able to retain at home.[3]

Marx, too, noted the flow, and surprisingly not only was his analysis similar to Mill's, but so were his conclusions.

> If capital is sent to foreign countries, it is not done because there is absolutely no employment at home. It is done because it can be employed at a higher rate in the foreign country .... These higher rates of profits ... sent home ... enter into the equalization of the general rate of profit and keep it up to that extent.[4]

Nor did Marx argue that the increased foreign rate was necessarily dependent on exploitation. While such exploitation was one possible cause, there was also, he argued, a substantial probability that the difference was due merely to the transitory monopoly profits attributed to the innovation of new production techniques in the underdeveloped country, 'in the same way a manufacturer who exploits a new invention before it becomes general undersells his competitors and yet sells his commodities above their individual value'.[5]

Alfred Marshall shared the view of Mill and Marx that foreign investment contributed positively to domestic welfare, although he admitted that there were numerous advantages to domestic commitments. On balance, it was clear to Marshall that overseas investment (in particular investment in the colonies) was very attractive since 'Capital is abundant in England; and she has few openings in which it can be made to yield a very high return'.[6] Like Marx, Marshall saw the high overseas rates as a temporary phenomenon resting on rents attached to new lands and new processes.

As the relative position of the British economy shifted, so economists' views on the utility of capital exports also changed. Few, however, doubted that the exports redounded to the benefit of the recipients; their concerns were with the impact of those transfers on the domestic economy. It was not until the present century that such investments came to be viewed by some as an unmitigated evil, injuring both the lender and the borrower.

Hardly had the Boer War ended than J.A. Hobson launched an attack on all things imperial. Beginning with the oft-quoted remark that 'Although the new Imperialism has been bad business for the nation, it has been good business for certain classes and certain trades within the nation',[7] Hobson's conclusions have provided the basis for three-quarters of a century of neo-Marxist rhetoric. Engels wrote: ' ... colonization today is merely a subsidiary of the stock exchange'; Rosa Luxenburg argued that: 'Imperialism is the political expression of the accumulation of capital'; but it was Lenin whose definition of imperialism included, ' ... the merging of bank capital with industrial capital. and the creation on the basis of this 'finance capital' of a financial oligarchy, [and] the export of capital which has been extremely important as distinguished from the export of commodities ...'.[8] It was also Lenin who focused his attention on the concentration of British overseas finance in the empire. He argued: 'The principal sphere of investment of British capital are the British colonies', and he put the empire's share at almost 50 per cent.[9]

Recognition of the importance of capital outflows was not limited to academic economists and critics of the system. Contemporary politicians took note of the phenomenon and speculated about its impact on the British economy. Joseph Chamberlain, for example, was convinced that capital transfers were the sinews of empire, and that prosperity both overseas and at home rested on a continuation of those flows. Lenin may have gone too far when he concluded that, 'leading British bourgeois politicians fully appreciated the connection between what might be called purely economic and the political–social roots of imperialism'.[10] Chamberlain, however, certainly espoused the principle that empire should be a source of monetary profit to the mother country; and he believed that those profits should be supported by substantial capital transfers, even if those transfers had to be subsidized. In a famous Birmingham address he laid the basis for the policy of that 'creative imperialism' that he attempted to effect during his tenure at the Colonial Office. To Chamberlain it was

> not enough to occupy certain great spaces of the world's surface unless you can make the best of them, unless you are willing to develop them. We are the landlords of a great estate; it is the duty of the landlord to develop his estate .... In my opinion, it would be the wisest course for the government of this country to use British capital and British credit in order to create an instrument of trade in all ... new important countries.[11]

Of course, Treasury objections severely constrained official actions, but the issue was important and it did produce policy recommendations and at least some subsidies.[12]

In the absence of a firm statistical base, it was clearly impossible for

Hobson, Lenin or even Chamberlain to provide an accurate assessment of the role of the London capital market. In 1914 C.K. Hobson in his analysis of financial exports provided a partial foundation. Since that time understanding of the subject has been advanced by the endeavours of Feis, Jenks, Cairncross, Segal and Simon.[13] While others have also concerned themselves with the level of capital export, this group has approached the question through examinations of the issues of financial instruments. To Jenks this implied the detailed study of hundreds of individual issues, but to Segal and Simon, as to Hobson, it involved the scrutiny of the financial press, which for nineteenth-century Britain meant the *Investor's Monthly Manual, The Stock Exchange Yearbook* and *Burdett's Official Intelligencer.*

This article reworks those sources, provides some substantial revisions of the general conclusions of the earlier work, and, more important, extends those previous studies in several new directions. Since there is no straightforward relationship between financial issues and capital transfers, any approach presuming such a relationship has been severely criticized; and as research produced more direct estimates of capital transfers, academic interest has shifted away from the scrutiny of financial issues. For this article, however, the criticism is irrelevant, since the focus is on the financial investments actually made by the British; and the new issues series do provide a record of the actual composition of new paper investment.

The shift in economists' attention from finance to capital is not surprising. For the great majority of questions it is the level of the real flows that is important; and the earlier excursion into finance was engendered almost solely by a desire to acquire an adequate proxy for those real transfers. From the point of view of certain questions in economic history, however (and the political economy of imperialism is one of those questions), it is the financial rather than the real flows that are more relevant. For economists the most important questions concern the magnitude of the transfers from the United Kingdom to the rest of the world. For questions involving finance capitalism as outlined by Lenin and Hobson, the central issues involve the financial relations between the domestic and overseas sectors. Use of real rather than financial data for this latter purpose raises at least two serious problems.

First, use of real flows may distort the analysis because of the way investments are distributed between the home and overseas markets. Consider two firms. Both raise £1,000,000 on the London capital market; however, one invests the entire amount in tea plantations in Assam, while the other divides its new resources between similar plantations and distribution facilities in the United Kingdom. The first firm has invested twice as much overseas as the second, but an analysis based on capital transfers would miss the fact that *ceteris paribus* both firms have an equal interest in maintaining an empire connection (i.e. both have £1,000,000 at risk and the level of that risk may be related to the strength of the empire connection).

A second source of distortion rests on the treatment of 'rolling over' in the calculation of capital transfers. Consider a firm that sells shares worth £100,000 in a Colorado cattle ranch in the 1870s. A few years later the enterprise is sold to American interests, and the proceeds are invested in a new enterprise in the Canadian prairies. The real capital series show an overseas transfer at the time of the first investment, but the figures are not affected by the second transaction. From the point of view of British–Empire relations, however, it is only the latter transaction that is relevant. The financial data, on the other hand, would reflect both stock issues, and, although overstating the total amount of capital transferred, provide an accurate assessment of the amount of finance made available to the US in the 1870s and to the empire a few years later. From the point of view of this work, it matters little whether the source of those funds was new savings or disentanglements from past accumulations, whether it represented new overseas transfers or merely the rolling over of funds long since in place outside the British Isles.

The new issues series provides an imperfect but superior index of imperial economic activity, and probably a better measure of the connections between Britain and the empire. Some feeling for the differences between the two measures can be obtained by a comparison of the net foreign lending figures used by Edelstein with the annual series of capital called up.[14]

Reliance on the financial series is not to deny that for some purposes the length of the investment may well be important; this point has recently been made somewhat obliquely by D.C.M. Platt.[15] If the financial series are used to estimate the amount of portfolio finance in place at any one time, it is necessary to know not only the annual volume but the maturity of those issues as well. The amount of American railroad finance held by the British public in 1914 is not the sum of the issue from 1830 to 1914, but that total *less* repayments. To the extent that there were significant differences in the maturities of home, foreign, and empire issues, it is misleading to use the simple sum as an index of the total finance transferred. External evidence, however, suggests that to the degree there were significant differences, it was domestic issues that had the longest maturities.[16] Thus such summary totals, although inflated, minimize the importance of the domestic component and provide a maximum estimate of the proportion of foreign and empire transfers. It is in this latter context that they are used in this analysis.

The figures cited in this study do not include the finance transferred by non-public companies, by some public companies floating issues on provincial exchanges, and by direct investment; it is possible that their inclusion might have changed the results. Subsidiary evidence, however, indicated that the omissions tended to be concentrated in domestic issues. The provincial exchanges were inclined to specialize in domestic securities, and the bulk of private offerings were domestic. Taken together, these factors suggest that the estimates on the proportion of foreign and empire securities can be viewed as providing a maximum evaluation of their actual importance to the British market. Moreover, what overseas flows there were appear to have been relatively small and fairly closely correlated with the reported measure. Thus, it appears unlikely that the general conclusions would have been much altered if allowance for them had been made. Still the caveat remains: this article is entitled 'The Export of Finance', not 'The Export of Capital'. It focuses on the spatial and industrial distribution of finance, not on the amount raised from the British savers nor on the level of the accumulated total of overseas finance.

The series are drawn from the same financial press on which C.K. Hobson and Segal and Simon based their work, but some earlier errors have been corrected. Both spatial and industrial distributions have been analysed and the empire has been divided into those colonies with responsible government and the dependent empire. The series should be viewed as an index of the capital calls, and the actual totals are almost certainly higher than the figures reported.

The basic tables provide three alternative measures of the financial flows. The 'minimum' series includes only those issues that are (1) actually reported and (2) reported as taken up entirely within the United Kingdom. The 'intermediate' series is also limited to 'entirely taken up in the UK' issues, but in addition to those enumerated in the 'minimum' series includes adjustments for calls whose presence can be inferred from existing reports.[17] Finally the 'maximum' series includes calls reported as 'partly abroad' issues, adjusted for inferred non-reported calls.

Given the focus on the spatial and industrial distribution of finance, no attempt has been made to adjust these figures either for those portions of issues reported as sold on the UK market alone that were purchased by overseas residents, nor for the foreign and empire securities initially held in the United Kingdom but later repatriated. D.C.M. Platt has recently concluded that these omissions were important for a study of capital transfer, particularly after the turn of the century, and that a correction for them could reduce the estimates of the British holdings of overseas symbolic capital at the outbreak of the First World War by more than 40 per cent.[18] Neither omission is directly relevant for this study, and the latter not at all. To the extent that a portion of the initial offerings passed immediately into colonial or foreign hands, the British contribution (as opposed to that of the London capital market) to colonial and foreign finance is overstated. A study of the stockholders of a sample of such corporations suggests that about 16 per cent of foreign securities were foreign-held, and about 2.5 per cent of colonial shares were held by foreigners and an additional 8 per cent by empire residents.[19] Such purchases do not, however, appear to have biased the conclusions about the spatial and industrial distributions of 'British' funds.

While the data thus produced differ in some ways from the general outlines proposed first by Hobson and revised by Segal-Simon and Simon, the primary purpose of this exercise is not to replace one set of estimates with another – the differences are relatively minor – but to expand the coverage of those earlier series, and so make it possible to provide a quantitative estimate of the extent and character of 'Financial Imperialism'. Simon and Segal extended Hobson's aggregate by providing a continent-by-continent breakdown of financial flows, and some estimates of the industrial composition of those flows. It is possible to refine those estimates further and provide: (1) a measure of the industrial distribution of the flows to each continent, and (2) a measure of the size and the industrial composition of the financial transfers to the UK domestic market and to each part of the empire (that is, to the colonies with responsible government, dependent colonies, and to India). This latter breakdown is a necessary prerequisite if the goal is an accurate assessment of the neo-Marxist view of the late nineteenth century.

Since C.K. Hobson's estimates are based on 'capital created' rather than 'capital called', it is difficult to provide an exact comparison; however, a simple regression suggests that there is a high degree of association between Hobson's figures and all of the three new series (depending on the series chosen the correlation coefficients range from .77 to .83). A more direct comparison is available with the Segal-Simon/Simon estimates. The correlation coefficients for the minimum and intermediate series are .92 and .93 respectively, but the maximum series suggests a slightly lower degree of association (.82). Since Simon has allocated the 'partly abroad' issues between Britain and the rest of the world, it is probably not surprising that his estimates fall, in general, between the minimum and maximum estimates. Over the entire 50 years, although subject to substantial year-to-year variation, the minimum estimate is something more than three-quarters of the Segal-Simon/Simon figure, the intermediate about equal (97 per cent, but almost exactly equal after 1885), and the maximum about 17 per cent higher (only three per cent after 1885). The differences between these and the earlier estimates appear significant only in two half-decades, 1895–99 and 1910–14, In the former instance the Segal-Simon/Simon figures are about 12 per cent above the 'maximum' figure, and in the latter about half that amount. Although the way in which the Simon data are reported makes direct comparisons difficult, it appears that the major source of the differences in the period 1895–99 rests in the empire agriculture and extractive estimates, particularly those for North America but to a lesser extent those for Africa, Asia, and Australasia as well. In the last quinquennium the major differences appear to have been in the estimates for Europe and North America (the differences are about the same for empire and foreign sectors), and about half of the total discrepancy can be accounted for by the estimate for the agriculture and extractive sector.[20]

II

The Data: Gross Flows

With the exception of the 1870s, when French War Loans and US Treasury borrowing bloat the 'maximum' series, the three estimates indicate similar trends in the volume of total finance.[21] In the interest of simplicity and given the underlying similarity, the remainder of this discussion is cast largely in terms of the minimum series. Annual flows averaged something less than £40 million per year in the late 1860s, rose to about £55 million in the early 1870s, and to more than £90 million between 1875 and 1884. From then until the end of the century the annual total fluctuated between £70 and £85 million, but thereafter increased steadily. It was more than £130 million in 1900–04, £145 million in 1905–09 and £175 million in 1910–14. In 'real' pounds of 1913, those total flows averaged £40 million over the decade 1865–74; £76 million in 1875–84; £98 million in 1885–94; £130 million in 1895–1904; and £173 million over the last pre-war decade.

Clearly, the British market directed a vast quantity of finance into a myriad of activities throughout the world. To put these aggregate figures in perspective, during the peak years (the late 1880s, and the immediate pre-war period) the market handled about £4.5 each year for every man, woman and child in England, Scotland and Wales; and, even in the periods of low activity, the figure was in excess of £2. Since national income amounted on average to only about £40 per person per year, it is easy to see why Lenin spoke of 'Finance Capitalism'.

Europe may well have been the world's banker, but Britain was the majority stockholder in that enterprise. For capital as opposed to finance, it is estimated that Britain accounted for 75 per cent of all international movements in 1900, and although its share declined thereafter, it was still in excess of 40 per cent in 1913. In the case of foreign investment in the United States, for example, the United Kingdom's share of total foreign investment is estimated to have been 80 per cent in 1880, 72 per cent in 1900 and 59 per cent in 1913.[22] Despite these figures, it is necessary to examine the spatial and industrial composition of the financial flows before it is possible to conclude that *Empire* finance either played an important role in underwriting British prosperity or served to drain funds from the domestic enterprise, or provided the foundation of finance imperialism in the Hobson–Lenin–Chamberlain sense of the word.

Table 1 (page 50) divides the total flows into their domestic, foreign and empire components. Over the entire 50-year period, about 42 per cent of the 'minimum' total went to the foreign sector, somewhat less than a third remained at home, and the remaining quarter supported empire activities. The distribution between home and overseas finance is quite consistent with C.K. Hobson's earlier estimate of one-third home and two-thirds abroad. There are, however, probably some differences in the foreign–empire distribution of the overseas component between these estimates and those of other authors. Lenin put the empire's share at just less than 50 per cent, while Simon places the figure at slightly more than 40 per cent. That latter figure is not far different from the 'minimum' estimate (39 per cent), but it is substantially higher than the one-third figure implied by the intermediate and maximum estimates.

The overall averages, while providing some feeling for magnitudes, mask some important facets of the transfer process. Traditional historiography, for example, asserts that late Victorian industry was starved by lack of new investment, as the nation's capital streamed abroad. While there is no simple relation between finance and capital, there is still no evidence in these data to indicate that the domestic economy suffered financial deprivation because of overseas demand. From 1880 to 1904 the domestic economy received more than 35 per cent of the total available finance and for the last decade the fraction was almost one-half. Moreover, in the private sector (domestic private industry is, after all, the subject of the conventional interpretation), the result is even clearer: the domestic average for the entire period is nearly 40 per cent. The variety of enterprises funded suggests that the market was at least as willing to finance the new growth industries as the traditional iron and textile firms; and an examination of domestic borrowing suggests that they were able to borrow at rates only slightly above the consol rate – rates that were much below the charges levied on overseas or empire firms.

It must be remembered that arguments based on the concept of finance imperialism concentrate on the fraction of British finance that went into the empire.[23] Over the entire 50 years, the proportion is about 25 per cent, but the average is biased upwards by the transfers made during the last decade. For the period before 1900 about which Hobson wrote and Lenin paraphrased, the proportion is only about one in five. Furthermore, of either fraction, only one-third went to the dependent empire. In terms of private finance, while foreign firms received almost 45 per cent and domestic 40, *all* empire firms absorbed less than one-fifth of the total, and only about one pound in eight in the year before 1900. Moreover, the dependent governments received only about a third of that empire total. The domestic share, on the other hand, was above 60 per cent in the years 1875–79 and more than 55 per cent in the quinquennium 1895–99. In the case of government finance the story is different. The foreign sector received something less than 40 per cent; the empire's share ballooned to about the same level; but that of the domestic economy fell to just less than a quarter. Of the government total about one pound in eleven went to India and the dependent colonies.

The picture is clear. Britain was indeed a major supplier of the world's finance; but, apart from the last decade, the empire was not a major recipient of those funds. Despite the more significant role played by empire in the area of government finance, there is little evidence that at any time, at least before 1905, it provided a significant alternative for private funds pushed out of Britain by low domestic returns, or a fertile ground for investment at high 'exploitative monopolistic' rates.

These observations are confirmed by a closer examination of the funds that did move into the empire. Of that total the regions with responsible government received over 70 per cent.[24] Of the remaining fraction, India received about two-thirds and the dependent colonies the remainder. As a fraction of all (home, foreign and empire) finance, the colonies with responsible government gained about 20, India five, and the dependent possessions less than three per cent. Limiting observation to private finance reduces further the role of the empire in general, and of the dependent empire in particular. The share of the colonies with responsible government falls to 13 per cent, India to less than four and the dependent colonies to under three per cent of the total.

III

The Data: Geographic Distribution

Table 2 (page 52) provides a geographic breakdown of the financial flows, and Table 3 (page 53) shows the distribution between the empire and foreign sectors for each continent.[25] Overall, the allocation of finance by continent is similar to that of Simon's earlier study; however, there are some noticeable differences. As one would expect, the treatment of 'partially called' issues produces some substantial differences in Europe (and to a lesser extent in North America in the late 1870s). There are, however, other differences as well. In particular, the Simon series appears to underestimate somewhat the proportion of finance flowing to South America and to overestimate the proportion directed towards Asia and Africa. Analysis suggests that these differences may be explained in part by the taxonomy, although Simon is not clear on his methods. In the present study Asiatic Russia was assigned to Europe and Central America placed in the Southern Hemisphere. A rough reassignment of those two areas (Central America is easily shifted, but the Russian adjustment was limited to a transfer of the Trans-Siberian Railroad from Europe to Russia) reduces much of the South American and Asiatic discrepancy, but it still leaves the problem of Africa unresolved. In that case the differences are concentrated in the decade 1895 to 1904, but the source of that difference is not easily discovered.[26]

The United Kingdom aside, the North American continent was the most important recipient of British finance; it attracted a quarter of all British finance and slightly more than a third of the overseas total. It was, however, the foreign sector (largely the United States) that early drew the bulk of the funds, although that domination all but disappeared in the present century. The USA and Mexico accounted for more than three-quarters of the total before 1905, but only about half thereafter.

Of the empire total, almost all went to what is now Canada. The increase in the empire's share during the late 1880s and again in the last decade was largely associated with increased investment in Canadian railroads. In the 1880s the Canadian Pacific and the Grand Trunk of Canada were the major recipients of London funds, but a number of smaller lines, including the Atlantic and Northwestern, the Midland of Canada, the Ontario and Quebec, the Qu'Appelle, Long Lake and Saskatchewan, the Quebec Central, the Quebec and St. John, and the Western Counties (Nova Scotia) also funded issues in excess of £100,000. After the turn of the century, the largest volume of securities was issued by the Canadian Pacific, the Grand Trunk of Canada, the Grand Trunk

Pacific and the Canadian Northern. Again, however, access to the London market was not limited to those firms. Railroads such as the Edmonton, Dunvegan and British Columbia, the Pacific Great Eastern, the Terminal Cities, and the Atlantic, Quebec and Western also received substantial transfusions.

The history of Canadian growth after Confederation is well known; and Edelstein's penetrating study neatly summarizes the interaction between international capital movements and Canadian development. All that need be emphasized here is that the financial data provide vivid support for the picture he provides. Edelstein concludes that throughout the period 1867 to 1915 Canada depended very heavily on foreign capital imports. His estimates indicate that at the time of Confederation one-half of gross domestic capital formation was financed from abroad, that the fraction declined to approximately one-third by 1890, but then rose again to its previous peak by the outbreak of the First World War. The latter surge was triggered off by the opening of commercial wheat production on the prairies, but was reinforced by a wave of industrial investment resting on Canadian tariff and patent policy, and by investment in the second and third transcontinental railroads – the latter apparently absorbing between 7 and 8 per cent of Canadian GNP in the immediate pre-war decades.[27] The financial data mirror and flesh out these results. They pinpoint the railroad finance in the late 1870s and 1880s that tied the prairies to Eastern and European markets as well as the later massive outpouring of railroad and industrial issues that flooded the London market after 1902.

Below the border, the development of the USA's capital markets reduced that country's dependence on British finance, and contributed to the decline in the continent's receipt. The North American total had reached about £18 million a year in the decade 1880–89, but it had fallen to less than half that amount ten years later. In the last pre-war decade, however, the United States and Mexico received £272 million, and the Canadians tapped the British markets for an additional £257 million; together these amounted to an average of almost £53 million a year.

In terms of the total volume of overseas finance, South and Central America (including the Caribbean) ranked second. As early as 1873, British companies controlled almost three-quarters of the Argentine railway network; and over the full period the southern continent received about 14 per cent of all finance.[28] That proportion was, however, subject to wide variation. After absorbing almost a quarter of all finance in the late 1880s, for example, it received only seven per cent in the decade of the 1890s. Of either amount, however, the formal empire received only a tiny fraction (one per cent). Taking the two continents together, the Western Hemisphere absorbed about two-fifths of all London-based finance and more than half of the overseas total. Of that total, the foreign sector received more than three-quarters and Canada almost a third. The dependent colonies together drew about half of one per cent.

'Europe' stood fifth among the continents, if the 'minimum' measure is employed. For the entire period, even by the latter measure, it drew about £1 in 12 of the total volume of identified finance. Of that £350 million only £1.3 million went to Britain's European colonies (Gibraltar, Cyprus and Malta). Thus, of the three 'western' continents (regions that accounted for almost two-thirds of overseas finance), the foreign sector received about four-fifths of the total. Canada (and the colonies that went to make up Canada) was the destination of an additional 20 per cent, and the dependent empire drew far less than one per cent.

On the three remaining continents, regions that absorbed less than 25 per cent of all (and slightly over a third of overseas) finance, the story was somewhat different. Of the three, Asia received the largest share, and although the foreign sector could hardly be termed insignificant, more than 60 per cent went to the empire. India was the major empire beneficiary, although the subcontinent's share declined from almost the entire empire total to less than £3 in four as the tin and rubber industries on the Malay peninsula began to tap the London market.

The development of Japan, together with China's increasing attractiveness as an area for foreign investment, reduced the empire's dominance of the continent's total. The foreign sector accounted for only about £1 in eight between 1865 and 1885, but for almost half in the last pre-war decade. In the later period government borrowing involved the national governments of Japan, China, Siam and Indo-China, and cities like Tokyo, Nagoya, Osaka and Yokahama. In the private sector there were railroad issues of the Imperial China, the Manila, and the Philippines; financial issues from the Industrial Bank of Japan and the National Bank of China; and the Agriculture and Extractive issues of firms like the Anglo-Dutch plantations of Java, the Chinese Engineering and Mining Company, the Hayeop (Dutch Borneo) Rubber Estates, the Mendaris (Sumatra) Rubber and Produce Estates and the Royal Dutch Company for the Working of Petroleum Wells in the Netherlands Indies.

Of all the continents, none was more clearly a British financial preserve than Oceania (Australia, New Zealand, etc.). Although only sparsely populated, it received almost eight per cent of all finance, a figure that by some measures was equal to Europe's. From the 1860s to the 1890s investment boomed and a large portion of that new capital (a fraction ranging from about a quarter in the 1870s and 1890s to almost a half in the 1860s and 1880s) was financed by loans and other financial transfers from the UK. The financial flow rose to more than £13 million a year in the latter half of the 1880s and in that peak decade accounted for more than one-eighth of all finance. On a per capita basis, Britain contributed more to Oceania than to any other continent; and almost all was directed into the empire. Unlike Canada, in Australasia, while there were some private issues, the majority of the transfers were public. In the Dominion about one-third of the total was governmental; in the Commonwealth the total was more than three-quarters and in the boom decade of the 1880s it was over four-fifths. Given the independent attitude of the Australasian governments and the horror with which the British government greeted each new financial issue, it can hardly be argued that it was the British who were forcing their savings on an unwilling set of colonists. In 1875 Lord Carnarvon, Secretary of State for the Colonies, wrote to W.H. Smith: 'I am not surprised that you are rather startled at the Treasury at the financial speed at which New Zealand is travelling. At the same time the crisis may not come yet ... '.[29] Of the empire's share, however, the dependent empire received very little; £39 of every £40 went either to colonies with responsible government, or to those (like Western Australia) about to achieve that status.

Finally there is Africa, along with India the inspiration for most of the imperial rhetoric. Imperialism there may well have been, but it does not appear to have been 'finance imperialism'. The continent ranks last among the recipients, and the figure is as large as it is only because of the heavy flows between 1895 and 1909. Nor were the bulk of the flows directed towards the dependent empire. While the reshuffling of allegiances that followed the Boer War blurs the distinctions between foreign, responsible and dependent regions, some trends can be distinguished. For the entire period, the foreign sector received almost 40 per cent of African finance – a total that would have been even higher had the Transvaal and the Orange Free State not been absorbed into the empire in 1902.[30] The empire portion was divided between responsible and dependent governments in a ratio of two to one, if the two newly-acquired colonies are classified as responsibly governed in the years from 1902 to 1906. In no year before 1895 did the dependent empire in Africa absorb as much as £1 million and the average for the entire period was only about a third of that figure.

Europe, the western hemisphere and Australasia provide little comfort to the prophets of finance imperialism, if that term is understood to imply major financial transfers to parts of the dependent empire. Only Lenin even among the neo-Marxists argues that Britain had substantial 'exploitative control' over the self-governing colonies. Certainly the British were under no illusion about their ability to affect governmental policy in the self-governing colonies, even when those policies directly affected the mother country. As early as 1871 Kimberley lamented that 'the effect of the New Zealand [tariff] Bill would undoubtedly be that New Zealand might admit Sydney-made shoes free and charge any duty she pleased on shoes from Northampton',[31] but admitted nothing could be done. Similar comments are frequent not only on tariff issues but on such widely diverse enterprises as loan repayments, provision for the common defence, and attempts by those colonial governments to expand their economic and political power into neighbouring territories. If any evidence is to be found to support the concept of financial imperialism, it is in Asia and Africa. Yet little more than 16 per cent of all finance was transferred to these two continents; and of that amount, well under half was directed towards India and the dependent colonies. Even in the twentieth century when those latter flows peaked, they accounted for only one-tenth of all finance passing through the British capital market. If, as Hobson argued, 'final determination rests with the financial power', or, as Lenin concluded, 'British bourgeois politicians fully appreciated the connection between what might be called the purely economic and the political-social roots of imperialism', it is unclear why the empire developed as it did.[32]

IV

The Data: Industrial Composition

How did British finance distribute itself across the industrial spectrum? Neither Jenks nor C.K. Hobson made a systematic attempt to answer this question, but Segal and Simon made a first hesitant step in this direction. In their 1961 article they provide an industrial profile drawn across eight industries for the total of all issues covered by their 30-year study. In his extension of their joint work, Simon provides annual estimates from 1865 to 1914 but, unfortunately, adopts a different taxonomy – one that includes only three sectors (social overhead, extractive, and manufacturing) and explicitly excludes 'real estate, defence, and miscellaneous'. Both Segal/Simon and Simon alone include both private and government issues in their industrial classification; the inclusion of the latter class raises severe technical problems.

The classification scheme adopted for this study is narrower, but, it is hoped more easily comprehensible. First, at the highest level issues were classified either as public or private. There was no attempt to include a 'mixed' category since it appeared impossible to delineate such a class of securities with any precision. Any issue emanating from any level of government was classified as 'government', but any issue originating in the private sector (even issues with government guarantees) was termed a private one. Secondly, no attempt was made to classify government issues by use; they were termed government whether the funds were 'used' to pay public servants, to build railways or to fight wars.[33] Finally, the private sector was further subdivided into six super industries: agriculture and extractive, manufacturing, trade and services, finance and real estate, public utilities and transportation.

Because of the different bases of classification it is impossible to compare these estimates with Simon's series, and a comparison with the Segal/Simon 'all years all issues' estimate should be accompanied by a set of clear caveats. If, for example, it is assumed that the public works sector is entirely government and that nine-tenths of the 'All Other' sectors should be similarly assigned, then the two sets appear to yield quite similar results for the 30-year period 1865–94.[34] The current study permits a more detailed analysis of the industrial composition of the flows by political sector – a classification that has not previously been available.

About two-thirds of all issues were private, and more than half of private finance went into transport, a figure that translates into about one-third of all finance.[35] The proportions were even higher in the first two decades, as the British financed not only European and American railroads but domestic lines as well. The list of the world's railways that turned to the London market for financial support is very long. Between 1865 and 1880, for example, it included such famous names as the Caledonian, the three Greats (Eastern, Northern, Western), the Manchester, Sheffield and Lincolnshire, the Midlands, the North British, and the South Eastern in the United Kingdom; the B & O, the Erie, the Milwaukee, the New York Central, the Katy, the Pennsy, the Reading, the Southern Pacific, and the Union Pacific in the United States; and the Charkof–Azoff, the Dutch Rhenish, the Orel–Vitebsk, the Roumanian, the Southern Austria, and the Orléans and Chalons in Europe. The market also provided substantial funds for railways whose names were never household words and which have long since faded into history; for example, the Cuxhaven, the Des Moines Valley, the Dunaburk and Witepsk, the Edinburgh and Bathgate, the Keokuk and Kansas City, the Plymouth, the Kankakee and Pacific, and the Taff Vale.

The fraction of total finance accounted for by transportation declined somewhat as those networks neared completion, and then rose once again as construction boomed in the parts of the empire with responsible government. That growth was largely concentrated in Canada, but there were major issues from Australia (the Midlands and Western Australia) and South Africa (the New Cape Central and the Vryheid). Over the 50-year period hardly less than £1.6 billion were directed towards the transport sector, and of that total almost all (97 per cent) went to railways.

No other industry attracted nearly as much private capital as the railways, although 'Finance' did command about one-fourth as much. In terms of volume, 'Manufacturing' ranks third. Relatively unimportant until the mid-1880s, it represented a substantial draw on the total thereafter; and in the late 1890s manufacturing averaged £16 million a year (just less than a fifth of all finance). The sector's importance declined in the first decade of the present century, but rose again just before the outbreak of the First World War. Of the other three private industrial sectors, 'Agriculture and Extractive' absorbed approximately eight per cent; 'Public Utilities' some five per cent; and 'Trade and Services' about four per cent of the private total.

In contrast to the one-quarter figure in the domestic sector, the foreign sector proportion of government finance averaged about one-third while in the empire that figure was well above 50 per cent. The explanation for the comparatively high proportion of government in total overseas finance reflects in part the relative difficulty of marketing foreign private issues, and, in part, marked differences in the composition of demand. The former is, however, a consideration that must have had implications for the public–private mix in both countries and colonies far removed from the London financial centre.

There are, however, some important contrasts between the composition of the total financial flows and the streams received by the domestic, foreign and empire sectors and even within the empire itself. These differences are important for any understanding of the financial roots of imperialism, but they have not previously been examined systematically. In the domestic market, the 'Agriculture and Extractive' category was only about one-fourth as important as it was in the 'All Finance' total and over time the domestic index fell. Similarly, 'Transport's' share of the home market was substantially below the 'All Finance' average total, and it is marked by a strong negative trend, a trend that reflected the virtual completion of the domestic railway network. Before 1890 domestic public utilities issues appeared less frequently than the 'All Finance' averages, but over the succeeding two decades they became much more prominent. Much of domestic gas and water investment antedates 1865; however, the diffusion of electricity, slow by US and German but fast by world standards, raised the domestic sector's share in the first decade of the twentieth century. In the home country three other industries all reflect proportions well in excess of the average: 'Finance' almost half as much again, and 'Trade and Services' and 'Manufacturing' more than twice that.

In the foreign sector, the indices for 'Finance', 'Manufacturing', and 'Trade and Services' are well below the average, and none appears to have been increasing. 'Public Utilities' stand almost at the 'All Finance' average; and the Agriculture and Extractive industry only slightly above, a bias which seems to reflect popular perceptions of the latter industry's position at the time. In the years after the American Civil War, British investors, it is alleged, proved particularly susceptible to the lure of the American West. Any Englishman interested in Western mining – so the story goes – was considered a sitting duck by native sharpshooters. After one particularly shady transaction, a noted London financial journal wrote that the British investors involved had fallen victim to 'gold extracting with a vengeance'.[36] The *Statist* of 18 July 1885 noted that, 'When novices meddle with foreign or colonial mines, they play to lose. American mines', the journal continued, 'were not very remunerative. They are got up exclusively for export'.[37]

American cattle-ranching, too, seemed to have fired the British investor's imagination. Profitable in the late 1870s and early 1880s, British-owned cattle companies had by the end of the century suffered major financial reverses. The loss to British investors between 1884 and 1900 has been placed at about $18,000,000.[38]

In the case of 'Transport', the foreign sector received more than what could be termed its fair share. The index rose from 1880 to the mid-90s, but declined somewhat after 1905. Again, American railways exerted an almost hypnotic effect on the British investor. As late as 1865 there had not been an American railway stock or bond on the British market, but 20 years later British involvement was so great that a collapse in American railway securities resulted in a depression throughout Britain.[39]

Railway investment in South America was also heavy, particularly in Argentina and Peru.[40] The Peruvian Corporation, a British firm, for example, counted among its holdings no less than eight of the nation's railways. As in the United States, investment patterns were often more enthusiastic than wise. In reference to the Chimbote Railway, the Corporation's records point out:

> In the early days of the Corporation hope was always held out that as soon as various coal deposits were reached there would be immediate traffic for the railway. In practice, however, the first coal deposit reached ... proved quite worthless and the same was found to be the case with the coal deposits at Huallancana .... [41]

Again, the Central Railway was conceived in part to serve the Cerro de Pasco silver mines, but due to wrong-headed intransigence the Corporation lost that concession even before the line was completed. As the company records admit:

> It is evident that the Corporation had abundant opportunity and power to retain this concession to construct the railway and open up the mines but all this was allowed to fall in other hands. [To add insult to injury copper was discovered] ... the existence of which the original concessionaires had no idea .... [42]

In the empire, 'Manufacturing' and 'Trade and Services' both received substantially smaller fractions of total finance than 'world' levels. Empire 'Transport', however, received funds in proportions that were more or less 'typical' and the sector's share of 'Finance' stood above the general average. The latter figure reflects in large part the issues of the financial, land, and investment companies that inflated the industry total, particularly in the last three decades of the century. Those firms were closely tied to land and depended for their profits on well-defined property rights. Similarly, empire 'Agriculture and Extractive' firms received much more than their proportionate shares, particularly in the years from 1880 to 1905. The late-nineteenth-century surge was associated not with agriculture but with mining (particularly gold mining). Although the list of firms included those as familiar as De Beers, it was dominated by names with a 'get rich quick' aura, including, for example, the Ivanhoe, the World's Treasure and the Corsair.

While the empire played third fiddle to the home and foreign sectors in terms of total resources drawn from the Victorian financial markets, it displayed a greater than average affinity for 'Finance' and for 'Agriculture and Extractive' issues. In the colonies with responsible government, the 'Agricultural and Extractive' industries drew above average proportions of finance, but these indices were substantially below those of the dependent colonies. In the case of 'Finance', the self-governing colonies received somewhat more than average amounts; however, that inflated figure largely reflects the boom in Australasian land and development companies in the decade and a half after 1875, and the similar activities in South Africa in the 1890s. In 'Transport', those self-governing colonies received about 'typical' proportions, and while somewhat above all-empire averages in 'Manufacturing' they were below that figure for

'Trade and Commerce'. For 'Public Utilities', on the other hand, the fractions received were below both the all-empire and the foreign average. In summary, it appears that in the areas of the empire with responsible government (and they were parts of the empire that attracted the greatest absolute levels of finance), the stream of private finance tended to be directed towards the 'Agricultural and Extractive' industries, towards 'Finance' and, to a lesser degree, towards 'Transport'.

Although the dependent colonies received only 2.5 per cent of all private finance, the industrial composition was quite different from the patterns prevailing either in the self-governing portions of the empire or in India. In 'Manufacturing', 'Trade and Services', and 'Transport', the dependent colonies received substantially less than normal proportions, and there is no evidence of an upward trend in any of the three series. In the 'Agriculture and Extractive' industries, in the 'Public Utilities' and in 'Finance', the dependent colonies drew proportions well above empire and 'all world' levels. For 'Finance' the 50-year average was almost two and a half times, and for 'Agriculture and Extractive' it was more than four times typical proportions; and those levels were almost as high at the end of the period as they had been at the beginning. Intra-sectoral analysis indicates that it was the financial, land and development component that produced the inflated 'Finance' figure. Thus, it appears that in the dependent colonies, finance imperialism, to the degree that it existed, was intimately connected to the possession of land and a legal structure that gave British investors the right to relatively unfettered exercise of their ownership privileges.

In India, the other part of the dependent empire, 'Transport' and the 'Agriculture and Extractive' industries drew proportions of finance almost 50 per cent above the world average. In the latter industry, the major inflows occurred during the two and a half decades between 1880 and 1905; but at both the beginning and the end of the period, the subcontinent drew less than normal proportions. While tea, rubber and even oil companies contributed to that rise, the greatest impetus came from the financial demands of the Indian gold fields. Thus, while firms like the Assam Oil Company, the Consolidated Tea and Lands Company, the Imperial Tea Company, and the India Rubber Estates all managed to market issues with values between £100,000 and £1,000,000, the Gold Fields of Mysore drew £691,000, the Mysore Reef Gold £500,000, the Kempinkote Gold Field £275,000, and even firms with names like Coromandel, Dharwai and Jibutil floated issues of over £100,000.

Transport remained vital throughout the period; and railroads were almost as important a component of private finance in India as they were in the foreign sector. On the subcontinent, railroad finance was bolstered immeasurably by government's guarantee of interest payments. From 1859 to 1869 the guarantee stood at five per cent, and even the modified scheme initiated in 1879 left the figure at four per cent, no mean inducement to a potential investor.

To summarize: finance imperialism, in so far as it had substance, was linked to the 'Agriculture and Extractive' industries throughout the dependent empire, to the financial, land and development component of the finance industry in the dependent colonies, and to railroads in India.

Relative measures suggest something about tendencies, and perhaps about relative profit rates; but the Hobson–Lenin argument hinged not on such tendencies, but on the alleged magnitudes committed to the empire. From the relative measure it may be possible to infer that some empire activities were more profitable than others (and those inferences may suggest something about the nature of imperialism), but the total magnitude of the transfers must be examined if one is to conclude that exploitative profits drove the imperial engine. It is after all total profit, not the rate of profit, that is relevant to the argument; and there the evidence is more ambiguous. In the case of the Agriculture and Extractive industries, while almost half of the total flow went into the foreign sector, the empire's share was just above 40 per cent. Of that figure, about two-fifths went to the dependent empire and India, and the proportion shows some tendency to increase, although those gains were concentrated in the dependent colonies. Still, the amount of 'Agriculture and Extractive' finance channelled to colonies with responsible government was substantial, and the foreign sector's share was larger than the entire empire total. Thus, while the dependent empire may well have been a lucrative area for such investment, it is clear that political dominance, although perhaps useful, was not a necessary prerequisite.

In the case of 'Finance', the home market received more than half the total funds, the foreign sector about a quarter, and the empire the remainder divided in a proportion of three to two between self-governing and dependent sectors. For 'Manufacturing' finance, the empire was unimportant, and the dependent portion insignificant. The empire drew hardly more than five per cent, although that fraction tripled in the last pre-war decade. Of that total, nine-tenths went to the colonies with responsible government, leaving hardly more than one-half of one per cent for both India and the dependent colonies. Even in the final decade, when the empire's fraction was almost one fifth, it was Canada growing behind substantial tariff barriers that drew the major share. While both the Australian Smelting Company and Ohlssons' Cape Brewery appear on the list of empire firms issuing blocks of securities valued at more than £100,000 in the years after 1905, 36 of those 38 firms are located in the North American dominion. The Imperial Tobacco Company of Canada by itself attracted £2,635,000; and, although no other firm received as much, a greater total was received by the Dominion's steel industry (Algoma Steel, Canada Iron, Dominion Iron and Steel and the Steel Company of Canada). The empire's share of all 'Trade and Service' finance was less than 10 per cent, but of that sum, the dependent empire drew more than half. The dependent colonies received only a tiny fraction, but India drew more than all of the colonies with responsible government. That latter surprising result was the product of the last five years of the study when the subcontinent's trade sector (Shell was particularly important) drew over £3,000,000.

The home market absorbed about two-fifths of the funds destined for the public utilities, and the foreign sector somewhat more. Of the remaining fifth, the self-governing colonies received about 60 per cent and the dependent regions the remainder. If, however, the years 1910–14 are excluded – a quinquennium that saw the colonies with responsible government absorbing an eighth of all 'Public Utility' finance – the 'dependent' empire outdrew its self-governing equivalent.[43]

For 'Transport', foreign sector demand was by far the most important. It accounted for about a third of the total before 1880, and over 60 per cent thereafter. United Kingdom receipts averaged another 25 per cent, but still the empire received almost one-fifth, and that share increased substantially after the turn of the century. While the bulk went to colonies with responsible government, something less than a third went to the dependent empire, almost all of the latter being to India.

The empire received almost 40 per cent of all government finance, and while most was accounted for by the issues of responsible governments, almost £1 in ten was destined for the dependent empire. Of that sum India received somewhat less than eight per cent and the dependent colonies slightly less than two. As with the 'Agriculture and Extractive', 'Transport' and 'Public Utility' industries in the private sector, it appears that government finance in the dependent empire may have been an important consideration for the few, if not the many, British investors.

V

The Data: The Industrial Composition of Regional Finance

The examination of the industrial and geographic composition of the flows of finance has indicated that at some times, in some places, and in some industries, the dependent empire may have exerted noticeable pressure on British investors and the financial community. A more detailed examination of the data makes it possible to localize the times and places where arguments about the exploitative nature of 'finance capitalism' may not be patently false.

Although the total level of African finance was not high, there were important differences between the flows destined for the dependent empire and those that went to the other sectors. In the case of the 'Agricultural and Extractive' industries, the relative proportions received by the dependent colonies were, the first decade aside, well below continent-wide and even further below the proportions received by the colonies with responsible government. Although the totals were not large, the shares of 'Finance', 'Public Utilities' and 'Transport' received by those dependent colonies were above the 'all continent' average and that of 'Trade and Services' was nearly equal to it. It should, however, be remembered that the 'finance' totals are in Africa, as elsewhere, inflated by receipts of the financial, land, and development firms.

In Asia, the dependent colonies and India developed differently. For the former, the proportion of 'Agriculture and Extractive' finance was high, almost three times the continent average, and it accounted for almost half of all the finance received by those colonies. 'Finance', too, was well above continent averages and accounted for about a fifth of the total transfers to those colonies. Again, it was land and the land-related industries that inflated the total.

The flows to the 'Agriculture and Extractive' sector were a much smaller proportion of the total finance in India than elsewhere in the Asian dependent empire (only one pound in five as compared with almost one-half). Although India's total private receipts were five times those of the dependent colonies, the total amount of 'Agriculture and Extractive' finance was only about three-quarters of that received by those colonial possessions. The 'Trade and Services' proportion, was however, more than one and a half times the Asian average; and perhaps most important, the fraction flowing to transport finance was one and a quarter times the foreign and almost six times the dependent colonial shares. Lastly, the proportion of government issues in total Indian finance was almost twice the level that prevailed in the dependent colonies of Asia and Africa.

VI

Conclusion

If the 'old' empire attracted traders and planters who left Britain to earn their fortunes in the far-flung corners of the imperial domain, its later incarnation is alleged to have appealed to investors who supported entrepreneurs in their attempts to open new markets for the products of British industry and who organized new sources of raw materials for the factories at home. No doubt the romance of empire and the lure of distant places played their part; and it is not possible to deny that to many the 'City', with its satchel of empire securities, appeared far more dynamic and exciting than the bicycle factories of the Midlands. With few exceptions, however, the dependent empire did not draw large quantities of British finance.

By almost any standards, the London securities market was remarkable for the scale of its activity. The sales of new issues alone amounted to £34 billion in 1865 and £192 billion in 1914: £1.5 in 1865 and £4.5 in 1914 for every man, woman and child in the United Kingdom. Over that 50 year period, the British markets directed close to £5 billion of new finance to government and businesses throughout the globe. While Britain itself was the recipient of almost one-third of the total, the remainder poured across the seas. The question, however, still remains: granted that finance was important both to the British economic process and to the psychological well-being of the middle and upper classes, how important was the empire to economy and policy? To answer this question, attention should be directed to those flows that might have been affected by the imperial connection and should exclude the fraction of foreign and domestic finance. The British economy's share was about 30 per cent of the total for the entire period. The foreign portion comes to at least another 45 per cent.

Nevertheless, the £1.2 billion that did go to the empire was no small sum. It is, however, a figure that cannot be taken at face value. Given the ability of the colonies with responsible government to bend the political process for their own benefit, there was little chance for British capitalists to garner more than competitive returns. Those colonies consistently refused to pay for even their share of imperial expenditures, they failed to favour British imports, and they continually pressed the British government to engage in political adventures where the economic profits, if they existed at all, redounded to the benefit of the colonies. The self-governing colonies together accounted for an additional 17 per cent of all new issues. Thus, taken together, the domestic economy, foreign governments and colonies with responsible government accounted for more than 90 per cent of the new funds that passed through the British capital markets. Less than 10 per cent went to the dependent empire. That sum was not, however, distributed evenly across the globe. Of £355 million, Asia drew more than three-quarters and Africa an additional sixth. Oceania absorbed only about two per cent, if Western Australia and the Northern Territories are included among colonies with responsible government; and the dependent colonies in North, Central and South America, the Caribbean and Europe together received about the same share. In aggregate terms, it appears that the dependent empire received such a small share of the capital flow that, under any reasonable set of assumptions, a redirection of those resources to other parts of the world would have only trivially affected the realized rate of return. Moreover, even if those dependent areas had been independent, they would have continued to attract some British finance.

If the dependent empire was alluring to British financiers and savers, the attraction was clearly limited. To the degree that it existed at all, it appears to have been connected in India with 'Transport' and, to a lesser degree, with government finance. In the dependent colonies, the appeal appears to have been associated with investments in the 'Agriculture and Extractive' industries, with 'Finance' and 'Government' of lesser importance. There are, however, no grounds for thinking that, in terms of the volume of finance alone, the dependent empire could have played an important role in shaping the British economy. For some few persons it might well have been important, but those few investments would have had to yield spectacular profits to have provided the engine to drive either the domestic economy or the British political machine.

California Institute of Technology
and
University of California, Santa Barbara

TABLE 1
CAPITAL CALLED UP 1865–1914
(£ thousands)

	UNITED KINGDOM			FOREIGN			EMPIRE		
	Total	Private	Govt	Total	Private	Govt	Total	Private	Govt
							(1) MINIMUM ESTIMATE		
1860-2	91,964	90,530	1,434	64,315	34,782	29,533	41,126	29,332	11,794
1870-1	106,634	99,487	7,147	127,526	86,789	40,737	45,029	21,566	23,463
-2	88,874	70,016	18,858	56,093	27,332	28,761	86,465	13,355	73,110
1880-1	119,433	94,299	25,134	188,669	113,271	75,398	115,334	38,926	76,408
-2	142,396	126,122	16,274	241,012	163,431	77,581	132,928	46,419	86,509
1890-1	109,164	90,256	18,908	153,444	97,953	55,491	82,507	24,938	57,569
-2	176,743	155,036	21,707	143,992	75,189	68,803	81,004	50,571	30,433
1900-1	331,604	152,975	178,629	179,597	139,180	40,417	142,400	58,006	84,349
-2	135,774	96,984	38,790	361,762	247,334	114,428	221,008	134,203	86,805
1910-1	184,921	113,431	71,490	422,090	296,937	125,153	278,443	144,667	133,776
TOTAL	1,487,507	1,089,136	398,371	1,938,501	1,282,198	656,302	1,226,239	561,983	664,261
							(2) INTERMEDIATE ESTIMATE		
1860-2	129,449	128,015	1,434	87,192	50,031	37,161	53,172	41,295	11,877
1870-1	113,634	106,487	7,147	131,288	90,551	40,737	46,257	22,794	23,463
-2	106,328	87,470	18,858	61,967	28,673	33,294	88,813	15,541	73,272
1880-1	135,537	106,871	28,666	224,020	124,163	99,857	122,532	41,258	81,274
-2	171,554	151,973	19,581	290,443	195,731	94,712	148,458	53,494	94,964
1890-1	151,089	127,440	23,649	219,323	143,835	75,488	113,002	44,523	68,479
-2	231,638	202,811	28,827	184,895	99,976	94,919	113,103	72,815	40,288
1900-1	396,715	199,712	197,003	216,181	157,256	58,925	179,031	78,750	100,281
-2	173,902	127,081	46,821	483,503	320,555	162,948	270,991	162,983	108,008
1910-1	218,547	143,922	74,625	558,670	377,301	181,369	352,494	185,818	166,676
TOTAL	1,828,393	1,381,782	446,611	2,467,481	1,588,072	879,410	1,148,851	719,271	768,582
							(3) MAXIMUM ESTIMATE		
1860-2	129,449	128,015	1,434	188,527	64,792	123,735	53,397	41,520	11,877
1870-1	113,700	106,553	7,147	494,971	130,035	364,936	47,014	23,551	23,463
-2	106,328	87,470	18,858	303,422	34,970	268,452	91,313	15,541	75,772
1880-1	135,537	106,871	28,666	262,303	134,628	127,675	122,555	41,281	81,274
-2	171,691	151,973	19,718	307,127	198,274	108,853	148,583	53,619	94,964
1890-1	151,089	127,440	23,649	233,633	148,804	84,829	113,188	44,624	68,564
-2	231,759	202,932	28,827	209,731	103,865	105,866	113,536	73,229	40,307
1900-1	396,765	199,762	197,003	218,846	157,604	61,242	179,160	78,863	100,297
-2	173,911	127,090	46,821	493,569	327,519	166,050	281,609	170,009	111,600
1910-1	218,624	143,999	74,625	560,954	379,118	181,836	355,137	185,835	169,302
TOTAL	1,828,853	1,382,105	446,748	3,273,083	1,679,609	1,593,474	1,505,488	728,072	777,420

ALL CAPITAL

| | | | EMPIRE | | | | | | | | |
| TOTAL | | | RESPONSIBLE GOVERNMENT | | | DEPENDENT GOVERNMENT | | | INDIA | | |
Total	Private	Govt	Total	Private	Govt	Total	Private	Govt	Total	Private	Govt
197,405	154,644	42,761	14,144	3,962	10,182	4,539	2,927	1,612	22,443	22,443	0
279,189	207,842	71,347	30,910	13,069	17,841	2,248	1,701	547	11,871	6,796	5,075
231,432	110,703	120,729	62,338	9,460	42,878	1,219	521	698	22,908	3,374	19,534
423,436	246,496	176,940	85,628	24,882	60,746	7,131	3,773	3,358	22,575	10,271	12,304
516,336	335,972	180,364	100,356	33,812	66,544	6,804	5,093	1,711	25,768	7,514	18,254
345,115	213,147	131,968	57,478	19,820	37,658	4,407	2,275	2,132	20,622	2,843	17,779
401,739	280,796	120,943	45,234	24,151	21,083	16,271	14,387	1,884	19,499	12,033	7,466
653,601	350,161	303,440	105,533	33,537	71,996	16,959	12,957	4,002	19,908	11,512	8,396
718,544	478,521	240,023	162,720	104,856	67,864	20,870	14,053	6,817	37,418	15,294	22,124
885,454	555,035	330,419	207,836	101,866	105,970	34,550	26,396	8,154	36,057	16,405	19,652
4,652,244	2,933,317	1,718,934	872,174	369,415	502,762	114,998	84,083	30,915	239,069	108,485	130,584
269,813	219,341	50,472	16,326	6,061	10,265	5,885	4,273	1,612	30,961	30,961	0
291,179	219,832	71,347	31,172	13,331	17,841	2,383	1,836	547	12,702	7,627	5,075
257,108	131,684	125,424	63,038	9,998	53,040	1,219	521	698	24,556	5,022	19,534
482,089	272,292	209,797	91,207	26,525	64,682	7,364	3,976	3,388	23,961	10,757	13,204
610,455	401,198	209,257	110,071	37,874	72,197	8,258	6,426	1,832	30,129	9,194	20,935
483,414	315,798	167,616	82,411	36,331	46,080	6,926	3,770	3,156	23,665	4,422	19,243
539,636	375,602	164,034	63,139	37,190	25,949	22,750	19,346	3,404	27,214	16,279	10,935
791,927	435,718	356,209	128,987	43,229	85,758	25,082	20,058	5,024	24,962	15,463	9,499
928,396	610,619	317,777	195,481	122,207	73,274	28,862	20,076	8,786	46,648	20,700	25,948
1,129,711	707,041	422,670	263,418	127,918	135,500	47,384	37,198	10,186	41,692	20,702	20,990
5,783,725	3,689,125	2,094,603	1,045,251	460,664	584,586	156,113	117,480	38,633	286,489	141,127	145,363
371,373	234,327	137,046	16,326	6,061	10,265	6,110	4,498	1,612	30,961	30,961	0
655,685	260,139	395,546	32,729	13,888	17,841	2,583	2,036	547	12,702	7,627	5,075
501,063	137,981	363,082	63,038	9,998	53,040	1,219	521	698	27,056	5,022	22,034
520,395	282,780	237,615	91,230	26,548	64,682	7,364	3,976	3,388	23,961	10,757	13,204
627,401	403,866	223,535	110,196	37,999	72,197	8,258	6,426	1,832	30,129	9,194	20,935
497,910	320,868	177,042	82,562	36,432	46,130	6,961	3,770	3,191	23,665	4,422	19,243
555,026	380,026	175,000	63,538	37,589	25,949	22,765	19,361	3,404	27,233	16,279	10,954
794,771	436,229	358,542	129,116	43,342	85,774	25,082	20,058	5,024	24,962	15,463	9,499
949,089	624,618	324,471	196,822	123,548	73,274	38,139	25,761	12,378	46,648	20,700	25,948
1,134,715	708,952	425,763	263,435	127,935	135,500	50,010	37,198	12,812	41,692	20,702	20,990
6,607,424	3,789,786	2,817,642	1,047,991	463,340	584,652	168,490	123,605	44,886	289,009	141,127	147,882

TABLE 2

PERCENTAGE OF PUBLIC AND PRIVATE OF ALL CAPITAL CALLED UP 1865–1914

(1) MINIMUM ESTIMATE

	United Kingdom		Foreign		Total Empire		Total		Responsible Government		Dependent Government		India	
	Private	Govt	Private	Govt	Private	Govt	Private	Govt	Private	Govt	Private	Govt	Private	Govt
1860-2	98.4	1.6	54.3	45.7	71.3	28.7	78.4	28.0	72.0	84.6	64.5	35.5	100.0	0.0
1870-1	93.3	6.7	68.1	31.9	47.9	52.1	74.4	25.6	42.3	57.7	75.7	24.3	57.2	42.8
-2	78.8	21.2	48.7	51.3	15.4	84.6	47.8	52.2	15.2	84.8	42.7	57.3	14.7	85.3
1880-1	79.0	21.0	60.0	40.0	33.8	66.2	58.2	41.8	29.1	70.9	52.9	47.1	45.5	54.5
-2	88.6	11.4	67.8	32.2	34.9	65.1	65.1	34.9	33.7	66.3	74.8	25.2	29.2	70.8
1890-1	82.7	17.3	63.8	36.2	30.2	69.8	61.8	38.2	34.5	65.5	51.6	48.4	13.8	86.2
-2	87.7	12.3	52.2	47.8	62.5	37.5	69.9	30.1	53.4	46.6	88.5	11.5	61.7	38.3
1900-1	46.1	53.9	77.5	22.5	40.7	59.3	53.6	46.4	31.8	68.2	76.4	23.6	57.8	42.2
-2	71.4	28.6	68.4	31.6	60.7	39.3	66.6	33.4	64.4	35.6	67.3	32.7	40.9	59.1
1910-1	61.3	38.7	70.3	29.7	52.0	48.0	62.7	37.3	49.0	51.0	76.4	23.6	45.5	54.5

(2) INTERMEDIATE ESTIMATE

	United Kingdom		Foreign		Total Empire		Total		Responsible Government		Dependent Government		India	
	Private	Govt	Private	Govt	Private	Govt	Private	Govt	Private	Govt	Private	Govt	Private	Govt
1860-2	98.9	1.1	57.9	42.1	77.7	22.3	81.4	18.6	37.1	62.9	72.6	27.4	100.0	0.0
1870-1	93.7	6.3	69.0	31.0	49.3	50.7	75.5	24.5	42.8	57.2	77.0	23.0	60.0	40.0
-2	82.3	17.7	46.3	53.7	17.5	82.5	51.2	48.8	15.9	84.1	42.7	57.3	20.5	79.5
1880-1	78.9	21.1	55.4	44.6	33.7	66.3	56.5	43.5	29.1	70.9	54.0	46.0	44.9	55.1
-2	88.6	11.4	67.4	32.6	36.0	64.0	65.3	34.7	34.4	65.6	77.8	22.2	30.5	69.5
1890-1	84.3	15.7	65.6	34.4	39.4	60.6	69.6	30.4	44.1	55.9	54.4	45.6	18.7	81.3
-2	87.6	12.4	51.3	48.7	64.4	35.6	55.0	45.0	58.9	41.1	85.1	14.9	59.8	40.2
1900-1	50.3	49.7	72.7	27.3	44.0	56.0	65.8	34.2	33.5	66.5	80.0	20.0	61.9	38.1
-2	73.1	26.9	66.3	33.7	60.1	39.9			62.5	37.5	69.6	30.4	44.4	55.6
1910-1	65.9	34.1	67.5	32.5	52.7	47.3	62.6	37.4	48.6	51.4	78.5	21.5	49.7	50.3

(3) MAXIMUM ESTIMATE

	United Kingdom		Foreign		Total Empire		Total		Responsible Government		Dependent Government		India	
	Private	Govt	Private	Govt	Private	Govt	Private	Govt	Private	Govt	Private	Govt	Private	Govt
1860-2	98.9	1.1	34.8	65.2	77.8	22.2	63.2	36.8	37.1	62.9	73.6	26.4	100.0	0.0
1870-1	93.7	6.3	26.3	73.7	50.1	49.9	39.7	60.3	43.8	56.2	78.8	21.2	60.0	40.0
-2	82.3	17.7	11.5	88.5	17.0	83.0	27.5	72.5	15.9	84.1	42.7	57.3	18.6	81.4
1880-1	78.9	21.1	51.3	48.7	33.7	66.3	54.3	45.7	29.1	70.9	54.0	46.0	44.9	55.1
-2	88.5	11.5	64.6	35.4	36.1	63.9	64.4	35.6	34.5	65.5	77.8	22.2	30.5	69.5
1890-1	84.3	15.7	63.7	36.3	39.4	60.6	68.5	31.5	44.1	55.9	54.2	45.8	18.7	81.3
-2	87.6	12.4	72.0	28.0	64.5	35.5	54.9	45.1	59.2	40.8	85.1	14.9	59.8	40.2
1900-1	50.3	49.7	72.0	28.0	44.0	56.0	65.8	34.2	33.6	66.4	80.0	20.0	61.9	38.1
-2	73.1	26.9	66.4	33.6	60.4	39.6			62.8	37.2	67.5	32.5	44.4	55.6
1910-1	65.9	34.1	67.6	32.4	52.3	47.7	62.5	37.5	48.6	51.4	74.5	25.6	49.7	50.3

TABLE 3
ALL CAPITAL CALLED UP BY CONTINENT
(£ thousands)

	United Kingdom	Europe	North America	South America & Caribbean	Africa	Asia	Australia & Pacific	Unknown	Total
				(1) MINIMUM ESTIMATE					
1860-2	91,964	20,036	19,049	16,896	11,702	26,366	11,714	2,001	199,728
1870-1	106,634	20,584	70,484	46,702	2,803	19,578	15,200	2,641	284,626
-2	88,873	11,185	40,913	12,601	16,349	26,434	35,075	1,122	232,552
1880-1	119,432	73,349	85,583	41,275	18,814	27,581	57,451	3,381	426,866
-2	142,396	29,767	90,914	128,895	20,266	36,017	68,251	4,177	520,683
1890-1	109,164	27,013	77,900	42,589	20,254	33,224	34,944	1,298	346,386
-2	176,757	42,930	32,894	29,304	33,823	51,639	34,494	1,983	403,824
1900-1	331,604	19,003	113,869	34,326	89,082	39,137	26,580	553	654,154
-2	135,774	41,307	241,281	124,717	56,207	96,634	22,576	2,181	720,677
1910-1	184,921	64,800	286,910	153,930	40,898	85,908	68,119	3,463	888,949
TOTAL	1,487,519	349,974	1,059,797	631,235	310,198	442,518	374,404	22,800	4,678,445
				(2) MAXIMUM ESTIMATE					
1860-2	129,449	105,826	30,130	23,084	24,291	46,605	13,111	2,489	374,985
1870-1	113,700	172,092	195,840	70,028	35,505	56,115	15,200	2,641	661,121
-2	106,328	43,909	251,374	13,833	16,349	33,645	35,625	1,152	502,215
1880-1	135,537	124,152	95,286	53,223	21,477	30,567	60,203	3,527	523,972
-2	171,691	54,353	103,546	158,214	23,244	41,540	74,983	4,212	631,783
1890-1	151,089	48,649	113,794	60,965	27,798	44,440	51,148	1,652	499,535
-2	231,773	52,561	56,500	42,470	44,923	76,216	50,686	2,497	557,626
1900-1	396,765	30,395	122,242	47,670	112,117	48,889	36,692	567	795,337
-2	173,911	58,318	303,734	168,998	75,587	137,953	30,535	3,072	952,108
1910-1	218,624	107,644	353,636	205,080	52,464	112,862	84,441	5,531	1,140,282
TOTAL	1,828,867	797,899	1,626,082	843,565	433,755	628,832	452,624	27,340	6,638,964

TABLE 4

CAPITAL CALLED UP BY CONTINENT AND TYPE OF GOVERNMENT (MINIMUM)
(£ thousands)

	FOREIGN			TOTAL EMPIRE			TOTAL		
	Total	Private	Govt	Total	Private	Govt	Total	Private	Govt
									AFRICA
1860-2	10,000	1,267	8,733	1,702	306	1,396	11,702	1,573	10,129
1870-1	2,041	1,956	85	763	619	144	2,804	2,575	229
-2	7,254	454	6,800	9,095	80	9,015	16,349	534	15,815
1880-1	3,992	3,892	100	14,822	3,109	11,713	18,814	7,001	11,813
-2	15,722	4,902	10,820	4,545	2,567	1,978	20,267	7,469	12,798
1890-1	12,894	5,249	7,645	7,360	2,080	5,280	20,254	7,329	12,925
-2	17,020	15,404	1,616	16,803	10,678	6,125	33,823	26,082	7,741
1900-1	9,564	7,738	1,826	79,518	26,740	52,778	89,082	34,478	54,604
-2	19,604	16,533	3,071	36,600	15,937	20,663	56,204	32,470	23,734
1910-1	21,774	13,784	7,990	19,100	12,535	6,565	40,874	26,319	14,555
TOTAL	119,865	71,179	48,686	190,308	74,651	115,657	310,173	145,830	164,343
									ASIA
1860-2	2,854	1,036	1,818	23,513	23,314	199	26,367	24,350	2,017
1870-1	7,009	3,626	3,383	12,569	7,494	5,075	19,578	11,120	8,458
-2	3,044	169	2,875	23,390	3,649	19,741	26,434	3,818	22,616
1880-1	1,779	1,688	91	25,802	11,734	14,068	27,581	13,422	14,159
-2	8,680	4,945	3,735	27,337	8,792	18,545	36,017	13,737	22,280
1890-1	10,148	4,527	5,621	23,077	4,143	18,934	33,225	8,670	24,555
-2	30,384	1,461	28,923	21,256	13,396	7,860	51,640	14,857	36,783
1900-1	15,207	1,450	13,757	23,930	14,211	9,719	39,137	15,661	23,476
-2	51,653	8,927	42,726	44,981	21,619	23,362	96,634	30,546	66,088
1910-1	35,670	13,964	21,706	50,239	28,882	21,357	85,909	42,846	43,063
TOTAL	166,428	41,793	124,635	276,094	137,234	138,860	442,522	179,027	263,495
								AUSTRALIA/PACIFIC	
1860-2	0	0	0	11,704	1,860	9,844	11,704	1,860	9,844
1870-1	0	0	0	12,405	3,013	9,392	12,405	3,013	9,392
-2	0	0	0	35,075	3,897	31,178	35,075	3,897	31,178
1880-1	0	0	0	57,401	11,344	46,057	57,401	11,344	46,057
-2	259	63	196	67,972	13,456	54,516	68,231	13,519	54,712
1890-1	40	40	0	34,904	9,519	25,385	34,944	9,559	25,385
-2	375	375	0	34,106	21,357	12,749	34,481	21,732	12,749
1900-1	86	86	0	26,494	6,545	19,949	26,580	6,631	19,949
-2	13	13	0	22,563	6,286	16,277	22,576	6,299	16,277
1910-1	360	360	0	67,731	11,226	56,505	68,091	11,586	56,505
TOTAL	1,133	937	196	370,355	88,503	281,852	371,488	89,440	282,048

RESPONSIBLE GOVERNMENT			DEPENDENT GOVERNMENT			INDIA		
Total	Private	Govt	Total	Private	Govt	Total	Private	Govt
173	60	113	1,529	246	1,283			
192	98	94	571	521	50			
8,965	50	8,915	130	30	100			
13,658	1,945	11,713	1,164	1,164	0			
2,330	625	1,705	2,215	1,942	273	N O T		
6,251	1,577	4,674	1,109	503	606			
7,179	1,587	5,592	9,624	9,091	533	A P P L I C A B L E		
67,419	17,215	50,204	12,099	9,525	2,574			
24,362	9,208	15,154	12,238	6,729	5,509			
1,371	953	418	17,729	11,582	6,147			
131,900	33,318	98,582	58,409	41,333	17,075			

RESPONSIBLE GOVERNMENT			DEPENDENT GOVERNMENT			INDIA		
			1,070	871	199	22,443	22,443	0
			698	698	0	11,871	6,796	5,075
			482	275	207	22,908	3,374	19,534
N O T			3,227	1,463	1,764	22,575	10,271	12,304
			1,569	1,278	291	25,768	7,514	18,254
A P P L I C A B L E			2,455	1,300	1,155	20,622	2,843	17,779
			1,757	1,363	394	19,499	12,033	7,466
			4,022	2,699	1,323	19,908	11,512	8,396
			7,563	6,325	1,238	37,418	15,294	22,124
			14,182	12,477	1,705	36,057	16,405	19,652
			37,025	28,749	8,276	239,069	108,485	130,584

RESPONSIBLE GOVERNMENT			DEPENDENT GOVERNMENT			INDIA		
10,756	912	9,844	948	948	0			
12,405	3,013	9,392	0	0	0			
34,703	3,720	30,983	372	177	195			
55,976	10,558	45,418	1,425	786	639			
66,042	12,190	53,852	1,930	1,266	664	N O T		
34,904	9,519	25,385	--	--	0			
31,474	19,038	12,436	2,632	2,319	313	A P P L I C A B L E		
26,277	6,328	19,949	217	217	0			
22,344	6,067	16,277	219	219	0			
67,361	10,856	56,505	370	370	0			
362,242	82,201	280,041	8,113	6,302	1,811			

TABLE 4 *(Continued)*

	FOREIGN			TOTAL EMPIRE			TOTAL		
	Total	Private	Govt	Total	Private	Govt	Total	Private	Govt
							CARIBBEAN & SOUTH AMERICA		
1860-2	16,270	5,258	11,012	420	390	30	16,690	5,648	11,042
1870-1	46,083	17,416	28,667	619	122	497	46,702	17,538	29,164
-2	12,406	4,215	8,191	196	0	196	12,602	4,215	8,387
1880-1	40,058	29,629	10,429	1,217	262	955	41,275	29,891	11,384
-2	127,969	82,788	45,181	927	443	484	128,896	83,231	45,665
1890-1	42,009	28,317	13,692	581	210	371	42,590	28,527	14,063
-2	27,488	16,854	10,634	1,816	1,172	644	29,304	18,026	11,278
1900-1	33,706	24,642	9,064	620	515	105	34,326	25,157	9,169
-2	124,532	87,206	37,326	185	115	70	124,717	87,321	37,396
1910-1	152,924	103,738	49,186	1,007	704	303	153,931	104,442	49,489
TOTAL	623,445	400,063	223,382	7,588	3,933	3,655	631,033	403,996	227,037
									EUROPE
1860-2	19,363	13,054	6,309	360	360	0	19,723	13,414	6,309
1870-1	20,224	16,690	3,534	360	360	0	20,584	17,050	3,534
-2	11,147	3,011	8,136	39	39	0	11,186	3,050	8,136
1880-1	73,289	8,780	64,509	60	60	0	73,349	8,840	64,509
-2	29,480	14,069	15,411	137	137	0	29,617	14,206	15,411
1890-1	26,750	5,226	21,524	263	263	0	27,013	5,489	21,524
-2	42,931	18,075	24,856	0	0	0	42,931	18,075	24,856
1900-1	19,003	3,632	15,371	0	0	0	19,003	3,632	15,371
-2	41,276	17,060	24,216	32	32	0	41,308	17,092	24,216
1910-1	64,800	22,263	42,537	0	0	0	64,800	22,263	42,537
TOTAL	348,263	121,860	226,403	1,251	1,251	0	349,514	123,111	226,403
									NORTH AMERICA
1860-2	15,623	13,962	1,661	1,315	990	325	16,938	14,952	1,986
1870-1	52,170	47,102	5,068	18,314	9,959	8,355	70,484	57,061	13,423
-2	22,242	19,483	2,759	18,670	5,690	12,980	40,912	25,173	15,739
1880-1	69,551	69,282	269	16,033	12,418	3,615	85,584	81,700	3,884
-2	58,903	56,665	2,238	32,012	21,025	10,987	90,915	77,690	13,225
1890-1	61,604	54,595	7,009	16,296	8,698	7,598	77,900	63,293	14,607
-2	25,796	23,021	2,775	7,098	4,044	3,054	32,894	27,065	5,829
1900-1	102,032	101,632	400	11,837	9,994	1,843	113,869	111,626	2,243
-2	124,686	117,596	7,090	116,595	90,163	26,432	241,281	207,759	33,522
1910-1	146,564	142,829	3,735	140,346	91,299	49,047	286,910	234,128	52,782
TOTAL	679,171	646,167	33,004	378,516	254,280	124,236	1,057,687	900,447	157,240

RESPONSIBLE GOVERNMENT			DEPENDENT GOVERNMENT			INDIA		
Total	Private	Govt	Total	Private	Govt	Total	Private	Govt
			420	390	30			
			619	122	497			
			196	0	196			
			1,217	262	955			
N O T			927	443	484	N O T		
			581	210	371			
A P P L I C A B L E			1,816	1,172	644	A P P L I C A B L E		
			620	515	105			
			185	115	70			
			1,007	704	303			
			7,588	3,933	3,655			
			360	360	0			
			360	360	0			
			39	39	0			
			60	60	0			
N O T			137	137	0	N O T		
			263	263	0			
A P P L I C A B L E			0	0	0	A P P L I C A B L E		
			0	0	0			
			32	32	0			
			0	0	0			
			1,251	1,251	0			
1,102	877	225	213	113	100			
18,314	9,959	8,355	0	0	0			
18,670	5,690	12,980	0	0	0			
15,995	12,380	3,615	38	38	0			
31,984	20,997	10,987	28	28	0	N O T		
16,296	8,698	7,598	0	0	0			
6,581	3,527	3,054	517	517	0	A P P L I C A B L E		
11,837	9,994	1,843	0	0	0			
115,963	89,531	26,432	632	632	--			
139,099	90,052	49,047	1,247	1,247	0			
375,841	251,705	124,136	2,675	2,575	100			

TABLE 5

CAPITAL CALLED UP BY INDUSTRY (ALL LOCATIONS)

(MINIMUM)

(1,000s £'s)

	A&E	Finance	Mfg	Public Utilities	T&S	Transp	Unknown	Total Private	Total Govt	Total
1860-2	5,604	28,570	9,836	8,291	4,773	95,508	1,755	154,337	42,761	197,098
1870-1	16,721	30,982	20,329	15,580	5,146	123,024	1,497	213,279	71,348	284,627
-2	1,842	16,759	5,703	6,057	3,621	76,984	859	111,825	120,728	232,553
1880-1	20,354	37,140	14,345	10,051	7,099	159,059	1,879	249,927	176,940	426,867
-2	29,698	52,338	62,053	11,556	11,524	169,336	3,814	340,319	180,364	520,683
1890-1	16,917	40,035	31,639	7,022	15,203	100,766	2,836	214,418	131,969	346,387
-2	40,436	36,754	80,450	10,649	27,223	83,864	3,424	282,800	120,943	403,743
1900-1	25,198	45,765	47,457	17,475	13,812	199,419	1,589	350,715	303,440	654,155
-2	38,059	53,917	32,078	27,685	16,082	309,277	3,558	480,656	240,023	720,679
1910-1	65,730	87,969	61,350	37,063	18,777	282,427	5,214	558,530	330,419	888,949
TOTAL	260,559	430,229	365,240	151,429	123,260	1,599,664	26,425	2,956,806	1,718,935	4,675,741

(Percents)

	A&E	Finance	Mfg	Public Utilities	T&S	Transp	Unknown	Total Private	Total Govt
1860-2	2.8	14.5	5.0	4.2	2.4	48.5	0.9	78.3	21.7
1870-1	5.9	10.9	7.1	5.5	1.8	43.2	0.5	74.9	25.1
-2	0.8	7.2	2.5	2.6	1.6	33.1	0.4	48.1	51.9
1880-1	4.8	8.7	3.4	2.4	1.7	37.3	0.4	58.5	41.3
-2	5.7	10.1	11.9	2.2	2.2	32.5	0.7	65.4	34.7
1890-1	4.9	11.6	9.1	2.0	4.4	29.1	0.8	61.9	38.1
-2	10.0	9.1	19.9	2.6	6.7	20.8	0.8	69.9	30.1
1900-1	3.9	7.0	7.3	2.7	2.1	30.5	0.2	53.6	46.3
-2	5.3	7.5	4.5	3.8	2.2	42.9	0.5	66.7	33.3
1910-1	7.4	9.9	6.9	4.2	2.1	31.8	0.6	62.8	37.1
TOTAL	5.6	9.2	7.8	3.2	2.6	34.2	0.6	63.2	36.8

A&E: Agriculture & Extractive
Govt: Government
Mfg: Manufacturing
T&S: Trade & Services
Transp: Transportation

TABLE 6

CAPITAL CALLED BY TYPE OF GOVERNMENT AND INDUSTRY (MINIMUM)

(£ thousands)

	A&E	Finance	Mfg	Public Utilities	T&S	Transp	Unknown	Total Private	Total Govt	Total
					UNITED KINGDOM					
1860-2	1,564	18,929	8,442	1,310	3,610	55,617	1,060	90,532	1,434	91,966
1870-1	4,315	16,875	15,531	3,129	4,337	54,415	885	99,487	7,147	106,634
-2	572	11,497	4,715	2,012	3,161	47,816	242	70,015	18,858	88,873
1880-1	2,325	17,481	10,436	3,974	5,560	53,890	633	94,299	25,134	119,433
-2	6,149	29,872	49,354	2,623	9,138	27,215	1,771	126,122	16,274	142,396
1890-1	3,224	18,656	24,638	4,589	14,035	23,629	1,485	90,256	18,908	109,164
-2	2,773	13,477	68,007	7,695	24,388	36,565	2,131	155,036	21,707	176,743
1900-1	1,082	27,950	41,303	14,290	11,136	56,680	535	152,976	178,629	331,605
-2	1,214	23,292	22,053	10,600	8,984	29,168	1,674	96,985	38,790	135,775
1910-1	2,957	42,291	33,247	7,335	11,454	14,519	1,626	113,429	71,490	184,919
TOTAL	26,175	220,320	277,726	57,557	95,803	399,514	12,042	1,089,137	398,371	1,487,508
					FOREIGN					
1860-2	1,526	5,141	548	4,345	580	22,427	10	34,577	29,533	64,110
1870-1	10,336	9,438	3,975	9,371	736	52,902	32	86,790	40,737	127,527
-2	791	1,661	863	2,880	307	20,799	30	27,331	28,761	56,092
1880-1	8,119	10,202	2,496	3,145	584	88,603	123	113,272	75,398	188,670
-2	15,186	11,152	10,828	7,001	1,866	116,947	452	163,432	77,581	241,013
1890-1	10,076	12,271	6,266	1,468	558	66,807	507	97,953	55,491	153,444
-2	20,340	6,991	10,714	2,108	1,158	33,702	176	75,189	68,803	143,992
1900-1	4,547	7,927	3,710	1,507	625	120,603	261	139,180	40,417	179,597
-2	19,516	18,884	5,421	13,556	5,751	183,593	613	247,334	114,428	361,762
1910-1	32,890	23,230	16,322	21,692	2,896	197,836	2,073	296,939	125,153	422,092
TOTAL	123,327	106,897	61,143	67,073	15,061	904,219	4,277	1,281,997	656,302	1,938,299
					ALL EMPIRE					
1860-2	2,160	4,323	335	2,523	584	17,275	20	27,220	11,794	39,014
1870-1	1,436	640	662	3,050	72	15,706	0	21,566	23,464	45,030
-2	303	3,280	65	1,157	35	8,343	172	13,355	73,120	86,465
1880-1	9,014	9,076	791	2,826	745	16,241	233	38,926	76,408	115,334
-2	7,197	10,740	869	1,863	394	25,174	181	46,418	86,509	132,927
1890-1	3,281	9,005	527	916	556	10,330	324	24,939	57,569	82,508
-2	17,065	15,858	1,367	834	1,466	13,598	383	50,571	30,433	81,004
1900-1	19,490	9,853	2,382	1,673	2,042	22,136	431	58,007	84,394	142,401
-2	17,023	11,451	4,191	3,513	1,331	96,407	287	134,203	86,805	221,008
1910-1	28,107	21,849	11,719	7,871	4,402	69,879	839	144,666	133,776	278,442
TOTAL	105,076	96,075	22,908	26,226	11,627	295,089	2,870	559,871	664,262	1,224,133

A&E: Agriculture & Extractive
Govt: Government
Mfg: Manufacturing
T&S: Trade & Services
Transp: Transportation

TABLE 6 *(Continued)*

	A&E	Finance	Mfg	Public Utilities	T&S	Transp	Unknown	Total Private	Total Govt	Total
				RESPONSIBLE GOVERNMENT						
1860-2	134	775	60	0	60	821	0	1,850	10,182	12,032
1870-1	1,201	231	589	1,200	0	9,849	0	13,070	17,841	30,911
-2	98	2,936	10	685	0	5,560	172	9,461	52,878	62,339
1880-1	4,858	6,741	504	1,867	695	10,144	73	24,882	60,746	85,628
-2	4,444	8,587	677	859	323	18,870	52	33,812	66,544	100,356
1890-1	1,969	7,442	499	916	543	8,127	324	19,820	37,658	57,478
-2	10,272	8,594	1,142	315	1,235	2,251	344	24,153	21,083	145,236
1900-1	14,637	3,324	2,164	1,495	810	10,753	353	33,536	71,996	105,532
-2	10,028	4,906	3,803	1,950	548	83,416	205	104,856	57,864	162,720
1910-1	12,896	16,018	11,187	6,247	1,062	53,701	756	101,867	105,970	207,837
TOTAL	60,537	59,554	20,635	15,534	5,276	203,492	2,279	367,307	502,762	870,069
				DEPENDENT GOVERNMENT						
1860-2	1,338	701	176	400	0	293	20	2,928	1,612	4,540
1870-1	149	209	45	844	12	442	0	1,701	547	2,248
-2	105	344	0	7	30	35	0	521	698	1,219
1880-1	877	1,833	56	48	50	760	149	3,773	3,358	7,131
-2	1,670	1,507	0	864	71	943	39	5,094	1,711	6,805
1890-1	558	1,121	0	0	7	588	0	2,274	2,132	4,406
-2	3,902	7,128	125	260	232	2,710	29	14,386	1,884	16,270
1900-1	2,970	6,322	100	92	242	3,154	77	12,957	4,002	16,959
-2	5,559	5,545	61	1,006	100	1,699	82	14,052	6,817	20,869
1910-1	14,195	5,831	329	1,460	290	4,216	74	26,395	8,154	34,549
TOTAL	31,323	30,541	892	4,981	1,034	14,840	470	84,081	30,915	114,996
				INDIA						
1860-2	689	2,847	100	2,123	524	16,161	0	22,444	0	22,444
1870-1	86	200	29	1,006	60	5,415	0	6,796	5,075	11,871
-2	100	0	55	465	5	2,748	0	3,373	19,534	22,907
1880-1	3,279	502	231	911	0	5,337	11	10,271	12,304	22,575
-2	1,084	646	193	140	0	5,361	90	7,514	18,254	25,768
1890-1	753	441	28	--	6	1,614	0	2,842	17,779	20,621
-2	2,891	136	100	258	0	8,637	10	12,032	7,466	19,498
1900-1	1,884	206	118	85	990	8,229	0	11,512	8,396	19,908
-2	1,435	1,000	326	558	682	11,293	0	15,294	22,124	37,418
1910-1	1,016	0	204	164	3,049	11,963	9	16,405	19,652	36,057
TOTAL	13,217	5,978	1,384	5,710	5,316	76,758	120	108,483	130,584	239,067

Dash (--) = No Data

	A&E	Finance	Mfg	Public Utilities	T&S	Transp	Unknown	Total Private	Total Govt	Total
				UNKNOWN						
1860-2	355	178	511	113	0	190	665	2,012	0	2,012
1870-1	634	4,030	161	30	0	0	581	5,436	0	5,436
-2	176	322	59	8	117	25	415	1,122	0	1,122
1880-1	895	382	623	106	210	325	890	3,431	0	3,431
-2	1,166	575	1,002	69	126	0	1,410	4,348	0	4,348
1890-1	337	103	208	50	54	0	520	1,272	0	1,272
-2	258	428	362	13	211	0	733	2,005	0	2,005
1900-1	79	35	62	5	9	0	362	552	0	552
-2	307	290	413	16	16	108	984	2,134	0	2,134
1910-1	1,776	599	63	165	25	193	676	3,497	0	3,497
TOTAL	5,983	6,942	3,464	575	768	841	7,236	25,809	0	25,809
				ALL EMPIRE - AFRICA						
1860-2	48	169	0	0	60	30	0	307	1,396	1,703
1870-1	61	62	0	100	12	384	0	619	144	763
-2	0	50	0	0	30	0	0	80	9,015	9,095
1880-1	1,035	356	68	473	75	970	133	3,110	11,713	14,823
-2	772	333	86	773	85	493	26	2,568	1,978	4,546
1890-1	1,216	554	67	234	3	5	0	2,079	5,280	7,359
-2	1,929	6,322	179	106	399	1,726	16	10,677	6,125	16,802
1900-1	11,895	8,879	2,139	188	934	2,437	269	26,741	52,778	79,519
-2	7,455	5,615	863	1,083	153	683	86	15,938	20,664	36,602
1910-1	3,730	3,484	324	1,358	258	3,373	9	12,536	6,565	19,101
TOTAL	28,141	25,824	3,726	4,315	2,009	10,101	539	74,655	115,658	190,313

TABLE 7*

INDUSTRY RELATIVES BY TYPE OF GOVERNMENT

	UNITED KINGDOM						FOREIGN						EMPIRE					
	A&E	Finance	Mfg	PU	T&S	Transp	A&E	Finance	Mfg	PU	T&S	Transp	A&E	Finance	Mfg	PU	T&S	Transp
1860-2	50	112	152	27	125	98	128	80	26	231	53	104	230	85	20	183	75	101
1870-1	56	131	161	42	165	92	154	84	47	144	32	103	86	23	32	189	32	123
-2	54	109	131	53	130	98	192	40	62	193	33	109	151	215	10	158	26	90
1880-1	31	124	199	104	202	89	91	60	40	69	18	121	293	156	36	180	89	65
-2	57	154	212	61	209	43	109	44	36	125	33	142	183	150	11	117	29	108
1890-1	46	110	183	154	219	55	132	67	43	45	8	144	169	193	16	122	31	88
-2	13	67	154	131	157	79	189	72	50	74	15	150	236	242	9	44	38	90
1900-1	10	140	199	187	185	65	46	44	20	22	11	152	468	130	30	58	89	67
-2	16	214	344	189	276	47	100	68	33	95	69	115	161	76	47	45	30	111
1910-1	23	230	265	97	299	25	96	48	50	110	29	131	169	105	73	82	90	95

	RESPONSIBLE GOVERNMENT						DEPENDENT COLONIES						INDIA					
	A&E	Finance	Mfg	PU	T&S	Transp	A&E	Finance	Mfg	PU	T&S	Transp	A&E	Finance	Mfg	PU	T&S	Transp
1860-2	209	225	53	0	102	71	1,326	129	98	251	0	16	89	68	7	174	73	115
1870-1	119	14	46	122	0	127	113	95	27	663	27	44	16	23	4	198	33	135
-2	69	203	2	132	0	85	1,344	431	0	23	166	10	198	0	32	252	4	117
1880-1	247	182	36	186	96	63	295	326	26	32	45	31	404	33	40	220	0	81
-2	155	165	11	74	28	111	386	192	0	496	40	37	170	56	14	55	0	142
1890-1	128	200	17	140	39	87	316	263	0	0	4	55	341	83	7	0	3	120
-2	297	275	17	34	51	31	190	383	3	48	16	63	168	9	3	57	0	240
1900-1	608	76	48	89	61	56	320	374	6	14	47	43	228	14	8	15	218	126
-2	121	42	55	32	16	123	501	352	7	124	21	19	119	58	32	63	133	114
1910-1	110	97	99	92	31	104	467	136	11	83	33	31	54	0	11	15	550	143

*% in government noted

% in total

A&E: Agriculture & Extractive
Mfg: Manufacturing
PU: Public Utilities
T&S: Trade & Services
Transp: Transportation

NOTE: Issues recorded with no amount called have been excluded.

TABLE 8
CAPITAL CALLED UP BY INDUSTRIES AND BY TYPE OF GOVERNMENT (MINIMUM)
(£ thousands)

	United Kingdom	Foreign	Total Empire	Responsible Government	Dependent Government	India	Total
	(A) AGRICULTURE & EXTRACTIVE						
1860-2	1,564	1,526	2,160	134	1,338	689	5,250
1870-1	4,315	10,336	1,436	1,201	149	86	16,087
-2	572	791	303	98	105	100	1,666
1880-1	2,325	8,119	9,014	4,858	877	3,279	19,458
-2	6,149	15,186	7,197	4,444	1,670	1,084	28,532
1890-1	3,224	10,076	3,281	1,969	558	753	16,581
-2	2,773	20,340	17,065	10,272	3,902	2,891	40,178
1900-1	1,082	4,547	19,490	14,637	2,970	1,884	25,119
-2	1,214	19,516	17,023	10,028	5,559	1,435	37,753
1910-1	2,957	32,890	28,107	12,896	14,195	1,016	63,954
TOTAL	26,175	123,327	105,076	60,537	31,323	13,118	254,578
	(C) MANUFACTURING						
1860-2	8,442	548	335	60	176	100	9,325
1870-1	15,531	3,975	662	589	45	29	20,168
-2	4,715	863	65	10	0	55	5,643
1880-1	10,436	2,496	791	504	56	231	13,723
-2	49,354	10,828	869	677	0	193	61,051
1890-1	24,638	6,266	527	499	0	28	31,431
-2	68,007	10,714	1,367	1,142	125	100	80,088
1900-1	41,303	3,710	2,382	2,164	100	118	47,395
-2	22,053	5,421	4,191	3,803	61	326	31,665
1910-1	33,247	16,322	11,719	11,187	329	204	61,288
TOTAL	277,726	61,143	22,908	20,635	892	1,384	361,777
	(E) TRADE & SERVICES						
1860-2	3,610	580	584	60	0	524	4,774
1870-1	4,337	736	72	0	12	60	5,145
-2	3,161	307	35	0	30	5	3,503
1880-1	5,560	584	745	695	50	0	6,889
-2	9,138	1,866	394	323	71	0	11,398
1890-1	14,035	558	556	543	7	6	15,149
-2	24,388	1,158	1,466	1,235	232	0	27,012
1900-1	11,136	625	2,042	810	242	990	13,803
-2	8,984	5,751	1,331	548	100	682	16,066
1910-1	11,454	2,896	4,402	1,062	290	3,049	18,752
TOTAL	95,803	15,061	11,627	5,276	1,034	5,316	122,491

United Kingdom	Foreign	Total Empire	Responsible Government	Dependent Government	India	Total
(B) FINANCE						
18,929	5,141	4,323	775	701	2,847	28,393
16,875	9,438	640	231	209	200	26,953
11,497	1,661	3,280	2,936	344	0	16,438
17,481	10,202	9,076	6,741	1,833	502	36,759
29,872	11,152	10,740	8,587	1,507	646	51,764
18,656	12,271	9,005	7,442	1,121	441	39,932
13,477	6,991	15,858	8,594	7,128	136	36,326
27,950	7,927	9,853	3,324	6,322	206	45,730
23,292	18,884	11,451	4,906	5,545	1,000	53,627
42,291	23,230	21,849	16,018	5,831	0	87,370
220,320	106,897	96,075	59,554	30,541	5,978	423,292
(D) PUBLIC UTILITIES						
1,310	4,345	2,523	0	400	2,123	8,178
3,129	9,371	3,050	1,200	844	1,006	15,550
2,012	2,880	1,157	685	7	465	6,049
3,974	3,145	2,826	1,867	48	911	9,945
2,623	7,001	1,863	859	864	140	11,487
4,589	1,468	916	916	0	--	6,973
7,695	2,108	834	315	260	258	10,637
14,290	1,507	1,673	1,495	92	85	17,470
10,600	13,556	3,513	1,950	1,006	558	27,669
7,335	21,692	7,871	6,247	1,460	164	36,898
57,557	67,073	26,226	15,534	4,981	5,710	150,856
(F) TRANSPORTATION						
55,617	22,427	17,275	821	293	16,161	95,319
54,415	52,902	15,706	9,849	442	5,415	123,023
47,816	20,799	8,343	5,560	35	2,748	76,958
53,890	88,603	16,241	10,144	760	5,337	158,734
27,215	116,947	25,174	18,870	943	5,361	169,336
23,629	66,807	10,330	8,127	588	1,614	100,766
36,565	33,702	13,598	2,251	2,710	8,637	83,865
56,680	120,603	22,136	10,753	3,154	8,229	199,419
29,168	183,593	96,407	83,416	1,699	11,293	309,168
14,519	197,836	69,879	53,701	4,216	11,963	282,234
399,514	904,219	295,089	203,492	14,840	76,758	1,598,822

TABLE 9a

CAPITAL CALLED UP, INDUSTRIES BY CONTINENTS – ALL GOVERNMENTS

(£ thousands)

	A&E	Finance	Mfg	PU	T&S	Trans	Unknown	Total Private	Govt	Total
					AFRICA					
1860-2	78	709	0	0	560	227	0	1,574	10,129	11,703
1870-1	117	1,349	0	510	12	586	0	2,574	229	2,803
-2	54	250	0	200	30	0	0	534	15,815	16,349
1880-1	1,827	2,576	104	688	194	1,400	213	7,002	11,813	18,815
-2	3,113	1,860	153	998	135	1,154	56	7,469	12,798	20,267
1890-1	4,731	1,451	91	271	170	603	13	7,330	12,926	20,256
-2	9,916	9,781	376	300	698	4,899	111	26,081	7,741	33,822
1900-1	12,839	13,782	3,006	396	934	3,248	274	34,479	54,604	89,083
-2	12,052	14,570	1,207	1,181	251	2,976	236	32,473	23,735	56,208
1910-1	13,782	6,747	481	1,579	258	3,439	58	26,344	14,554	40,898
TOTAL	58,509	53,075	5,418	6,123	3,242	18,532	961	145,860	164,344	310,204
					ASIA					
1860-2	1,394	2,997	275	2,693	524	16,467	0	24,350	2,017	26,367
1870-1	149	2,187	74	2,564	98	6,049	0	11,121	8,458	19,579
-2	206	170	141	513	5	2,784	0	3,819	22,616	26,435
1880-1	3,685	1,688	355	946	0	6,721	27	13,422	14,159	27,581
-2	2,050	2,058	233	213	40	9,050	93	13,737	22,280	36,017
1890-1	1,561	2,161	44	4	10	4,793	96	8,669	24,556	33,225
-2	3,881	491	297	258	11	9,909	10	14,857	36,782	51,639
1900-1	2,986	1,388	118	85	990	9,955	140	15,662	23,476	39,138
-2	5,811	3,928	483	558	702	18,939	126	30,547	66,087	96,634
1910-1	15,846	2,177	1,922	873	3,086	18,880	61	42,845	43,063	85,908
TOTAL	37,569	19,245	3,942	8,707	5,466	103,547	553	179,029	263,494	442,523
					AUSTRALIA/PACIFIC					
1860-2	443	1,180	60	0	0	168	20	1,871	9,844	11,715
1870-1	436	3,004	349	540	0	1,479	0	5,808	9,392	15,200
-2	80	2,947	10	688	0	0	172	3,897	31,178	35,075
1880-1	3,155	4,887	412	1,019	670	1,178	73	11,394	46,058	57,452
-2	3,193	7,896	200	384	264	1,591	12	13,540	54,711	68,251
1890-1	921	6,325	406	452	456	685	314	9,559	25,385	34,944
-2	10,063	8,841	725	66	731	1,008	311	21,745	12,749	34,494
1900-1	3,448	656	98	1,391	108	844˙	86	6,631	19,949	26,580
-2	3,941	1,504	149	60	496	149	1	6,300	16,277	22,577
1910-1	3,158	6,307	84	399	113	1,476	76	11,613	56,505	68,118
TOTAL	28,838	43,547	2,493	4,999	2,838	8,578	1,065	92,358	282,048	374,406

A&E: Agriculture & Extractive
Mfg: Manufacturing
PU: Public Utilities
T&S: Trade & Services
Trans: Transportation

A&E	Finance	Mfg	PU	T&S	Trans	Unknown	Total Private	Govt	Total
					NORTH AMERICA				
573	1,052	0	1,858	32	11,437	0	14,952	1,986	16,938
5,324	2,322	2,508	2,122	0	44,785	0	57,061	13,423	70,484
238	819	320	2,261	38	21,498	0	25,174	15,739	40,913
5,572	7,718	984	736	110	66,570	10	81,700	3,884	85,584
5,096	6,006	8,839	2,214	87	55,106	342	77,690	13,225	90,915
3,929	7,927	5,096	287	64	45,687	303	63,293	14,607	77,900
4,588	2,166	2,620	817	343	16,471	58	27,063	5,829	32,892
2,871	1,918	374	596	178	105,604	85	111,626	2,243	113,869
6,876	3,354	4,386	12,026	453	180,472	193	207,760	33,522	241,282
18,406	14,460	20,376	18,201	1,104	160,525	1,057	234,129	52,781	286,910
53,473	47,742	45,503	41,118	2,409	708,155	2,048	900,448	157,239	1,057,687
				SOUTH AMERICA, CENTRAL AMERICA & CARIBBEAN					
839	466	355	461	0	3,517	10	5,648	11,042	16,690
1,341	889	193	3,359	25	11,709	20	17,536	29,165	46,701
141	599	350	177	84	2,864	0	4,215	8,387	12,602
1,758	1,154	646	636	145	25,540	13	29,892	11,384	41,276
7,080	3,640	821	4,742	1,265	65,564	120	83,232	45,665	128,897
1,530	3,413	322	658	143	22,386	75	28,527	14,063	42,590
3,001	305	1,981	1,209	221	11,233	0	17,950	11,278	29,228
756	21	982	494	15	22,783	106	25,157	9,169	34,326
3,639	6,812	718	1,746	338	74,035	34	87,322	37,396	124,718
4,371	10,299	2,330	5,839	2,246	78,989	368	104,442	49,488	153,930
24,456	27,598	8,698	19,321	4,482	318,620	746	403,921	227,037	630,958
					EUROPE				
360	3,071	193	1,856	48	7,886	0	13,414	6,309	19,723
4,404	3,120	1,514	3,326	674	4,001	11	17,050	3,534	20,584
375	155	108	198	186	1,996	30	3,048	8,136	11,184
1,187	1,254	787	1,947	210	3,436	20	8,841	64,509	73,350
1,852	452	1,602	315	470	9,657	8	14,356	15,411	29,767
685	0	834	712	244	2,983	31	5,489	21,524	27,013
5,957	1,277	6,082	291	621	3,779	69	18,076	24,856	42,932
1,138	15	1,515	218	441	305	0	3,632	15,371	19,003
4,221	167	2,670	1,449	4,841	3,430	314	17,092	24,216	41,308
5,419	5,117	2,873	2,666	491	4,405	1,293	22,264	42,537	64,801
25,598	14,628	18,178	12,978	8,226	41,878	1,776	123,262	226,403	349,665

TABLE 9b

CAPITAL CALLED UP, INDUSTRIES BY CONTINENT & GOVERNMENT

(£ thousands)

	A&E	Finance	Mfg	PU	T&S	Trans	Unknown	Total Private	Govt	Total
					ASIA - FOREIGN					
1860-2	150	150	0	530	0	206	0	1,036	1,818	2,854
.1870-1	30	1,819	0	1,208	38	532	0	3,627	3,383	7,010
-2	0	0	86	48	0	36	0	170	2,875	3,045
1880-1	96	50	124	35	0	1,384	0	1,689	91	1,780
-2	323	908	40	57	15	3,599	3	4,945	3,735	8,680
1890-1	468	875	16	4	0	3,068	96	4,527	5,621	10,148
-2	226	25	180	0	0	1,030	0	1,461	28,923	30,384
1900-1	8	1,069	0	0	0	233	140	1,450	13,757	15,207
-2	1,080	1,021	156	0	19	6,576	75	8,927	42,726	51,653
1910-1	4,686	131	1,582	710	4	6,831	20	13,964	21,706	35,670
TOTAL	7,067	6,048	2,184	2,592	76	23,495	334	41,796	124,635	166,431
					ASIA - INDIA					
1860-2	689	2,847	100	2,123	524	16,161	0	22,444	0	22,444
1870-1	86	200	29	1,006	60	5,415	0	6,796	5,075	11,871
-2	100	0	55	465	5	2,748	0	3,373	19,534	22,907
1880-1	3,279	502	231	911	0	5,337	11	10,271	12,304	22,575
-2	1,084	646	193	140	0	5,361	90	7,514	18,254	25,768
1890-1	753	441	28	0	6	1,614	0	2,842	17,779	20,621
-2	2,891	136	100	258	0	8,637	10	12,032	7,466	19,498
1900-1	1,884	206	118	85	990	8,229	0	11,512	8,396	19,908
-2	1,435	1,000	326	558	682	11,293	0	15,294	22,124	37,418
1910-1	1,016	0	204	164	3,049	11,963	9	16,405	19,652	36,057
TOTAL	13,217	5,978	1,384	5,710	5,316	76,758	120	108,483	130,584	239,067
					ASIA - DEPENDENT GOVERNMENT					
1860-2	555	0	176	40	0	100	0	871	199	1,070
1870-1	33	169	45	350	0	102	0	699	0	699
-2	105	170	0	0	0	0	0	275	207	482
1880-1	310	1,136	0	0	0	0	16	1,462	1,764	3,226
-2	644	504	0	16	25	90	0	1,279	291	1,570
1890-1	341	844	0	0	4	111	0	1,300	1,155	2,455
-2	763	330	16	0	11	243	0	1,363	394	1,757
1900-1	1,094	112	0	0	0	1,493	0	2,699	1,323	4,022
-2	3,297	1,907	0	0	0	1,070	51	6,325	1,238	7,563
1910-1	10,144	2,046	136	0	33	86	32	12,477	1,705	14,182
TOTAL	17,286	7,218	373	406	73	3,295	99	28,750	8,276	37,026

A&E: Agriculture & Extractive
Mfg: Manufacturing
PU: Public Utilities
T&S: Trade & Services
Trans: Transportation

A&E	Finance	Mfg	PU	T&S	Trans	Unknown	Total Private	Govt	Total
				AFRICA - FOREIGN					
30	540	0	0	500	197	0	1,267	8,733	10,000
56	1,288	0	410	0	203	0	1,957	85	2,042
54	200	0	200	0	0	0	454	6,800	7,254
792	2,221	36	215	119	430	80	3,893	100	3,993
2,341	1,528	67	225	50	661	30	4,902	10,820	15,722
3,515	897	23	37	167	598	13	5,250	7,645	12,895
7,987	3,459	198	194	299	3,173	95	15,405	1,616	17,021
944	4,904	867	208	0	811	4	7,738	1,826	9,564
4,597	8,956	344	99	99	2,293	146	16,534	3,071	19,605
10,053	3,263	132	221	0	67	48	13,784	7,990	21,774
30,369	27,256	1,667	1,809	1,234	8,433	416	71,184	48,686	119,870
				AFRICA - RESPONSIBLE GOVERNMENT					
0	0	0	0	60	0	0	60	113	173
0	22	0	0	0	76	0	98	94	192
0	50	0	0	0	0	0	50	8,915	8,965
831	278	68	473	25	270	0	1,945	11,713	13,658
341	68	86	40	39	50	0	624	1,705	2,329
998	277	67	234	0	0	0	1,576	4,674	6,250
199	834	179	0	209	166	0	1,587	5,592	7,179
10,174	2,723	2,039	137	692	1,259	192	17,216	50,204	67,420
5,322	2,129	856	98	53	683	67	9,208	15,154	24,362
374	40	164	0	0	375	0	953	418	1,371
18,239	6,421	3,459	982	1,078	2,879	259	33,317	98,582	131,899
				AFRICA - DEPENDENT COLONIES					
48	169	0	0	0	30	0	247	1,283	1,530
61	40	0	100	12	308	0	521	50	571
0	0	0	0	30	0	0	30	100	130
204	78	0	50	700		133	1,165	0	1,165
430	264	0	733	46	443	26	1,942	273	2,215
218	277	0	0	3	5	0	503	606	1,109
1,730	5,488	0	106	190	1,560	16	9,090	533	9,623
1,721	6,156	100	51	242	1,179	77	9,526	2,574	12,100
2,134	3,486	6	985	100	0	19	6,730	5,509	12,239
3,356	3,444	160	1,358	258	2,998	9	11,583	6,147	17,730
9,902	19,402	266	3,333	931	7,223	280	41,337	17,075	58,412

TABLE 9b (Continued)

	A&E	Finance	Mfg	PU	T&S	Trans	Unknown	Total Private	Govt	Total
					AUSTRALIA/PACIFIC - FOREIGN					
1860-2	--	--	--	--	--	--	--	--	--	--
1870-1	--	--	--	--	--	--	--	--	--	--
-2	--	--	--	--	--	--	--	--	--	--
1880-1	--	--	--	--	--	--	--	--	--	--
-2	0	0	0	0	0	63	0	63	196	259
1890-1	40	0	0	0	0	0	0	40	0	40
-2	375	0	0	0	0	0	0	375	0	375
1900-1	38	0	0	49	0	0	0	87	0	87
-2	13	0	0	0	0	0	0	13	0	13
1910-1	360	0	0	0	0	0	0	360	0	360
TOTAL	826	0	0	49	0	63	0	938	196	1,134
				AUSTRALIA/PACIFIC - RESPONSIBLE GOVERNMENT						
1860-2	98	750	60	0	0	5	0	913	9,844	10,757
1870-1	436	209	349	540	0	1,479	0	3,013	9,392	12,405
-2	80	2,773	10	685	0	0	172	3,720	30,983	34,703
1880-1	2,946	4,305	367	1,019	670	1,178	73	10,558	45,418	55,976
-2	2,954	7,137	200	384	264	1,253	0	12,192	53,852	66,044
1890-1	881	6,325	406	452	456	685	314	9,519	25,385	34,904
-2	8,810	7,528	616	66	700	1,008	311	19,039	12,436	31,475
1900-1	3,289	602	98	1,301	108	844	86	6,328	19,949	26,277
-2	3,860	1,429	94	39	496	149	1	6,068	16,277	22,345
1910-1	2,775	5,978	51	386	113	1,476	76	10,855	56,505	67,360
TOTAL	26,129	37,036	2,251	4,872	2,807	8,077	1,033	82,205	280,041	362,246
				AUSTRALIA/PACIFIC - DEPENDENT GOVERNMENT						
1860-2	345	420	0	0	0	163	20	948	0	948
1870-1	--	--	--	--	--	--	--	--	--	--
-2	0	174	0	3	0	0	0	177	195	372
1880-1	160	581	45	0	0	0	0	786	639	1,425
-2	239	739	0	0	0	275	12	1,265	664	1,929
1890-1	--	--	--	--	--	--	--	--	--	--
-2	878	1,301	109	0	31	0	0	2,319	313	2,632
1900-1	122	55	0	41	0	0	0	218	0	218
-2	68	75	55	21	0	0	0	219	0	219
1910-1	23	301	33	13	0	0	0	370	0	370
TOTAL	1,835	3,646	242	78	31	438	32	6,302	1,811	8,113
				SOUTH AMERICA - FOREIGN						
1860-2	449	466	355	461	0	3,517	10	5,258	11,012	16,270
1870-1	1,286	889	193	3,295	25	11,707	20	17,415	28,667	46,082
-2	141	599	350	177	84	2,864	0	4,215	8,191	12,406
1880-1	1,554	1,154	635	588	145	25,540	13	29,629	10,429	40,058
-2	6,751	3,640	821	4,628	1,265	65,564	120	82,789	45,181	127,970
1890-1	1,530	3,413	322	658	143	22,176	75	28,317	13,692	42,009
-2	2,489	297	1,981	1,140	221	10,726	0	16,854	10,634	27,488
1900-1	723	21	982	494	15	22,301	106	24,642	9,064	33,706
-2	3,578	6,809	718	1,746	338	73,996	21	87,206	37,326	124,532
1910-1	3,794	10,294	2,330	5,750	2,246	78,989	334	103,737	49,186	152,923
TOTAL	22,295	27,582	8,687	18,937	4,482	317,380	699	400,062	223,382	623,444
				SOUTH AMERICA - DEPENDENT GOVERNMENT						
1860-2	390	0	0	0	0	0	0	390	30	420
1870-1	55	0	0	64	0	3	0	122	497	619
-2	0	0	0	0	0	0	0	0	196	196
1880-1	204	0	11	48	0	0	0	263	955	1,218
-2	329	0	0	114	0	0	0	443	484	927
1890-1	0	0	0	0	0	210	0	210	371	581
-2	512	8	0	69	0	507	0	1,096	644	1,740
1900-1	33	0	0	0	0	482	0	515	105	620
-2	61	3	0	0	0	39	12	115	70	185
1910-1	577	5	0	89	0	0	33	704	303	1,007
TOTAL	2,161	16	11	384	0	1,241	45	3,858	3,655	7,513

Dash (--) = No Data

A&E	Finance	Mfg	PU	T&S	Trans	Unknown	Total Private	Govt	Total
NORTH AMERICA - FOREIGN									
537	914	0	1,858	32	10,621	0	13,962	1,661	15,623
4,560	2,322	2,268	1,462	0	36,490	0	47,102	5,068	52,170
220	707	320	2,261	38	15,938	0	19,484	2,759	22,243
4,491	5,523	914	361	110	57,873	10	69,282	269	69,551
3,919	4,624	8,447	1,778	67	37,539	290	56,664	2,238	58,902
3,839	7,086	5,070	58	4	38,245	293	54,595	7,009	61,604
3,307	1,933	2,273	483	18	14,994	13	23,021	2,775	25,796
1,696	1,918	346	538	169	96,954	10	101,631	400	102,031
6,029	1,932	1,532	10,263	453	97,330	56	117,595	7,090	124,685
8,578	4,426	9,404	12,345	155	107,543	378	142,829	3,735	146,564
37,176	31,385	30,574	31,407	1,046	513,527	1,050	646,165	33,004	679,169
NORTH AMERICA - RESPONSIBLE GOVERNMENT									
36	25	0	0	0	816	0	877	225	1,102
764	0	240	660	0	8,295	0	9,959	8,355	18,314
18	113	0	0	0	5,560	0	5,691	12,980	18,671
1,081	2,158	70	375	0	8,697	0	12,381	3,615	15,996
1,149	1,382	392	436	20	17,567	52	20,998	10,987	31,985
90	840	26	230	60	7,442	10	8,698	7,598	16,296
1,262	233	347	249	326	1,077	33	3,527	3,054	6,581
1,175	0	27	58	9	8,650	75	9,994	1,843	11,837
847	1,347	2,853	1,763	0	82,584	137	89,531	26,432	115,963
9,748	9,999	10,972	5,856	949	51,849	679	90,052	49,047	139,099
16,170	16,097	14,927	9,627	1,364	192,537	986	251,708	124,136	375,844
NORTH AMERICA - DEPENDENT GOVERNMENT									
0	113	0	0	0	0	0	113	100	213
--	--	--	--	--	--	--	--	--	--
--	--	--	--	--	--	--	--	--	--
0	38	0	0	0	0	0	38	0	38
28	0	0	0	0	0	0	28	0	28
--	--	--	--	--	--	--	--	--	--
19	0	0	85	0	400	13	517	0	517
--	--	--	--	--	--	--	--	--	--
0	74	0	0	0	558	0	632	0	632
80	35	0	0	0	1,132	0	1,247	0	1,247
127	260	0	85	0	2,090	13	2,575	100	2,675
EUROPE - FOREIGN									
360	3,071	193	1,496	48	7,886	0	13,054	6,309	19,363
4,404	3,120	1,514	2,996	674	3,971	11	16,690	3,534	20,224
375	155	108	195	186	1,961	30	3,010	8,136	11,146
1,187	1,254	787	1,947	210	3,376	20	8,781	64,509	73,290
1,852	452	1,452	313	470	9,522	8	14,069	15,411	29,480
685	0	834	712	244	2,720	31	5,226	21,524	26,750
5,957	1,277	6,082	291	621	3,779	69	18,076	24,856	42,932
1,138	15	1,515	218	441	305	0	3,632	15,371	19,003
4,221	167	2,670	1,449	4,841	3,398	314	17,060	24,216	41,276
5,419	5,117	2,873	2,666	491	4,405	1,293	22,264	42,537	64,801
25,598	14,628	18,028	12,283	8,226	41,323	1,776	121,862	226,403	348,265
EUROPE - DEPENDENT GOVERNMENT									
0	0	0	360	0	0	0	360	0	360
0	0	0	330	0	30	0	360	0	360
0	0	0	4	0	35	0	39	0	39
0	0	0	0	0	60	0	60	0	60
0	0	0	2	0	135	0	137	0	137
0	0	0	0	0	263	0	263	0	263
--	--	--	--	--	--	--	--	--	--
--	--	--	--	--	--	--	--	--	--
0	0	0	0	0	32	0	32	0	32
--	--	--	--	--	--	--	--	--	--
0	0	0	696	0	555	0	1,251	0	1,251

TABLE 10

INDUSTRIAL PROFILES BY CONTINENT*

(Africa and Asia only)

	A&E	Finance	Mfg	Public Utilities	Trade & Services	Trans	Total Private	Govt
				AFRICA - FOREIGN				
1860-2	48	95	0	0	111	108	95	101
1870-1	64	126	0	106	0	46	104	51
-2	118	94	0	118	0	0	191	97
1880-1	78	155	60	56	111	55	262	4
-2	115	125	70	34	56	87	85	109
1890-1	104	86	33	19	139	139	112	93
-2	136	60	93	108	70	110	117	41
1900-1	33	159	129	245	0	112	209	31
-2	75	121	57	17	75	151	146	37
1910-1	139	93	56	27	0	4	98	103
TOTAL	106	105	62	600	77	93	126	77
				AFRICA - RESPONSIBLE GOVERNMENT				
1860-2	0	0	0	0	281	0	259	75
1870-1	0	43	0	0	0	340	56	598
-2	0	214	0	0	0	0	18	103
1880-1	164	39	233	248	46	70	38	137
-2	131	44	690	48	350	52	73	116
1890-1	98	89	358	400	0	0	70	117
-2	33	140	807	0	489	56	29	340
1900-1	159	40	136	73	148	78	66	122
-2	156	51	251	31	75	80	65	147
1910-1	75	16	56	0	0	300	108	86
TOTAL	136	53	281	69	145	68	54	141
				AFRICA - DEPENDENT COLONIES				
1860-2	388	152	0	0	0	84	120	97
1870-1	260	15	0	97	460	259	99	107
-2	0	0	0	0	1,786	0	700	80
1880-1	67	18	0	0	154	301	269	0
-2	53	55	0	281	133	147	238	19
1890-1	67	278	0	0	26	12	125	86
-2	50	161	0	100	78	91	123	24
1900-1	49	162	11	45	93	132	203	35
-2	85	115	3	406	188	0	95	107
1910-1	55	116	78	195	220	198	101	97
TOTAL	60	129	16	193	105	138	151	55

A&E: Agriculture & Extractive
Mfg: Manufacturing
Trans: Transportation
Govt: Government

A&E	Finance	Mfg	Public Utilities	Trade & Services	Trans	Total Private	Govt
			ASIA - FOREIGN				
254	118	0	461	0	29	39	838
62	255	0	144	111	27	91	112
0	0	1,368	210	0	29	39	110
21	24	281	30	0	163	195	10
44	123	47	75	100	110	150	69
57	78	80	192	0	123	171	75
59	52	615	0	0	106	17	134
3	828	0	0	0	25	24	151
64	88	106	0	9	119	55	121
91	18	251	255	0	111	78	123
80	136	236	127	6	97	62	126
			ASIA - INDIA				
54	103	36	86	105	107	108	0
100	15	57	64	100	147	101	99
56	0	43	103	100	112	102	100
116	39	85	127	0	104	93	106
97	57	153	119	0	108	77	114
147	62	200	0	200	103	53	117
92	33	40	124	0	108	214	54
86	20	125	140	137	112	145	70
49	50	131	200	196	119	129	86
17	0	27	50	258	165	91	109
58	51	59	108	158	122	112	92
		ASIA - DEPENDENT GOVERNMENT					
1118	0	1836	41	0	17	88	245
362	123	914	217	0	27	176	0
707	1373	0	0	0	0	397	50
77	617	0	0	0	0	93	107
338	263	0	81	667	11	214	30
146	261	0	0	300	15	203	64
215	733	60	0	800	27	269	· 31
212	46	0	0	0	87	168	55
274	234	0	0	0	27	265	24
220	322	24	0	4	2	176	24
286	235	59	29	10	20	192	38

FIGURE 1
CAPITAL CALLED UP – INTERMEDIATE ESTIMATE
Logarithmic scale
1,000s Constant £'s
1913 = 100
5 Year Moving Average

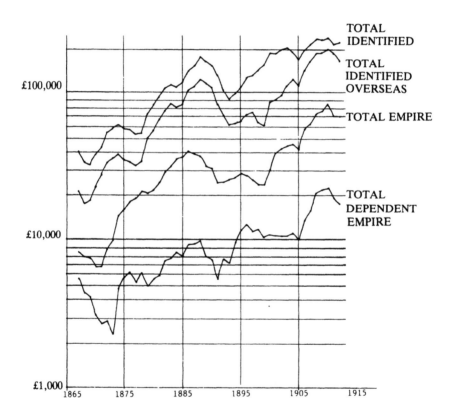

FIGURE 2

EMPIRE CAPITAL CALLED UP AS A FRACTION OF ALL OVERSEAS CAPITAL
CALLED

(5 Year Moving Average of a 5 Year Moving Average)

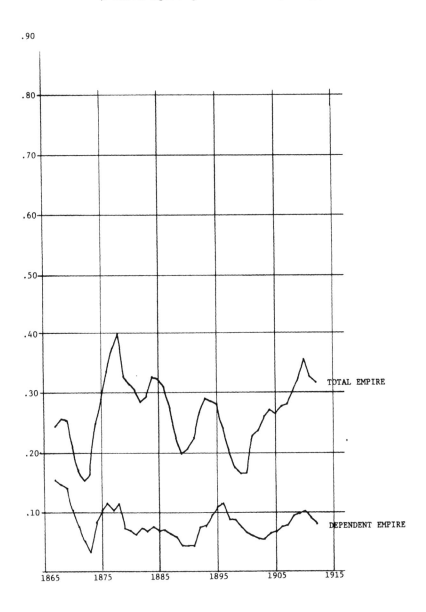

NOTES

1. J.A. Schumpeter, *Business Cycles: A Theoretical and Statistical Analysis of the Capitalist Process*, (New York, 1939) 2 vols., Vol. I, pp.398, 430–431.
2. Ibid., 430–431.
3. J.S. Mill, *Principles of Political Economy* (London, 1907 edition), p.739.
4. Karl Marx, *Capital: A Critique of Political Economy* (Chicago: 1909 edition), 3 vols., Vol. III, pp.278–9, 300.
5. Marx, *Capital*.
6. Alfred Marshall, *Memorials*, (London, 1890), pp.415–6.
7. J.A. Hobson, *Imperialism: A Study* (repro. Ann Arbor, 1967), p.40.
8. F. Engels, *Engels on Capital* (New York: International Publishers, 1937), p.117. Rosa Luxemburg, quoted in K.J. Tarbaum, *The Accumulation of Capital – An Anti-Critique* and Nicolai Bukharin, *Imperialism and the Accumulation of Capital* (New York, 1972), p.253. V.I. Lenin, *Imperialism. The Highest Stage of Capitalism* (New York, 1972), p.253.
9. Lenin, *Imperialism*, p.64.
10. Ibid., p.89.
11. Joseph Chamberlain, speech to the Birmingham jewellers and silversmiths, quoted in *The Times*, 1 April 1895.
12. R.V. Kubicek, *The Administration of Imperialism: Joseph Chamberlain at the Colonial Office* (Durham, 1969), pp.68–91. For a detailed discussion of British subsidies to the colonies see: Richard M. Kesner, *Economic Control and Colonial Development: Crown Colony Financial Management in the Age of Joseph Chamberlain* (Westport, 1981).
13. Matthew Simon, 'The Pattern of the British Portfolio Foreign Investment, 1865–1914', in A.R. Hall, *The Export of Capital from Britain* (London, 1968); Herbert Feis, *Europe, The World's Banker* (London, 1930); Leland Jenks, *The Migration of British Capital to 1875* (New York, 1927); Alexander Cairncross, *Home and Foreign Investment, 1870–1913* (Cambridge, 1953); Harvey Segal and Matthew Simon, 'British Foreign Capital Issues', *Journal of Economic History*, Dec. 1961. For a useful overview, consult J.C. Wood, *British Economists and the Empire* (New York, 1980).
14. M. Edelstein, *Overseas Investment in the Age of High Imperialism* (1982), pp.313–14. Depending on the measure chosen, the correlation between the series ranges from .74 to .80, with associated r^2s between .54 and .64.
15. D.C.M. Platt, 'British Investment Overseas at the End of 1913', *Economic History Review*, forthcoming.
16. An analysis of all bond issues for 18 of the 31 years between 1882 and 1912 shows that for government bonds there is little to choose between home, responsible colonies and the dependent empire. Maturities between 1885 and 1912 averaged about 34.5 years (the dependent empire was highest at 35.4 and the colonies with responsible government lowest at 33.4 years). Foreign government maturities were much lower (22.4 years). In the private sector, however, the United Kingdom aside, the results were very different. In the case of railroads, for example, maturities averaged 29.8 in the dependent Empire, 31.2 in the colonies with responsible government, 26.0 in India, but 56.2 in the foreign sector.
17. In the case of the inferred calls, if the first report is on the third call of an issue, we assume that the first and second calls were made in the months preceding. Similarly, if calls two and five are reported, we assume that calls three and four were made during the intervening period.
18. Platt, 'British Investment'.
19. Based on the records of 482 British firms dealing on the domestic, foreign and imperial markets.
20. It might be noted that both half decades fall in the period covered by Simon's extension.
21. It is very difficult to determine what fraction of these loans was actually financed by the British. C.K. Hobson, for example, reports that in the case of the indemnity loan of 1872 the amount was 'covered five times over by the French capitalists and seven times

over by foreign subscriptions, principally from England and Germany', *The Export of Capital,* (London, 1919), p.138. Simon claims his adjustments are more accurate, but does not explain how they were made. For the entire period the ratio of intermediate to minimum and maximum to minimum was:

	I/M	M/M
UK	123	123
For	126	153*
Emp	121	123
RG	119	120
DG	136	146
India	119	120

*122 without 1865–74

22. Peter J. Buckley and Brian R. Roberts, *European Direct Investment in the USA Before World War I,* (New York: 1982), pp.12–13.
23. Finance imperialism, in the context utilized in this article, refers to the Marxist formulations in which ever-increasing flows of capital pour into the colonies of the dependent empire as capitalists desperately seek new markets. In the familiar words of J.A. Hobson: ' . . . the financial interest has those qualities of concentration and clear-sighted calculation which are needed to set imperialism to work . . . '
24. The 'intermediate' measure indicates a slight increase in the share of the domestic and foreign sectors and a small decline in that of the empire sector. The maximum measure displays an overall increase of about five per cent for the foreign sector with a decline in domestic of 2.5, and in empire of about three, per cent.
25. The European sector includes all of Russia and excludes the United Kingdon and Ireland. Mexico is considered part of North America, and Africa is defined to include also the Ottoman Empire, Syria, Persia and Aden.
26.

SIMON RELATIVES BY CONTINENT
All continents AVG of Min. and Max. = 10

Year		Europe	N. America	S. America	Africa	Asia	Australasia
1860	2	86	103	92	101	125	93
1870	1	173	85	87	44	60	82
	2	187	54	138	139	101	145
1880	1	53	122	97	121	126	126
	2	74	98	141	74	102	86
1890	1	63	120	86	92	91	118
	2	49	144	66	125	109	105
1900	1	86	93	89	115	111 ·	87
	2	100	88	99	127	113	105
1910	1	114	113	86	99	93	72
Avg. All Yrs.		93	93	91	110	107	102

27. Edelstein, *Overseas Investment,* pp.270–87.
28. C. Lewis, 'British Railway Companies and the Argentine Government', in D.C.M. Platt (ed.), *Business Imperialism,* (Oxford: 1977), p.412.
29. Carnarvon Papers PRO 30/6 vol. 17 (6) no. 21, Carnarvon to W.H. Smith, 25 March 1877.
30. A correction for that political revision would raise the share of the foreign sector to something well in excess of one-half.
31. Gladstone Papers, British Library, Add. MS. 44224, f. 137, Kimberley to Gladstone, 22 May 1871.

32. Lenin, *Imperialism*, p.78.
33. For a government engaged in a wide variety of activities there is no clear connection between the funds received and the uses to which they were (or are) put. Since most governments are engaged in a great many activities it is simple to sell bonds for one purpose, use those funds to replace some existing expenditure, and utilize those released funds for any purpose at hand. A study of South American finance in the nineteenth century suggests just how creative those governments could be. Only a study of the government budgets can provide a clue as to the redirections of economic activity within the government sector. Of course, a similar shift within a budget can distort private allocation as well. However, it is only recently with the rise of the conglomerate that we have seen funds raised for the steel industry invested in petroleum production.
34.

PERCENTAGE OF PRIVATE FINANCE BY INDUSTRY 1865–94

	A & E	Mfg.	Transp.	Fin. and PU	All Else
Capital Call (Minimum)	10.0	4.1	66.3	18.3	1.3
Segal/Simon	9.4	3.5	68.3	17.4	1.3

35. As noted: many of the private issues had government guarantees. The history of the government guarantees of the railroads in India is well known; however, there was hardly a foreign railroad outside the United States that was not the recipient of some government guarantee or subsidy. Some lines even within the USA were assisted in this way. These arrangements were not always honoured; however, the pervasiveness of these guarantees is suggested by the fact that as late as 1903, of the 121 non-US foreign railways whose issues traded on the London exchange, 74 still had some official support.
36. Cited in Clark C. Spense, *British Investments and the American Mining Frontier 1860–1901*, (Ithaca, 1958), p.86. The firm was the Cassels Gold Extracting Company.
37. *The Statist*, 18 July 1885, cited in W. Turrentine Jackson, *The Enterprising Scot*, (Edinburgh, 1968), p.154.
38. Ibid., p.137.
39. Ibid., p.154.
40. Of the total foreign railroad investment, North America accounted for 44 per cent and South America for an additional 20 per cent.
41. Typescript manuscript, 'The Forty Years of the Peruvian Corporation, 1896–1936', deposited with the Records of the Peruvian Corporation at University College, London.
42. Ibid., pp.21–22.
43. That surge was attributable to the activities of Canadian telephone (particularly Bell of Canada) and electric utilities (including Toronto, Northern and Canadian Western).

Canada and Argentina: the First Preference of the British Investor, 1904–14

by

D. C. M. Platt

'With the exception of the United States,' said Sir George Paish shortly before the First World War, 'our greatest investments are in the daughter States of the Empire and in our great Indian possessions.'[1] His total of £3.7 billion for Britain's aggregate investment abroad on 31 December 1913 was distributed as follows: £754.6 million for the United States, £515 million for Canada and Newfoundland, £378 million for India and Ceylon, £370 million for South Africa, £332 million for Australia, and £320 million for Argentina.[2] These, Paish indicated, were the main targets for investment, and he supplied estimates for every other destination: Europe, the Americas, Africa, the Middle East, South Asia and the Far East. Paish's calculations were energetic and impressive, and his figures, compiled three-quarters of a century ago, have become the base for 'direct' estimates ever since – not only for the distribution of British investment by country, but also by function.

Yet it is one (among many) of the consequences of Paish's estimates that priorities in the destination and character of Britain's overseas investment during its Golden Age, 1904–12, have been misunderstood. Paish, when he made the claims quoted at the head of this article, was referring to the *aggregate* of British investment overseas right back into the nineteenth century. His prose is misleading, and he sometimes got it wrong himself. But his original intention was to produce an aggregate – what Britain had invested abroad since overseas investment began. He did not mean to suggest *net* figures for securities held at the time he delivered his papers, 1909, 1911 and 1914.[3]

Fashions change, securities move freely between investors, some investments are repatriated, others are sold, bought and re-sold, loans are repaid. Although it must have been true, for the half-century before 1914, that in aggregate the larger part of British investment found a home in the United States, India, and in the 'white' Dominions, it was no longer the case that *new* investment during the Golden Age followed the same path. It was also true, in aggregate and over Paish's 50–60 years (1865/70–1914) that the share of government bonds and railway securities in total investment was overwhelmingly large, but the distribution was no longer so obvious for the decade before the First World War. John Dunning followed Herbert Feis, who in turn followed (and misunderstood) Paish, when he claimed that, in 1913, 40 per cent of Britain's investment portfolio overseas was in railways, and 30 per cent in government and municipal securities.[4] This might have been correct for the accumulated figures of over half a century, but national, federal, state and municipal securities were always the first to return to the domestic investor, and it is unlikely that as much as 30 per cent of the British portfolio remained in these categories as late as the end of 1913.[5] By 1914 perhaps half of Britain's holdings of US railway securities had returned to the United States or were sold to other, non-British investors, and almost as much of the British railway system in India had been bought up by domestic investors, both native and foreign.

Many changes took place in the direction of the market that are concealed in aggregates. A list of portfolio and direct investment for the end of December 1913, net holdings, would show a distinctly different pattern. One figure (for aggregate investment) is not necessarily better or more useful than another (for net holdings on a particular date); it is just different. On 31 December 1913 investment portfolios might have shown traces of South African mines from the 'Kaffir Circus' of the mid 1890s, Japanese government loans from the Russo-Japanese war, Chinese bonds of the new Republic, Chilean, Mexican and Brazilian government stock, Russian national and municipal bonds, shares in new enterprises for the development of tea and rubber plantations and the extraction of oil. But it would no longer seem so evident that, from the turn of the century, 'the placements of U.K. financial savings abroad were first skewed so that the savings flowed towards the Empire'.[6] An automatic association of Britain's 'white' Dominions (Canada, Australia, New Zealand, South Africa) – as if each developed in the same way, at the same pace, and at the same time[7] – is perhaps rather old-fashioned, an imperial relic and less obvious than the association of the two new favourites on the London market, both temperate regions of recent European development, but one (Canada) a British Dominion and the other (Argentina) most certainly not.

I

It is not simply a question of the preference of British investors for such regions. Ragnar Nurkse includes within the category of regions of recent settlement the 'spacious, fertile and virtually empty plains of Canada, the United States, Argentina and other "new" countries in the world's temperate latitudes'.[8] At one time or another these countries, including Australia, South Africa, Chile, New Zealand and Southern Brazil, were immensely and obviously attractive to the British investor in search of political stability, economic security, protection within the law. But the United States had relatively less need for foreign capital from the last decades of the nineteenth century, and Australia was out of the market for two decades after the financial crisis of 1893. When so much money could be mobilised at home, neither the United States nor Australia looked first for their money abroad. On a smaller scale, the same could be said for New Zealand after the 1880s.[9] Australia did not return to the London financial market until 1912; Australia's capital imports, still only £1.2 million in 1911, rose to a total of £31.8 million over the next three years.[10] But for the longer period, back to the renewal of Britain's interest in overseas investment in 1904, it was Canada and Argentina that attracted the British investor. Furthermore, it was Canada and Argentina that actually took the trouble to ask for the money that the investor might have on offer.

Argentina's approach to the international money market gained substance only in the 1880s, and Canada followed nearly 20 years later. But the strength of their appeal (at the peak of renewed foreign investment) can be seen in Table 1. Habits and existing contacts kept investment flowing towards the United States, and there was a fashion for Brazil in 1911–13 (although some of the American securities and many of the Brazilian loans were sold in London merely for investment by Frenchmen, Belgians and Germans). British investors, on the other hand, looked more eagerly to Canada and Argentina. Canada, said J.A. Hobson as far back as 1906, was 'conscious, uproariously conscious, that her day has come ... The poor relation has come into her fortune'.[11] Did not Canada (in 1912) 'possess to a marked degree the three elemental forms of wealth, viz., material wealth, the wealth of labour, and the wealth of credit?'[12] Argentina's national ideal, as explained by Carlos Pellegrini, Senator, newspaper proprietor and former President (in his *North American Letters*, 1904), was 'to be tomorrow what the U.S. is today, and to occupy in the world some day the position which that country occupies already'. It was the rhetoric of a politician, but John Fogarty is right to describe the Argentine pampas before the First World War as a fast-growing region heavily dependent on imports of capital and labour which 'stood pre-eminent amongst the regions of recent settlement'.[13] When, by 1913, London's overseas investment had begun to fall off, Argentine securities still maintained their popularity in a generally suspicious market. A City of Buenos Aires issue (for £2.5 million) was 'largely oversubscribed ... a result which has not often been experienced during the past twelve months'.[14] The general decline in overseas investment was bound to affect Argentina as it did other major borrowers (including Canada), and 1913 was a relatively modest year for Argentina's foreign borrowing. But Argentina's credit was remarkably strong, 'exceeded by none', said Harold Peters, 'except the old nations of Europe', and Argentine public credit was such that money could be borrowed abroad at 4½ per cent.[15]

The contrast with Australia was remarkable. Australia drew heavily on the London market up to the financial crisis of 1893, but thereafter Australia had been thrown back on the sufficiently ample resources of the domestic investor; there was no room for British capital. Ultimately, the market for foreign capital revived. But as late as April 1913 Robert Lucas Nash, a distinguished London financial journalist who had become editor of the Sydney *Daily Telegraph,* reminded the Dominion Royal Commis-

TABLE 1

DESTINATION OF NEW CAPITAL ISSUES TO SELECTED FOREIGN COUNTRIES,
LONDON 1908–1913 (£ millions)

	Argentina	Australia and New Zealand	Brazil	Canada	India and Ceylon	United States
1908	15.0	4.0	13.0	27.8	13.1	21.5
1909	21.7	11.4	9.2	26.8	15.3	15.9
1910	22.9	13.4	11.8	36.9	18.0	39.6
1911	16.7	3.3	19.2	41.2	5.2	21.3
1912	20.1	13.5	14.4	47.0	3.7	23.6
1913	12.0	18.6	15.1	44.1	3.8	18.7

Source: *Investor's Monthly Manual*, annually. These figures have been much refined since then, but they remain useful for comparative purposes as they come (1908 onwards) from a single source and cover Britain's new portfolio investment in most countries. Matthew Simon has reworked the figures for Canada in 'New British Investment in Canada, 1865–1914', *Canadian Journal of Economics* 32 (1970), 248; Irving Stone has used Simon's data to rework the Argentine figures: 'British investment in Argentina', *Journal of Economic History* 3,2 (1972), 546; Simon, again, has produced a refined set of figures for Australia in his paper 'The pattern of new British Portfolio Investment 1865–1914' in J.H. Adler (ed.), *Capital Movements and Economic Development* (New York, 1967), p.56; and the best Australian figures were compiled by N.G. Butlin, *Australian Domestic Produce, Investment and Foreign Borrowing, 1861–1938/9* (Cambridge, 1962), pp.405–44. Unfortunately there are no directly comparable figures for Brazil, India and Ceylon, and the United States.

sion that the total amount of British capital in Australia – government and municipal loans and public companies – had actually *fallen* from £387 million in 1902 to £370 million in 1912.[16]

II

The great era for the Argentine economy was the first 30 years of the twentieth century, from the establishment of free convertibility of the paper peso into gold (in 1899) to the beginning of the slump in 1929. Back in the second half of the 1880s Argentina had enjoyed an investment boom for which borrowing reached some £140 million, about half raised through London.[17] But by 1889 European markets had grown suspicious, and credit collapsed altogether during and after the Baring Crisis of 1890–91. Recovery began in the mid 1890s, aided by a strongly favourable development in Argentina's terms of trade (129.7 for 1905–9 and 129.8 for 1910–14, calculated on the base year 1890).[18] Conditions were almost as favourable for the late 1920s (125.3 for 1925–9), and the areas both sown to wheat and turned over to cattle reached their peak just before the slump.[19] In 1910 skilled labour commanded a better wage in Argentina than in Southern Europe, more even than in most parts of Britain and the United States. Foreign borrowing was not restored until 1904, but interest rates fell from 6 per cent in the 1880s to 4.75 per cent in 1909 (and they were to fall even further by 1914). The Argentine population doubled from 3.9 million at the time of the census of 1895 to 7.9 million in the census of 1914. GNP, from the late 1890s to the outbreak of the First World War, increased at an annual rate of 6 per cent. David Rock explains how, for contemporaries just before the war, Argentina 'as a society of white immigrants undergoing almost breakneck economic growth ... no longer seemed part of Latin America',[20] and the point was not lost on the British investor.

During the decade leading up to the First World War, Argentina, although no member of the 'master race', enjoyed a place in the affections of the British investor superior to every part of the Empire other than Canada. In 1914 the population of Argentina was very similar to Canada's (7.2 million in 1911), although Buenos Aires (with a population of 1.6 million) was almost three times the size of Canada's largest city, Montreal. Argentina's net immigration for 1901–10 was 1,120,000,[21] and although Canada was to experience a very large increase in the three years 1911–13 (a net 0.6 million), the net increase over the whole of the previous decade was also only 600,000.[22]

However, whatever the differences in so many respects, both Argentina and Canada, as temperate regions of recent European settlement, stable in politics, vastly expanding, anxious for capital and ready to pay for it, were tailor-made for the British investor. Canada, bound by race and tradition to British investors and so prominently part of the British Empire, had advantages in London and in Britain's provincial money markets denied to Argentina, and it is a reflection of the remarkable strength of Argentina's position that, for a few years, independent Argentina was second only to Canada for new British investment overseas. Canada's success was overwhelming. Like Argentina at the time, Canada was at the peak of its performance. By the usual criteria for overall economic growth, Penelope Hartland found that Canada had 'grown faster between 1900 and the outbreak of World War I than in any other period since the Act of Confederation in 1867.'[23] The production of wheat, for example, rose from an annual average of 38.3 million bushels in 1885–9 to 197.1 million in 1909–14 (50 million more than Argentina's).[24]

Canada, like Argentina, built its boom on the back of improved communications (shipping and railways), more favourable terms of trade, and modern production techniques. Conditions were ideal in world markets, and money could be borrowed readily and at a low price. Argentina took full advantage, and less than a fifth of its funded debt in 1914 was held within the Republic.[25] Argentina's borrowing continued until the slump. Kenneth Buckley is right to identify a substantial decline after 1912/13 in the availability of outlets for imported capital in Canada.[26] Canadians must indeed have been surprised by the scale of domestic capital resources shown by the demands of war finance in 1914–18, a scale that another Dominion, Australia, had been driven to recognise and exploit ever since the cut-off in British investment after the financial crisis of 1893.

III

It would be right, then, to say that from 1904 the priorities of British investors had shifted. The notion that when foreign investment revived Britons simply resumed their previous preference for US and Empire lending, though commonly held,[27] is difficult to maintain. The United States, historically, had strong attractions for the British investor. But the huge figure attached to British holdings of US securities just before the war has much to do with the confusion that surrounds Paish's aggregate estimates. Herbert Feis, after all, who used Paish's figures, felt able to maintain that the volume of British capital invested in the United States 'was probably never greater than 1913 – well over a third of the whole British investment outside the empire',[28] and where Feis went the textbooks have followed.[29] It is not difficult to prove him wrong.[30]

If we were to consider not the aggregates of half a century but rather the pattern of preference and distribution of Britain's *new* overseas investment 1904–12, then Canada and Argentina, which were virtually unknown to the British investor before the 1880s, came close to the United States on the list. The reasons are sufficiently obvious, although they are highlighted by the scale of Britain's imports from both countries over the period (see Table 2). There were differences, however, in the

TABLE 2

TOTAL CONSIGNMENTS (IMPORTS), VALUES RETAINED IN THE UK
(£ millions)

	1909	1910	1911	1912	1913
Argentina	31.4	27.8	26.2	39.4	40.7
Canada	24.4	24.7	23.6	25.7	29.4

Source: U.K. Trade and Navigation Accounts, rounded to the nearest hundred thousand.

relationship between Britain, Canada and Argentina which, whatever the state of affairs in 1904–14, tended over a longer period to draw them apart. Most obviously, Canada was a British Dominion. Although autonomous in most respects, Canada did not have (or rather, did not feel itself to have) the same liberty of action as the independent republic of Argentina. Before 1914 the Canadian public authorities preferred to issue their loans through branches of Canadian financial institutions in London, notably the Bank of Montreal. This was to the exclusion even of the domestic investor. 'There is no doubt,' Ian Drummond explains, 'that, except for Ontario, when the Canadian provinces thought of borrowing they automatically thought of London.'[31] Even just before the slump, Canada was slow to take advantage of its domestic capital resources by contrast with others of the British Dominions. British residents still held over 50 per cent of the share capital of Canada and Newfoundland in 1930, at a time when they had as little as 21 per cent in Australasia.[32]

Argentina never felt the same constraint; the independent Republic borrowed when and where it felt best able. Out of a £10 million government loan issued internationally in February 1909, just under £3 million were reserved for London and the remainder allotted to Paris, Berlin and New York.[33] The 'New Argentine Loan' of 1911, which it was hoped (in London) would find a home with Barings, was bid for successfully by a rival group of Continental houses, French and Belgian, under the direction of the *Banco Español del Rio de la Plata*.[34] These were government issues, but the same was true of private approaches to the market. Argentine railways, traditionally the stronghold of British investors, were favourites also on the Continent. Continental investors had absorbed some of the government-owned railways transferred to the bondholders after the Baring Crisis in the early 1890s. By the mid-1900s it was 'generally understood' that a considerable part of the share capital of Argentine railways was held in Buenos Aires.[35] A second wave of Continental finance was generated shortly before the war by the operations of Percival Farquhar, the American financial entrepreneur; Farquhar's Argentine Railway Company, most active between 1913 and 1915, 'served as a channel for European finance into London-registered lines.'[36] Continental investors, in fact, were deeply interested in Argentine securities at a time when they gave little thought to Canadian.

Cornelius Rozenraad, President of the Federation of Foreign Chambers of Commerce (London), made some powerful points during the discussion that followed Paish's first paper to the Royal Statistical Society (1909). He asked how much of the £716 million of capital currently quoted for British portfolio investment in South and Central America was actually British.

> How many millions of this amount, how many shares in Argentine, Brazilian, Peruvian and other companies, which have their head offices in London, are now in the hands of foreigners? Great Britain acts only for those loans as intermediary, as honest broker working in all parts of the world ... Although the investment power of Great Britain is very great, London is the principal intermediary between Europe and other parts of the world for the placing abroad of foreign securities issued here.[37]

Quite obviously the activity on the London market tends to confuse and mislead. Equally obviously, if British investment alone is considered, the proportion of Canadian securities issued and actually taken in London was likely to have been far higher than Argentina's.

This was to be expected, and it had nothing to do with imperial preference. Government direction of overseas investment was unknown in London before the First World War. It is true that the Colonial Stock Act of 1900 made Dominion government stock eligible for inclusion among trustee securities; Indian government loans and railway debentures had enjoyed the same privilege for at least a decade. Trustee status increased the attractions and sales of Dominion stock, and was certainly an advantage to Canada that was denied to Argentina. *The Times,* in 1909, had drawn attention to the 'sentimental prejudice' cherished by a considerable class of British investors in favour of placing their savings within the bounds of the Empire.[38] Some years later the *Financial Times* advised investors to choose 'our leading colonies ... which enjoy the great advantage, from a British point of view, of being under practically the same laws as those which govern company enterprise in this country.'[39] The fact that Argentina, in spite of these handicaps and with so much of its capital supplied by the Continent, attracted British investment on such a large scale is yet another measure of the very special position that Argentina enjoyed as a favourite destination for British investment before 1914.

J.M. Keynes, as McCloskey suggests, may have exaggerated the effect of the Trustee Acts on diverting home investment to the Empire,[40] and it is improbable that the 'imperial piety' that Keynes denounced was of great effect before the First World War.[41] On the contrary, the distribution of investments simply by life insurance companies in Britain before the war suggests a drift to foreign securities. Lenfant quotes the *Statist* to the effect that whereas the share of foreign securities in life insurance funds rose nearly six per cent (from 1.3 per cent in 1894 to 7.1 per cent in 1913), Indian and colonial investment advanced only by one per cent (6.8 per cent in 1894 to 7.8 per cent in 1913).[42] It was different later, when inperial preference came to be practised from both ends – from the Dominions for Britain, as had existed in some form since well before the war, and now, after the war, from Britain for the Empire. Imperial preference, in Drummond's phrase, had become 'a kind of Imperial habit' by the 1930s.[43] Sheppard may be premature in dating imperial preference from the Colonial Stock Act of 1900, but he is on stronger ground when he draws attention to the phenomenon during the inter-war period:

> The abandonment of the Gold Standard and the establishment of the Sterling Area in 1931 accentuated the process which in turn was practically completed with the establishment of the [British] Government's Foreign Transactions Advisory Committee in 1936.[44]

As for Argentina, the Republic enjoyed a period of continued prosperity in the 1920s, and the links with Britain were still strong. Indeed there may even have been, as Guido di Tella suggests, a return to the traditional relationship during the 1930s when Argentina was 'thrown into a panic by the thought that if the British market were lost, disaster would follow'.[45] But by then Britain's capacity to invest abroad was much diminished, and British investment had become more channelled and less adventurous. Over the 1920s, 25 per cent of London's new capital issues were for the Empire, and only 15 per cent for foreign governments and companies elsewhere.[46]

IV

An element that distinguished British investment in Canada from investment in Argentina is clearly the attitude and performance of 'direct' investment (i.e. in the older definition, used here, investment that does not find a market through the Stock Exchange). Direct investment was an immensely important part of British investment in Canada. In all foreign markets, British and Continental, portfolio investment for Argentina may have been as strong as in Canada in the boom years 1910–11, and even superior for 1912 and much of 1913. But Argentina was never likely to attract, from Britain, a similar level of direct, non-Stock Exchange investment.

Immigrants were the source of some direct capital. The figures for British immigrant capital into Argentina before the First World War are not helpful. British immigrants were of a different class from Canada's – settlers with some capital of their own, engineers, bank clerks and office workers, business operatives, professionals and remittance men. These were first-class passengers whose arrival was not recorded at Argentine ports. The British community in Argentina was prosperous compared with the Italian and Spanish; and first-class travellers may well have been worth several hundred pounds per head. But the number of Britons in Argentina did not seem to vary much from around 50,000.[47] In fact, in the 1914 census Britons (but only first generation) were listed as 27,692, Spaniards as 892,701 and Italians as 929,863! Overall Argentina suffered more from the loss to the economy of re-exported capital earnings of returning immigrants (mainly to Spain and Italy) than it gained from immigrant capital. Martínez and Lewandowski calculated that in three years 1905–7 Argentina lost the equivalent of nearly £10 million,[48] and their estimate does not include the frequent and large remittances of resident immigrants and Argentine citizens, immigrants of the second generation or later.

For Canada, a clear majority of the gross immigration of 2.8 million between 1901 and 1913 was British. Immigrant capital is always a prob em, although Butlin, for British Australians, settles for £25 per head.[49] Pentland abandoned any hope of estimating for Canada,[50] but Viner, long before, had calculated as much as $500 (£100) per head for saloon immigrants, and $50 for steerage. This produces a total of $30 million brought in by saloon passengers (mainly British) for the years 1900–13, and $53.6 million by Britons travelling steerage.[51] Viner's estimates may in fact be too modest. His refined total for Britons alone is $63.8 million. Yet the minimum capital required to begin farming on the Canadian prairies (tools, animals, seeds and shelter) was reckoned to be between £1000 and £1500 in 1900,[52] and Buckley, in his discussion of farming in the west of Canada, gives examples which show that the personal funds of settlers supplied a significant part of the credit requirements when they arrived at the frontier, nearly $2,000 in the period 1911–16, and $5000 post-war.[53] Remittances were never the problem for Canada that they were for Argentina; Britons remitted far less than Southern Europeans, partly because conditions were better for those who remained at home, but perhaps more because British emigrants did not expect themselves to return. Viner's estimate of non-commercial remittances from Canada 1900–1913, both to Britain and to the United States, was only $55 million.[54]

In any case, immigrant capital and remittances do not amount to much, although capital imports were lower and remittances higher for Argentina than for Canada, and the phenomena throw light on national character. More important was the amount of direct investment in commercial and financial enterprise, manufacturing, urban real estate, the pastoral industry and agriculture. Britons were interested in some of these activities in Argentina before 1914. They owned large quantities of pastoral and agricultural land – some of the best land in the Republic. They were interested in the import/export business. They took a share in retailing, although nothing by comparison with the Italians. They had more than a foothold in domestic finance. One of the largest manufacturing plants, Alpargatas (shoes), was owned by a British family resident in Buenos Aires. But the scale of Britain's direct investment in Argentina, an alien country with a relatively small British community, was always far less than it was for Canada.

Direct investment in Canada was of real importance. Even as early as the 1870s the United States had become deeply interested, and in this sense Canada before the First World War was much different from Argentina. In the course of active and expanding business, US entrepreneurs were bound to take their interests over the frontier. The scale of foreign direct investment in Canada, mainly in manufacturing, mining, urban real estate, timber and farm land, was soon acknowledged; and it came, Meier says, mainly from the United States.[55] Hartland describes it, in fact, as 'more akin to domestic than to foreign investment', and gives a figure of about $630 million (£126 million) as the total for US capital entering Canada 1900–1913.[56] Buckley's figure for US direct investment in Canada up to 1914 is rather higher than Hartland's at $880 million (£176 million), rising to $2 billion (£400 million) by 1930.[57] All kinds of patent regulations, tariff restrictions and tax inducements, quite apart from the savings on transport costs, acted as incentive for US branch plants in Canada. The same incentive existed for British industry, but American firms were closer at hand and quicker to get behind the tariff wall.[58]

If the figures are confined to portfolio investment, British capital in Canadian manufacturing appears to have been quite inadequate – less than 4 per cent of total capital called.[59] But, at the time, capital was seldom raised on the Stock Exchange for industrial, agricultural and pastoral development. Viner was aware of this, and his aggregate figures for British investment in Canada before 1914 include a substantial allowance for 'direct' investments, explained as the investments of British insurance companies in Canada; British purchases of Canadian mining, agricultural, timber, and urban properties; the investments of British shipping companies in Canadian coastwise and internal shipping; direct investments in Canadian industrial plants and mercantile establishments; British money lent on mortgage in Canada; and British capital used in financing Canadian import and export trade.[60]

Viner's calculation ('a conservative guess') was that Britain's direct investment in Canada for the period 1900 to 1913, other than by insurance companies, amounted to at least $200 million (£40 million).[61] Although it was between a third and a quarter the size of US direct investment, it was still substantial.

Private, direct investment by Britons in Argentina can never have assumed this scale. Paish's estimates for the distribution of Britain's capital overseas are simply portfolio (new capital issues on the London Stock Exchange), and the peculiar strength and volume of British direct investment in a country like Canada, not included in Paish's estimates, throws further doubt on their value even as an approximate indication of distribution. The amounts in themselves are not decisive, but assuming that Viner's estimates are indeed 'conservative', the volume of direct investment in such a promising area as Canada – within the Empire, relatively near the UK, politically stable, well-endowed with natural resources – does help to establish the case for Canadian pre-eminence among promising markets for new British investment after 1904, ahead of more traditional destinations in the United States, British India, and some of the other, more distant, 'white' Dominions.

For Argentina, however, the relative absence of direct investment from Britain reflects what was coming to be the case – the lesser success of British exporters to Argentina than to Canada (see Table 3).

TABLE 3

TOTAL EXPORTS:PRODUCE AND MANUFACTURES OF THE UK
(£ millions)

	1909	1910	1911	1912	1913
Argentina	18.7	19.1	18.6	20.5	22.6
Canada	15.7	19.6	19.7	23.5	23.8

Source: U.K. Trade and Navigation Accounts, rounded to the nearest hundred thousand.

Furthermore it is hardly surprising that a noticeable expansion of overseas businesses and branch plants before 1914 should have brought more activity to an Empire country like Canada than it did to Argentina. I have referred to this elsewhere, and the substance of what I said was that the natural path of expansion for a high-quality producer was the formation of branch plants behind the tariff walls of Continental Europe, of branch plants and sales agencies in the United States, and of manufacturing, assembling and sales organisations in the British Empire, particularly the 'white' Dominions; it was the 1920s before a firm like Levers felt it worth establishing branch factories in Latin America.[62] Even then only three of the 21 leading British firms identified by Nicholas as having direct investments abroad before 1939 had interests *in any part* of South America, by comparison with six in the single Dominion of Australia and seven in Canada.[63]

It is true that, even before the War, Argentina attracted most of what modest development there was in direct investment in Latin America. Harrods opened a fine department store in Florida, the main shopping street in Buenos Aires; Maples, the London furniture store, had its own large outlet. Many of the best British names were to be seen in the Republic. But of the two favourite destinations for new British capital before 1914, Canada and Argentina, it must be acknowledged that Canada had the advantage, more particularly in direct investment. Advertising and brand names – Cadbury, Fry, Smedley, John Dickinson, Huntley and Palmer, Holling and Viyella, Dunlop, Jeyes, Yardley, even 'Camp Coffee' – could naturally expect a better response in English-speaking markets, and their success in the Dominions encouraged further British exports and investment. If anything, increased cartelisation and international marketing agreements between European and United States' manufacturers and traders during the inter-war period served to reinforce the tendency already so visible in capital exports – the retreat of British trade and investment into the arms of the Empire.

V

It would surely be true to say that the ten years before the war, and those which followed to 1929, marked an unnatural phase in the history of Argentina. The Republic found itself linked with a distant, alien economy. It was, of course, a marriage of convenience, a classic illustration of comparative advantage, during which Argentina, although an outsider, came to be more highly regarded by British investors than any part of Britain's Empire other than Canada. It can be argued that for a few years before the war, at any rate for portfolio investment, Argentina was *more* popular with the foreign investor than Canada, itself the most popular of the British Dominions.

There is something, indeed, to be said for the idea that Argentina, spared the position of neighbour to a powerful, rival economy, was of more interest to Britons than a Canada so closely bound to the United States. The advantage of the neighbour in international investment, both portfolio and direct, is unquestionable. In an era of sea transport, Britain was in many respects more of a neighbour to Argentina than the United States, and Argentine exports to Britain were much larger than Canada's.

Although Argentina remained in close association with British finance and trade until after the Second World War, the modern Republic has long since lost contact with the British economy. Canada, naturally, has strengthened its links with the United States. But the trend, although established before the First World War, was not as yet of fundamental importance, even if it already distinguished the Canadian economy – like Mexico's, so far from God, so close to the United States – from distant Argentina's.

The practice of taking Paish's aggregate figures to represent net holdings of overseas portfolio investment, 31 December 1913, has disguised the pattern of market preference during what was probably the most exciting period of Britain's overseas investment. It *may* be true that Britain had invested as much as £750 million in the United States over the 50 or 60 years before 1914. However, that figure, in its failure to allow more than marginally for foreign ownership of securities bought through London, its overestimation of the British share in loans partially issued in London and on the Continent, the absence of any allowance for the cost of issue and for the reduction in net proceeds therefrom, the incorporation of a number of issues which were evidently failures on the London market, does give some reason for doubt. It *may* be true, with similar reservations, that over the same span of years Britain had invested as much as £378 million in Indian and Ceylon, £370 million in South Africa and £332 million in Australia. But from the revival of overseas investment in 1904 the mood of the market had changed; old borrowers had gone and the new generation of borrowers, the darlings of Britain's overseas investors, were Canada and Argentina.

I have suggested elsewhere, very tentatively as yet, that the net sum of United States securities actually held by Britons just before the war might be taken more realistically to be £450 million, while substantial adjustments have to be made for most of the countries on Paish's list.[64] We are left with very respectable figures for portfolio investment retained, but to a great extent they reflect the history of British investment back into the nineteenth century, much as Paish's estimate for British investment in Australia dates back and incorporates a heavy injection of British capital before the financial crisis of 1893.It was not the United States, 'our great Indian possessions', or, necessarily, 'the daughter States of the Empire' that captured the taste and imagination of British investors in the decade leading up to the First World War. Nor did investors continue unthinkingly to display an unnatural, fearful and conservative preference for government bonds and railway securities, whatever the odds. Some of the old practices survived far longer than they should. But after 1904 there was an obvious home for money, at a better rate of interest than could be obtained on parallel investment at home. It was to be found, of course, in those safe, expanding, temperate regions of recent European settlement, Canada and Argentina.

St Antony's College, Oxford

NOTES

*I am grateful to the Economic and Social Research Council (London) for financing a research project on the broad theme of Britain's capital exports, 1870–1914, from which this article derives. Dr Rachel Whitehead, research officer under the ESRC grant, has contributed much valuable material.

1. George Paish, 'Great Britain's Capital Investments in Individual Colonial and Foreign Countries', *Journal of the Royal Statistical Society* 74, 2 (1911), 176.
2. Ibid., 'The Export of Capital and the High Cost of Living', *Statist* (Supplement), 14 Feb 1914, vi.
3. I have discussed this problem, the reestimation which it implies, and some of the likely consequences (including an alteration in ideas on distribution), in an article 'Britain's investment overseas at the end of 1913: a downvaluation' which is still lingering on the way towards publication.
4. John H. Dunning, *Studies in International Investment* (London, 1970), p.18.
5. As Paish suggested in 'The Export of Capital and the High Cost of Living', xiv.
6. David K. Sheppard, *The Growth and Role of U.K. Financial Institutions 1860–1962* (London, 1971), p.12.
7. For example, in A.F.W. Plumptre, 'The Nature of Political and Economic Development in the British Dominions', *Canadian Journal of Economics and Political Science* 3, 4 (1937), 489–507.
8. Ragnar Nurkse, 'International Investment Today in the Light of Nineteenth-Century Experience', *Economic Journal* 64 (1954), 745.
9. See, for example, W. Rosenberg. 'Capital Imports and Growth in the Case of New Zealand: Foreign Investment in New Zealand, 1840–1958', *Economic Journal* 71 (1961), *passim*.
10. I.M. Drummond, 'Capital Markets in Australia and Canada, 1895–1914' (unpublished Ph.D. thesis, Yale, 1952), 72.
11. J.A. Hobson, *Canada Today* (London, 1906), pp.3–4 (in the unexpected role of financial journalist and propagandist).
12. (Sir) F. William Taylor, 'Canadian Loans in London', *United Empire* (Journal of the Royal Colonial Institute), n.s.III (1912), 993.
13. John Fogarty, 'The Comparative Method and Nineteenth-Century Regions of Recent Settlement', *Historical Studies* (University of Melbourne) 19 (1981), 418.
14. *Financial News,* 31 Dec. 1913, 6.
15. Harold E. Peters, *The Foreign Debt of the Argentine Republic* (Baltimore, 1934), pp.48–9.
16. Minutes of evidence (taken in Sydney 22 April 1913): *Second Interim Report of the Dominion Royal Commission,* Parliamentary Papers (Britain), 1914, XVII, QQ.6485–90, 6495, 6542, 6550–2, 6558.
17. A.G. Ford, 'British Investment and Argentine Economic Development, 1880–1914', in David Rock (ed.), *Argentina in the Twentieth Century* (London, 1975), p.23.
18. H.S. Ferns, *The Argentine Republic* (Newton Abbot, 1973), pp.88–9.
19. Ibid., p.90.
20. David Rock, 'The Argentine Economy, 1890–1914', in Guido di Tella and D.C.M. Platt (eds.), *The Political Economy of Argentina, 1880–1946* (London:Macmillan, 1985).
21. Carlos F. Díaz Alejandro, *Essays on the Economic History of the Argentine Republic* (New Haven, 1970), p.424; net balance of overseas immigration and emigration, second and third class foreign passengers only.
22. John A. Stovel, *Canada in the World Economy* (Cambridge, MA, 1959), p.122.
23. Penelope Hartland, 'Factors in Economic Growth in Canada', *Journal of Economic History* 15, 1 (1955), 16.
24. Wilfred Mandelbaum, *The World Wheat Economy, 1885–1939* (Cambridge, MA, 1953), pp.238–9.
25. V.L. Phelps, *The International Economic Position of Argentina* (Philadelphia, 1938),

p.119.
26. Kenneth Buckley, *Capital Formation in Canada, 1896–1930* (Toronto, 1955), 63.
27. Most influentially by Sir Alexander Cairncross in his *Home and Foreign Investment, 1870–1913* (Cambridge, 1953), p.184, but up to the present day in the textbooks: e.g. 'The biggest change in Britain's overall investment position since 1914 was the decline in the importance of the United States as an area for British investment as a result of war-time liquidation': A.J.H. Latham, *The Depression and the Developing World, 1911–1939* (London, 1981), p.67.
28. Herbert Feis, *Europe the World's Banker, 1870–1914* (New York, 1960 edn.), 25.
29. For example, D.H. Aldcroft and H.W. Richardson, *The British Economy 1870–1939* (London, 1969), p.87.
30. Platt, 'Britain's investment overseas', *passim.*
31. Ian M. Drummond, 'Government Securities and Colonial New Issue Markets: Australia and Canada, 1895–1914', *Yale Economic Essays* I (Spring, 1961), 148.
32. *The Economist,* 28 Oct. 1930, 700.
33. Ibid., 27 Feb. 1909, 444.
34. Ibid., 17 June 1911, 1299.
35. E. Crammond, 'British Investment Abroad', *Quarterly Review* 412 (July, 1907) 248.
36. Personal communication from Dr C.M. Lewis, London School of Economics.
37. Discussion, Paish, 'Great Britain's Capital Investment', 485.
38. *The Times* (Financial and Commercial Supplement), 5 Feb. 1909, 1.
39. *The Financial Times Investor's Guide* (London, 1913), p.10.
40. Donald N. McCloskey, 'Did Victorian Britain Fail?', *Economic History Review* 2nd. ser., 23, 3 (1970), 452, fn.5.
41. Keynes explained his point very lucidly in his article 'Foreign Investment and National Advantage', *The World and the Athenaeum,* 9 Aug 1924, 584–6.
42. J.H. Lenfant, 'British Capital Export, 1900–1913' (unpublished Ph.D. thesis, University of London, 1949), 148, fn.50.
43. Ian M. Drummond, *British Economic Policy and the Empire, 1919–1939* (London, 1972), p.32.
44. Sheppard, *Growth and Role of UK Financial Institutions,* p.12.
45. Guido di Tella, 'Economic Controversies in Argentina from the 1920s to the 1940s', in di Tella and Platt, *Political Economy of Argentina.*
46. Drummond, *British Economic Policy,* 29.
47. I discuss British immigration and its effects in my *Latin America and British trade, 1806–1914* (London, 1972), pp.126–35.
48. Albert M. Martínez and Maurice Lewandowski, *The Argentine in the 20th Century* (London, 1911), p.120.
49. N.G. Butlin, *Australia, Domestic Produce, Investment and Foreign Borrowing, 1861–1938/9* (Cambridge, 1962), p.433.
50. H.C. Pentland, 'The Role of Capital in Canadian Economic Development Before 1875', *Canadian Journal of Economics and Political Science* 16, 4 (1950), 463.
51. Jacob Viner, *Canada's Balance of International Indebtedness, 1900–1913* (Cambridge, MA., 1924), pp.44, 46–7.
52. Carl Solberg, 'Land Tenure and Land Settlement: Policy and Patterns in the Canadian Prairies and the Argentine Pampas, 1880–1930', in D.C.M. Platt and Guido di Tella (eds.), *Argentina, Australia and Canada: Studies in Comparative Development, 1870–1965* (London, 1985), 71, fn.5.
53. Buckley, *Capital Formation in Canada,* p.68.
54. Viner, *Canada's Balance of International Indebtedness,* p.283.
55. G.M. Meier, 'Economic Development and the Transfer Mechanism: Canada, 1855–1913', *Canadian Journal of Economics and Political Science* 19, 1 (1953), 9.
56. Hartland, 'Factors in Economic Growth', 78–9.
57. Buckley, *Capital Formation in Canada,* p.66.
58. D.G. Paterson, *British Direct Investment in Canada, 1890–1914* (Toronto, 1976), p.108.
59. Matthew Simon, 'The Pattern of New British Portfolio Foreign Investment 1865–1914', in J.H. Adler (ed.), *Capital Movements and Economic Development* (New York, 1967),

p.42.

60. Viner, *Canada's Balance of International Indebtedness*, p.123.
61. Ibid., p.124.
62. Platt, *Latin America and British Trade*, 212.
63. S.J. Nicholas, 'British Multinational Investment Before 1939', *Journal of European Economic History* 11, 3 (1982), Table 4, 619.
64. Platt, 'Britain's Investment Overseas'.

Anglo-Indian Banking in British India: From the Paper Pound to the Gold Standard*

by

Amiya Kumar Bagchi

Anglo-Indian banking was almost coeval with British rule in India. The bank established by the East India Company's servants in Bombay in the eighteenth century probably had features which borrowed equally from British innovations and Indian customs.[1] Many agency houses dating from the late eighteenth century established their own banks (legally, partnership firms) and almost invariably had Indian *banians, shroffs* or *dubashes* attached to them. The first proper joint-stock bank in British India, the Bank of Bengal, had a separate *khazanchee's* (treasurer's) department, with an Indian in charge: the clerks and the cashkeepers were supposed to be, but were not always, recruited by the *khazanchee* and worked under the dual control of the *khazanchee* and the (British) secretary and treasurer of the bank.[2] Until the 1850s, the bank accounts were kept in Bengali, and figures were transferred to English account books from these *rokars,* on separate slips of paper called *chits.* While the Anglo-Indian banks primarily catered for a European clientele, they also dealt largely with Indian customers, and discounting of the Indian-style bill of exchange, the *hundi,* or *hoondee,* was a major source of income for them.

I

There were a number of features in common between the decision of the British Parliament to suspend the convertibility of the pound in 1797 and that of the Governor-General in India to launch the Bank of Bengal with private share-holding but with important government backing. Scarcity of silver and gold coins and bullion was a predisposing cause in both cases, and the need to shore up public credit in a period of large deficits in the government budget was also important. In both cases, major wars were disrupting government finance and regular transaction mechanism.[3] The convertibility of sterling remained suspended throughout the period of belligerency and was restored only in 1821. The government-sponsored bank in Bengal opened for business as the Bank of Calcutta in 1806, only after the period of the greatest budgetary stress was over. It was granted a charter in 1808 and started working as the Bank of Bengal in 1809. Within the territory ruled by the East India Company in India, regional factors decided whether or not a state-backed private joint-stock bank could be established in the first decade of the nineteenth century. In Bombay, the financial weakness of the government *vis-à-vis* a small group of substantial capitalists decided that there would be no attempt as yet to establish a private joint-stock bank with government backing. In Madras, the disappearance of any substantial group of private British capitalists after the removal of the ramp of Arcot, and the reforming zeal of the young Lord William Bentinck, were responsible for the foundation of a Government Bank without any participation by private shareholders.[4]

In both the Bank of Bengal and the Government Bank in Madras, the main base of operations was the capital subscribed plus the note issue. Deposits played only a small part in the operations of these banks until the 1860s. The bank notes were received in payment of government dues and circulated in the Presidency towns and in towns nearby, especially where there was a substantial European population. When the semi-private Banks of Bombay and Madras were founded in 1840 and 1843 respectively (the Government Bank in Madras was discontinued in order to make room for the Bank of Madras), their main base for advances and discounts was also the subscribed capital and the note issue rather than deposits.

In the early part of the nineteenth century (up to the 1840s) banking functions were performed in India by at least four sets of institutions and agents. First, there was the East India Company and its subordinate governments in the three Presidencies. Although formally the East India Company's monopoly of trade between India and other countries continued till 1813, in fact the Company had come to accept European agency houses as partners – if subordinate partners – in trade. The Company financed agency houses and individual traders when it was judged that their operations would facilitate exports. For exports from India were crucial in enabling the Company to transfer the profit on its commercial operations, and its territorial tribute from India, increasingly via China. Such transfers were essential for paying dividends to the Company's shareholders and for defraying the other charges in England.

The second set of bankers were the European agency houses which sprang up from the late eighteenth century onwards. Their base of operations consisted of deposits from European civil and military servants, the capital subscribed by the principals, and the loans given to them by their Indian *banians* (in Calcutta), guarantee brokers (in Bombay) and *dubashes* (in Madras).[5]

The third set were the joint-stock banks. Of these, only three were banks in which the liability of the shareholders was limited to the value of the shares owned by them. These were the Banks of Bengal, Bombay and Madras, chartered in 1809, 1840 and 1843 respectively. In the absence of any Act or Regulation conferring limited liability on shareholders of joint-stock companies, the other banks remained only extended partnerships. The oldest private, unchartered banks were practically the money-lending and deposit divisions of the major agency houses; many of these, especially in Madras, proved short-lived and went down after the removal of the ramp of Arcot. The others, based in Calcutta, collapsed in the major agency house crisis which occurred between 1829 and 1834. With the collapse of major agency houses new private banks appeared, led by the Union Bank and the Agra and United Services Bank, whose share-holding was more widely dispersed and which were not identified with particular agency houses (although the control of the Union Bank seemed to have remained vested in the former partners and *banians* of Mackintosh & Co.).[6]

Finally, the most widely diffused and the most pervasive banking functions were performed by the traditional Indian bankers. Most of the big bankers had had connections with the Mughals and their successor states, with the Marathas and other Indian rulers. British rule destroyed or impoverished many of the older banking houses, but probably a majority of them adapted successfully to the new dispensation. While they were no longer treasurers for the big Indian states, they still remained important for the collection of revenue in both British and native state territory. And in the port cities new groups of Indian financiers rose and fell or survived, according to whether they tied themselves too closely to their British principals or managed to diversify into other fields.

The big Indian banking houses financed the growing of crops, the payment of revenue, and movement of commodities over long or short distances, over land or across the oceans. They also financed the wars of the rapidly diminishing group of independent rulers, and the extravagance of the princes, the landlords and the swells of the British officer corps. For traditional Indian bankers or for the agency houses there was no real distinction between short-term and long-term loans: whether a loan could be extended over one, two or even three years depended on the closeness of connection between the banker and his clients and the solidity (real or imagined) of the security the borrower would offer. Such long-term lending was often forced on a banker. The Bank of Bengal had explicit rules prohibiting lending for a period longer than three months or against the security of illiquid assets such as land or buildings. But loans of privileged customers were regularly renewed. Moreover, when the agency houses failed in the early 1830s, the bank found itself holding the (often disputed) title deeds of a large number of indigo factories.

The other unchartered banks did not have such explicit rules about the securities or periods of lending. Nor did the big agency houses who resented the intrusion of new banks into their favoured territories.[7] In Bombay there was determined opposition to the setting up of the Bank of Bombay. A little later, a group of East India houses which were themselves engaged heavily in banking wanted the unchartered banks to be regulated.

However, such demands for regulation did not yield tangible results. As far as European-style banking was concerned, the trend between the 1850s and 1870s was towards less rather than more regulation. Starting with the Oriental Bank Corporation, a number of exchange banks came in to carve out among themselves (with a residue left for European agency houses) the field of foreign exchange banking which earlier on had been the exclusive preserve of the East India Company and a number of big European agency houses. The demand for regulation of such banks was no more than muted from the start. Following in the footsteps of the British Parliament, the Government of India first passed a Companies Act (in 1857) to confer limited liability on shareholders of joint-stock companies which did not engage in banking or insurance business, and followed it up (in 1860) with another Act which conferred limited liability on shareholders of joint-stock banks as well.[8] But there was no attempt to regulate domestic banks, let alone the Indian operations of foreign banks. Following a precedent set by the Bank of Bengal charter of 1839, the Government of India prohibited foreign exchange banking to the three Presidency Banks, mainly on the ground that this branch of banking was too risky a proposition to be handled by a set of quasi-government banks. The effect of this kind of selective *laissez faire* was to leave Indian joint-stock banking to fend for itself without much central supervision until the establishment of the Reserve Bank of India in 1935.

Once the foreign exchange banks came into the picture, the semi-government Presidency Banks which had presided over the banking system at its apex in the Presidency towns were themselves pushed into the role of intermediary bankers in many sectors of the money market. Since they were denied any direct share in foreign exchange banking, they had to act through the exchange bank for financing foreign trade. The companies that were floated in London, and controlled factories, plantations and mines in India, depended on London-based banks for their initial financial requirements, apart from the shareholders' and promoters' capital. When they began operating, for working capital they naturally looked towards the branches of the Agra Bank, the National Bank of India, the Chartered Mercantile Bank, the Chartered Bank of India, Australia and China, and other exchange banks.

The Presidency Banks supplied these exchange banks in turn with much of their working capital requirements. The funds of the Presidency Banks came from the government and, increasingly, from the general public. A major liquidity crisis was caused for the government by the New Bank of Bombay (which had risen in 1868 from the ashes of the old Bank of Bombay) in 1874. It lent out Rs.6.8 million to eight exchange banks in January 1874, at a time when the government needed the money for financing famine relief in Bengal and Bihar.[9] The Bank of Bengal also acted as a provider of funds to the exchange banks. The latter were known to switch funds from London to India and back in response to actual or anticipated exchange fluctuations, thus causing sudden changes in the state of the money market at the apex in India and embarrassment to the Government of India which had regularly to remit very large sums to London to cover the so-called Home Charges.

The Presidency Banks acted also as intermediaries in financing the Indian part of the money market. Money was regularly taken by Indian bankers for meeting payment on *hundis* which were discounted by all the joint-stock banks. Since the amount of credit that could be extended by the Presidency Banks to any single party was subject to an upper limit, whereas the banks did not feel confident about the credit rating of the smaller or less well-known Indian bankers, the credit of the latter would be guaranteed by the endorsements of some of the leading Indian banking firms. The indigenous bankers also often acted as *khazanchees* or head *shroffs* (cash-keepers and field officers rolled into one) to the branches of the Presidency Banks. In many cases, these *khazanchees* or other leading Indian bankers endorsed loans of joint-stock banks to landlords, since the latter did not have sufficient liquid security to pledge, and land was barred as security to the Presidency Banks.

II

The Indian joint-stock banks, of course, performed more direct banking functions, such as lending to traders or meeting the working capital requirements of mill-owners, planters or mine-operators. There is little doubt that European traders or, later on, industrial or mining firms collared the major part of such direct credit, especially in Bengal and Madras. In these two presidencies the credit to the European firms was in its turn concentrated in a few leading managing agency houses with headquarters in Calcutta and Madras. However, in northern India banks promoted by locally resident Europeans such as the Agra Bank or the Alliance Bank of Simla had probably a more dispersed, though predominantly European, clientele.

The connection between modern joint-stock banking and industrial enterprise was most direct in Bombay. This link somehow became most visible in the major banking crises. The crisis of 1865–66 which led to the downfall of the old Bank of Bombay and numerous other banks and financial institutions lending on unconventional security was doubtless caused mainly by speculation in cotton, land, and shares, and the subsequent collapse of the market at the end of the American Civil War.[10] But a good deal of infrastructural investment took place in the city in those heady days and assisted industrial growth once cotton mill-construction was resumed. Again, when W. Nicol & Co. and the enterprises of the major Indian associate of the Company, Kessowji Naik and his son, Nursey Kessowji, collapsed in 1879, it became clear that the (reconstituted) Bank of Bombay had been knowingly or unwittingly financing the long-term investment of the father and son. Many of the major cotton mill-owners of Bombay, such as the Petits, the Sassoons and George Cotton, were directors of the Bank of Bombay in the 1870s and 1880s, and their firms were among the favoured customers of the bank. Even in the 1840s and 1850s, the founding of banks, running of shipping companies and building of hydraulic presses or cotton mills had been combined by such men as Cowasji Nanabhoy Davar and Framji Cowasji Banaji.

Bombay businessmen also remained much more doughty champions of free enterprise than their counterparts in Bengal and Madras. The seat of the Government of India was in Bengal, and the British business community naturally looked to the government for various favours. At the same time, because of the large hinterland of the Calcutta port, and the growth of jute mills, tea plantations and coal mines and similar enterprises, the community was wealthy and powerful, and there was a clearly recognized *camaraderie* between the bureaucracy and the business magnates. In Madras, the British business community was more powerful than the Indian, of course, but it could not claim anything more than a subservient sociability with the paternalistic bureaucracy. In Bombay, the government had been dependent on financial help from the businessmen at the beginning of the century. Later on, the dynamism of the opium and cotton trades supported an aggressive business community which could often count on the support of the local government in any conflict with the Government of India. For example, during the struggle of local businessmen to found a new, government-supported Bank of Bombay, rather than allow the Bank of Bengal to absorb the bankrupt Bank of Bombay, the Government of the Presidency supported the lobbyists, Europeans and Indians.[11] However, once it was founded with government help, the businessmen wanted only a minimum of official control over the New Bank of Bombay.

Even a very brief survey of joint-stock banking in British India in the nineteenth century reveals two important traits: modernization of banking remained largely confined to the European quarters and to certain select Indian enclaves, but paradoxically enough there was no shortage of finance or banking capital for the few modern enterprises that were set up.

The joint-stock banks remained a thin veneer on the credit structure. Peasants and artisans obtained their credit from the smaller Indian moneylenders who might borrow in turn from large Indian banking houses, and indirectly from the banks. However, most of the resources of the smaller bankers or moneylenders came from their own savings or from the larger Indian bankers rather than the joint-stock banks. One can quote various contemporary documents to suggest that rates of interest ranging from six to 48 per cent were found in this so-called 'informal' credit market.[12] But in fact, such figures are seriously misleading if there is no further information about the economic and social status of the borrower and the value and nature of security offered. The big landlords and traders could often get loans at a rate of 12 per cent or lower per year. The rates of interest charged by one Indian banker to another were generally even lower – often amounting to as little as two or three per cent. But there was virtually no ceiling on the rate of interest that could be charged to the poorer farmers, to the ordinary artisans, or to the landless or near-landless labourers who could be, and were, made into bond-slaves for failure to pay their own or their fathers' debts.[13]

Rates of interest charged by the Presidency Banks and other joint-stock banks were lower than those at which Indian landlords or traders could normally borrow money. Until the abolition of the law prohibiting usury in the 1850s, there was a ceiling of 12 per cent on the rates of interest charged by joint-stock banks. After that, rates could shoot up to as much as 15 per cent or sink as low as three per cent. In general, the rates charged by the joint-stock banks were lower than the *bazaar* rates (that is, the rates charged by big Indian bankers for loans to their valued customers) when the money market was tight, and higher, when the money market was slack. The loans from the Presidency Banks were granted against the security of government bonds, and later on, securities of guaranteed railway companies or bonds floated by selected municipal bodies. The bills discounted had to have two good signatures, and as far as the Presidency Banks or most of the banks registered in Britain were concerned, this meant signatures of the partners of leading British firms. Only in Bombay were some Indian firms also considered as good enough for having their bills discounted. But generally the clean credit enjoyed by them was less than that granted to European firms such as Ralli Brothers, Volkart Bros., Sir Charles Forbes & Co., Greaves Cotton & Co. and others. There were several occasions on which this trust lodged in European firms caused embarrassment for the banks. Palmer & Co., Alexander & Co. and the other agency houses caught up in the agency house crisis of the 1830s were granted extended lines of credit by the Bank of Bengal long after they had ceased to be creditworthy. In Bombay, Ritchie Steuart & Co. was one of the major firms enjoying the overextended credit that led to the liquidation of the old Bank of Bombay, and the firm was rescued only with capital infused by business associates. Again in Bombay, the senior partner of W. Nicol & Co., Hamilton Maxwell, was President of the reconstituted Bank of Bombay when his firm went bankrupt in 1879, after enjoying one of the highest credit limits granted by the bank after its resurrection in 1868.

In the 1850s credit extended by the Bank of Madras was monopolized by just a handful of firms led by Binny & Co., Arbuthnot & Co., Parry & Co. and Lecot & Co. This led to a liquidity crisis (because one or another firm had locked up the loanable funds of the bank), and to protests by the Indian merchants and the lesser European firms, with the result that the government of Madras even recommended the withdrawal of the charter of the bank. However, lobbying in London by powerful shareholders and customers of the bank stayed the hands of the government.

Not only was the credit extended by the Presidency Banks unequally distributed among the borrowers, it was also distributed unequally between different locations. Until the opening of inland branches by the Presidency Banks in the 1860s, virtually all their credit had been enjoyed by the three Presidency towns of Calcutta, Bombay and Madras. When branches were opened in the inland towns, the latter often acted simply as a mopper-up of deposits – governmental and private – while the credit flowed primarily to firms established in the Presidency towns, the ports, or, more rarely, large cities in the interior. Much of this credit was linked to external trade. Not only did the inland branches mop up deposits; they also seemed to bear the brunt of the indiscretions committed by the managers of the head offices or branches located in London, Calcutta, or Bombay.[14] The asymmetrical flows of purchasing power and information were responsible for this state of affairs. It was the rich customers overseas or in the ports who appeared to be creditworthy until ambition, greed or misfortune betrayed them. The depositors in the inland branches or ordinary shareholders learned only too late that collapse of the property or export market had again made paupers of the valued customers of the banks or shown up the trusted London managers as incompetent or fraudulent or both, and had spirited away deposits or their invested capitals.

If the distribution of the credit extended by the joint-stock banks was rather skewed, the distribution of bank notes, or, later, the government paper currency, was no more equal. Until the Presidency Banks lost their right of note issue, most of the value of the note circulation was accounted for by higher denomination notes (Rs.100 and above) and these in their turn circulated chiefly in the Presidency towns. The low income of an average Indian and the rather high minimum value of bank notes (Rs.10 and above) meant that most Indians had no use for them in their day-to-day transactions.

Why did modern banking not percolate down to the level of small towns, let alone villages? Was there shortage of capital, or to use a more appropriate word (following Joan Robinson), finance? As is well known, in macroeconomic terms, British India was not short of capital in the nineteenth century. A very large part of the investible capital was remitted to England for the payment of Home Charges.[15] Another part was used to finance the import of precious metals for use as media of circulation. Even then, there was considerable liquidity available and bank flotation was quite a popular activity. However, the bankers wanted to lend large amounts on the basis of safe securities. Most prospective Indian borrowers were not rich in assets, nor could they promise a safe passage for the loan up to its maturity. In order to finance small peasants and artisans, the banker had to have an intimate knowledge of their daily activities, and exercise some degree of control over them. The Indian moneylender-cum-trader could acquire such information and such control, but not the European secretary of a bank sitting in style in an office guarded by a dozen factotums. Even with information supplied by the *khazanchee*, detailed supervision of thousands of borrowers could have been costly. Hence the joint-stock banks preferred to operate at the wholesale end of banking and leave the retail banking to Indian bankers and moneylenders who took care of the transactions costs lower down.

The major staple of business of Anglo-Indian banking was trade, and especially, trade connected with exports and imports. This was again not necessitated by a shortage of capital, for even after leakages abroad, extravaganzas of the rich and the costs of the financing of trade, there remained a residue which could have been productively invested if Indians or Europeans had found it profitable to invest in industry or agriculture on a large scale. The meagre volume of modern manufacturing investment and the still smaller fraction of it financed by joint-stock banks are a reflection of a *post facto,* downward adjustment of the supply of industrial finance to the demand for it, rather than of the smallness of the potential, or even the actual, savings of the wealthy Indians or Europeans with Indian connections.

The demand for industrial investment was affected by a number of factors, the most important of which was the low level of income of ordinary people. Nevertheless, the possibility of displacing handicrafts offered an important opportunity for investment, particularly in the area of cotton textiles. Much of this potential, however, leaked abroad, especially to the British cotton mill industry, and investors in India were left with only the residue.[16] The free trade, or near-free trade, conditions obtaining for much of the century, and the extremely limited facilities for training Indians in the operation of modern mills, severely limited the profitability of investment in modern industry beyond a certain point. The lists of potential investors were depleted in various ways. The disabilities from which Indians suffered in respect of their access to government patronage (which was needed for development of infrastructure but also, before the passing of the Indian Companies Acts in 1857 and 1860, for the formation of joint-stock companies with limited liability for shareholders) meant that many Indians with money were barred from potentially profitable fields. Europeans did not suffer from such disabilities. But many of them reckoned – rightly, from their point of view – that a minimum degree of processing of the locally abundant raw materials with marketing and financial controls firmly held by the parent firms in London or some other commercial centre in Europe offered better prospects of secure profit in the long run than investing in the full processing facilities in India. This calculation was strengthened by the fact that for many industries, the start-up costs would have been higher in India. The commitment of the government to pursuing free trade whenever it was fiscally convenient (or even when it was fiscally damaging) meant that the required degree of assurance needed for large-scale industrial investment was lacking. That any industrial investment took place at all indicates an overwhelming difference in costs despite all the disabilities mentioned above.

The separation of Indian and European business communities by various kinds of barriers depressed investment in long-term ventures where private capital had to be risked. In the first half of the nineteenth century, Indians had some capital for investment, but little knowledge as yet of modern industrial processes, for one Ardeshir Wadia, the first Indian Fellow of the Royal Society and specialist in steam engines, did not make an industrial revolution; most of the Europeans who went out to India apparently fared no better.[17] During this period, British manufacturers of cotton goods penetrated the Indian market on a wide arc and established themselves. Detailed knowledge of the Indian market was not needed for this penetration, and goods were often sold on a consignment basis. Anybody wanting to establish a large cotton textile mill catering to the Indian piecegoods market after the 1850s would have to displace British cotton goods with their established trade and financial channels, as well as traditional cotton goods. By that time, much of the wholesale trade in cotton goods in the interior had passed into Indian hands. Paradoxically enough, while Manchester flooded the Indian market with its products, Europeans resident in India probably did not know much about the detailed product composition of demand in particular regional markets in India. It is significant that when Europeans entered the cotton mill industry in India, with a few exceptions, they established primarily or exclusively spinning factories, exporting yarn of low counts abroad (as in Bombay) or producing such yarn for consumption by local hand looms (as in Madras and Bengal). It was left mainly to the Indians with knowledge of the local market to start and operate composite cotton mills in Bombay and Ahmedabad, or, later on, in Nagpur, Delhi and Kanpur.

The Europeans' comparative advantage lay in access to government patronage, technical developments in Europe and the USA, external markets and finance. Since few of them meant to settle down in India, few wanted to lock up their *personal* wealth permanently in an Indian enterprise. For them, the best option was to design the managerial apparatus (consisting of purchasing arrangements for machinery, manufacturing operations, factory and office management, sale of goods abroad, and financial arrangements for day-to-day operations, expansion or fire-fighting) so that either they or their designated successors from Britain, France, Switzerland, Germany or Italy would be sure of retaining the effective direction in their own hands. The managing agency system was designed to combine flexibility with exclusiveness. The same logic dictated that only the operations for which an Indian location conferred an overwhelming cost advantage – and that usually meant only the crudest of processing operations with unskilled or semi-skilled operatives – would be set up in India.

Thus the politically conditioned separation between the Indians and Europeans not only stunted the growth of the Indian capitalist class but also depressed the level of demand for industrial investment below even what was realizable under the free-trade regime operated by the British rulers.

III

The limited role of modern banking in such an environment is very well illustrated by the experience of the Bank of Madras. The Bank of Madras was established in 1843, right in the middle of the long depression of prices and output in the Madras Presidency which lasted from the 1830s down to the middle of the 1850s.[18] It had a capital of only Rs.3 million but found it difficult to employ even that capital profitably in commercial loans. On the other hand, it found itself periodically in a crisis of liquidity. In times of need, it could not easily dispose of the government securities in which a substantial fraction of its resources was invested. There was hardly a market for government securities in Madras, and they had to be sold in Calcutta or Bombay. Even in these cities the securities market in the 1840s was still rather rudimentary. On the other hand, the few large firms which controlled the Bank of Madras cornered most of the credit when the money market was tight, and this led to the complaints by the Indian and the smaller European merchants that we have already referred to.

Until 1860 the Bank of Madras, in common with the other two Presidency Banks, had the right to issue notes, but the value of its note issue rarely exceeded Rs.1.5 million. There were agitations by the Madras Chamber of Commerce and directors of the Bank of Madras in favour of allowing the bank notes to be considered as legal tender for all public payments,[19] but the potential note circulation met intransigent barriers in the illiteracy and small incomes of the ordinary people, and the tiny instalments in which revenues were paid in *ryotwari* areas. The Madras Presidency contained only a handful of *Zamindaris* with large revenue payments to be deposited in the government treasury.

When the move for opening branches was set afoot in the 1860s with government support, the Bank of Madras was more active in branch-opening than the Banks of Bengal and Bombay, if one judges by the number of branches in relation to the total capital deployed. This is explained by the fact that the profitability of the Bank of Madras was lower than that of the Banks of Bengal and Bombay, and the need to diversify the investment of its resources was greater, whereas the trade of the Madras Presidency was much more dispersed among a number of ports than the trades of Bengal and Bombay. Branch-opening, aided by the cotton boom of the early 1860s, certainly raised profitability for a time. But in the early 1870s there was a crisis, caused partly by the fall in cotton prices but partly also by mismanagement at the head office and some of the important branches. While mismanagement at the head office took the form of increased expenditure even as business was declining, mismanagement at branches such as Alleppey and Negapatam was caused by the excessive dependence of the agents on the information supplied by the Indian cashkeepers.[20]

The agents appointed by the Presidency Banks were Europeans (more specifically, British). Few of them knew the local language. Attempts were made to inculcate a knowledge of the relevant languages among them, but not with outstanding success. Even when they knew the language, they were not in a position to keep in daily touch with the standing of Indian traders at the branches because of the social distance everybody among the official or mercantile circles considered it essential to maintain as between Europeans and Indians. In order to redress the state of ignorance about Indian businessmen's affairs prevailing among the agents of the Bank of Madras, the Accountant General of Madras suggested that educated Indians could be recruited as bank agents.[21] He was supported by the Chief Secretary of the Madras Government, who wrote:

The Government believe that qualified persons, carefully selected from the upper classes of native society, and adequately remunerated, might from their facility to acquire exact information regarding the means, character, and position of the Bank's clients, render valuable service in the management of the branch banks.

However, this proposal was turned down by the board of directors of the Bank of Madras. The board argued that Indians were not appointed as agents by the other two Presidency Banks, that such appointments would be distasteful to a large section of shareholders, and that bank officers needed training which Indians were not in a position to secure.

Given this state of affairs, bank officers resorted to signalling devices, or 'probabilistic discrimination',[22] using race as the first screening or filtering agent to exclude most Indians. At the next stage they relied on Indian *khazanchees* or cash-keepers to screen the remaining Indians. Where the Indian subordinates were honest, or there was already an established and reliable network of Indian bankers, this screening procedure served quite well in normal times, except that many creditworthy borrowers were excluded, and had either to pay a higher rate of interest elsewhere or go without credit. (As mentioned earlier, the interest charged by the Presidency Banks was generally lower than the *bazaar* rate of interest when the money market was tight.) Where the cashkeepers were dishonest and had little means of their own, the mechanism broke down, for in cases of difficulty the agent could not (as he did when the *khazanchees* were substantial bankers) fall back on the assets of the cash-keepers to bail out the bank.

Some of the rules adopted by the Presidency Banks and other joint-stock banks also effectively discriminated against Indians and the smaller European borrowers. According to these rules, loans could not be advanced for a period exceeding three months, nor could bills with a maturity above 90 days be discounted by the banks. By contrast, traditional Indian bankers and even the Government Bank of Madras (which lasted from 1806 to 1843) extended loans for more than a year or even longer. In practice, favoured (generally European) borrowers of the Presidency Banks could get their loans renewed without any difficulty and thus circumvent the prohibition on long-term loans. But ordinary borrowers who switched from Indian bankers to the Presidency Banks often found themselves in difficulty because of the unaccustomed rigidity in lending rules. The greater flexibility of operation of Indian bankers naturally meant that they had customers who would rather borrow from them at a higher rate of interest than go to the Presidency Banks. Sometimes, as in Muzaffarpur in Bihar in the 1860s and 1870s, European planters also preferred to stay with Indian bankers for similar reasons.

The method of management of the Bank of Madras was reformed on lines suggested by R. Taylor, a senior official of the Accounts Department appointed by the government to look into the bank's affairs. The operations of the branches and head office of the Bank of Madras looked up after 1874. But the external environment deteriorated sharply. There were massive famines in southern India in the years 1876–78. The modern banks did not necessarily suffer a loss in a famine year, for they could make money financing grain movements either by private operators or by the government as part of its famine relief operations.[23] However, following these massive famines, agricultural and trading activities were depressed. Moreover, the exports of cotton from the Madras Presidency stagnated throughout the 1870s and 1880s, recovering only around the end of the 1880s.[24]

The troubles of the bank were compounded by the crisis in the coffee economy of Ceylon. Colombo had been the most profitable branch of the Bank of Madras since its opening and almost until the end of the 1870s. Its profits then declined steeply and its net income compared only with the incomes of medium-sized Indian branches. The coffee crisis caused the fall of the Oriental Bank Corporation which along with the Chartered Mercantile Bank of India, London and China acted as government bankers in Ceylon.[25] The immediate effect of this fall was to restrict further the business of the Bank of Madras, since many of the Indian *chettiars* who acted as intermediaries of both the Oriental Bank and the Bank of Madras were in trouble. Eventually the Bank of Madras gained from the failure of the Oriental Bank since it was entrusted with much of the business of the Ceylon government. But the cause of such amelioration in its condition was as much political as commercial.

The upshot of the troubles faced by the Bank of Madras was that the dividends it declared rarely rose above six or seven per cent in the 1880s. But with the recovery of cotton exports from India and of agricultural exports in general from Ceylon, and further strengthening of the position of the Bank of Madras in the Ceylonese economy, its fortunes improved dramatically at the beginning of the 1890s, only to go down again in the last few years of the century.

Was the Bank of Madras involved in any way in financing industrial investment? Binny & Co., Parry & Co., Stanes & Co. and one or two other British managing houses in Madras were concerned directly or indirectly with the setting up of the few cotton mills, sugar mills and distilleries in the Madras Presidency.[26] Most of these managing agency houses had a powerful voice in the running of the Bank of Madras. It was natural then that the bank should also have financed the working capital needs of these enterprises. Since the loans taken by the big managing agencies or their concerns were generally renewed without difficulty, the working capital credit could also be rolled over longer terms when the need arose. Again, we have to look towards the general environment for investment and the barriers against the entry of Indians into prized areas and positions of vantage, rather than to a binding constraint on finance, to explain the very slow growth of modern industry in Madras during the period in question.

IV

This article has outlined only some of the bare bones at the highest reaches of domestic banking in India. If we want to dig into the foundations of the credit system, we will have to delineate the structure of property-holding, of wage incomes and of production relations in general. Even at the surface, we have hardly touched the relations between foreign exchange banking and domestic banking, especially in the 20-year period over which the price of silver declined, and Indian mints were kept open for the unlimited coinage of silver into rupees. In 1893 Indian mints were closed to the free coinage of silver and the rupee was put on the Gold Exchange Standard or, more appropriately, the Sterling Exchange Standard; its official exchange value was fixed at 1s. 4d. This measure bound the Indian to the London money market even more firmly than before.[27] But the flow of capital and credit, apart from loans raised by the Government of India in London, largely remained a one-way affair, and the anticipated equalization of rates of interest in London and Bombay or Calcutta never took place.[28] For a proper assessment of the persistence of what are inadequately labelled as 'imperfections' in Indian capital markets, both internally and in relation to the international money market, we need to step across a purely monetary field of discourse, and look at the internal structure of India's political economy and its relation to the international economic order. This is outside the scope of the present study.

Centre for Studies in Social Sciences, Calcutta

NOTES

*I am indebted to members of the History Cell, State Bank of India, Calcutta, for help in preparing this article.

1. For a description of the institutional amalgam embodied in systems of Anglo-Indian banking, see A.K. Bagchi, 'Transition from Indian to British Indian Systems of Money and Banking', *Modern Asian Studies* (April 1985).
2. For details, see C.N. Cooke, *The Rise, Progress and Present Conditions of Banking in India* (Calcutta, 1863), pp.95–6; G.P. Symes Scutt, *The History of the Bank of Bengal* (Calcutta, 1904), pp.3–4; and A.K. Bagchi, *The Evolution of the State Bank of India*, Vol. I, *The Roots 1806–1876* (forthcoming), Ch. 4.
3. For the crisis leading to the suspension of payment of cash for notes by the Bank of England, see E. Cannan, *The Paper Pound of 1797–1821* (London, 1919), Introduction; A. Andreades, *History of the Bank of England, 1640 to 1903* (fourth edition, London, 1966), Part IV, Ch. III; and J. Clapham, *The Bank of England: A History* (Cambridge, 1944), Vol. I, Chs. V and VII. Silver coins were not legal tender in England above the value of £25, but there was a shortage of silver coins for daily transactions; so foreign silver coins were stamped with the King's head. Similar devices to alleviate coin shortages were suggested and acted on in Bombay and Madras. See Bagchi, *The Evolution of the State Bank of India*, Vol. I, Ch. 3.
4. For further details, see ibid.

5. On the history of the agency houses operating in India and China, up to the 1830s, see H. Furber, *John Company at Work* (Cambridge, MA, 1951); M. Greenberg, *British Trade and the Opening of China 1800–42* (Cambridge, 1951); and A. Tripathi, *Trade and Finance in the Bengal Presidency 1793–1833* (Calcutta, 1956).

6. On the history of the Union Bank, see Cooke, *Rise, Progress and Present Condition of Banking in India*, pp.177–200; and Blair B. Kling, *Partner in Empire: Dwaraknath Tagore and the Age of Enterprise in Eastern India* (Berkeley, CA, 1976), Ch. IX.

7. Around 1845–46, a group of East India merchants in London (including Crawford Colvin & Co., Forbes Forbes & Co., and Fletcher Alexander & Co.) petitioned the Court of Directors of the East India Company to bring the operations of unchartered banks under legislative control. This led to an enquiry into the operations of these banks, but no action was taken, although many of them crashed, especially in the wake of the commercial crisis of 1846–47. See Bombay Archives, letter dated 30 September 1846 from Acting Manager, Oriental Bank, to the Chief Secretary, Government of Bombay; and Tamil Nadu Archives, Financial Department Consultations, Fort St George, 4 May 1847, letter dated 1 March 1847 from Accountant General, Madras, to Chief Secretary, Government of Madras.

8. R.S. Rungta, *The Rise of Business Corporations in India 1851–1900* (Cambridge, 1970), Ch. 3.

9. Bagchi, *Evolution of the State Bank of India*, Vol. I, Ch. 29.

10. For a short account of the events leading to the collapse of the Bank of Bombay, see India Office Records, L/F/3/279, *Report of the Bombay Bank Commission* (London, 1869); see also *Minutes of Evidence taken in England and Proceedings there, before the Commissioners appointed to Inquire into the Failure of the Bank of Bombay* (London, 1869); D.E. Wacha, *A Financial Chapter in the History of Bombay City and Island* (Bombay, 1910); and Bagchi, *Evolution of the State Bank of India*, Vol. I, Chs. 25–6.

11. Much of this story can be followed day by day in the pages of *The Times of India*, 1867, whose editor, W.M. Wood, was a doughty champion of local autonomy in banking, at least in counter-position to the Bank of Bengal. See also W.M. Wood, *'Things of India' Made Plain*, Part II, Section 3 (London, 1885).

12. See, for example, Cooke, *Rise, Progress and Present condition of Banking in India*, p.27; and J. Crawfurd, *A Sketch of the Commercial Resources and Monetary and Mercantile System of British India, with Suggestions for their Improvement by means of Banking Establishments* (London, 1837).

13. For a preliminary discussion of the link between credit and production relations in the context of British India, see A.K. Bagchi, 'Reflections on Patterns of Regional Growth in India During the Period of British Rule', *Bengal Past and Present* (January–June 1976).

14. See for example, the accounts of the collapse of the North-Western Bank of India in Cooke, *Rise, Progress and Present Condition of Baning in India*, pp.222–3, and of the failure of the Agra Bank and Masterman's Bank in *Bankers' Magazine* (London, 1865 and 1866). The Agra Bank could be successfully reconstructed largely because the Indian branches of the bank were found to have conducted their business soundly, and had escaped the worst effects of cover-up and mismanagement in London.

15. For a recent estimate of the export surplus remitted from India to Britain in the latter half of the nineteenth century, see A.K. Banerji, *Aspects of Indo-British Economic Relations 1858–1898* (Bombay, 1982), Chs. 4 and 7. For evidence that most of the silver imported into India over the period 1870–92 was used for coinage, see *Minutes of Evidence taken before the Committee Appointed to Inquire into the Indian Currency together with an Analysis of the Evidence and Appendices,* (London, 1893), pp.237–8, 261.

16. The argument has been spelled out in A.K. Bagchi, 'De-industrialization in India in the Nineteenth Century: Some Theoretical Implications', *Journal of Development Studies* (January 1976). See also John Hicks, *A Theory of Economic History* (Oxford, 1969), Chs. VIII and IX.

17. The troubles a pioneering entrepreneur, Dwarkanath Tagore, and his enterprises faced in mastering new technology are described by Kling, *Partner in Empire*, Ch. VI.

In Ahmedabad, Ranchhodlal Chhotalal faced severe problems in setting up the first cotton mill in the city. See S.M. Edwardes, *Memoir of Rao Bahadur Ranchhodlal Chhotalal, CIE* (Exeter, UK, 1920). However, by the 1870s in Bombay and Calcutta, setting up cotton and jute mills no longer involved intractable technical problems.

18. For documentation of this phenomenon see the earliest book on the subject, S. Srinivasa Raghavaiyangar, *Memorandum on the Progress of the Madras Presidency during the Last Forty Years of British Administration* (Madras, 1893), pp.27–33.

19. *Report of the Madras Chamber of Commerce, 1837–53* (Madras, 1854), Appendix; and Bagchi, *Evolution of the State Bank of India,* Vol. I, Ch. 17.

20. See R. Taylor's report on the Bank of Madras operations in Tamil Nadu Archives, Proceedings of the Madras Government, Financial Department, 17 February 1874.

21. Tamil Nadu Archives, Confidential Proceedings of the Madras Government, Financial Department, 28 November 1871.

22. See A. Michael Spence, *Market Signalling: Informational Transfer in Hiring and Related Screening Processes* (Cambridge, MA, 1974), esp. Chs. 4, 9, and 13; Sayre P. Schatz: 'Development in an Adverse Economic Environment', in Sayre P. Schatz (ed.), *South of the Sahara: Development in African Economies* (London, 1972); and A.K. Bagchi, *The Political Economy of Underdevelopment* (Cambridge, 1982), Ch. 7. The role of racial discrimination in limiting entrepreneurial development and capital accumulation in India during the last 40 years or so of British rule has been highlighted in A.K. Bagchi, 'European and Indian Entrepreneurship in India 1900–1930', in E. Leach and S.N. Mukherjee (eds.), *Elites in South Asia* (Cambridge, 1970) and A.K. Bagchi, *Private Investment in India 1900–1939* (Cambridge, 1972), Ch. 6, but the argument applies *a fortiori* to nineteenth-century India. In one of the seminal articles in the new field of the economics (and sociology) of information (G. Akerlof, 'The Market for Lemons: Qualitative Uncertainty and the Market Mechanism', *Quarterly Journal of Economies,* 1970), the possible reluctance of wealthy landlords to invest in enterprises controlled by another community has been cited as an explanation for the low volume of industrial investment in British India.

23. See, in this connection, A.K. Bagchi, 'The Great Depression and the Third World with Special Reference to India', *Social Service Information,* 18, 2 (1979).

24. Raghavaiyangar, *Memorandum on the Progress of the Madras Presidency,* p.cxvi.

25. For brief accounts of the fall of the Oriental Bank, see 'Our Indian Banks in 1883', *Bankers' Magazine* (London, May 1884), and 'The Failure of the Oriental Bank', *Bankers' Magazine* (June 1884).

26. See Hilton Brown, *Parry's of Madras: A Story of British Enterprise in India* (Madras, 1954), Part Two; *The House of Binny* (Madras, 1969), Ch. III; and N.C. Bhogendranath, *The Development of the Textile Industry in Madras up to 1950* (Madras, 1957).

27. For accounts of the Gold Exchange Standard as it operated in British India, see. J.M. Keynes, *Indian Currency and Finance* (London, 1913), Ch. 2; and M. De Cecco, *Money and Empire: The International Gold Standard 1890–1914* (Oxford, 1974).

28. For an early discussion of why the expected equalization of interest rates did not take place, see G.J. Goschen, *Essays and Addresses on Economic Questions* (London, 1905), pp.7–8.

The Banking Community of London, 1890–1914: A Survey

by

Y. Cassis

The crucial importance of the City of London for the British Empire does not need to be demonstrated. It appears in the commercial relationships between the metropolis and the Empire: an important part of this trade passed through the Port of London and was dealt with by the merchant houses of the City.[1] At the financial level the bill of exchange on London was the medium of financing for international trade, and especially for trade between Britain and its colonies.[2] It was through the City of London that the countless commercial and industrial enterprises abroad were financed; this raises in its turn the whole problem of the export of British capital in the nineteenth century, at the heart of which the City is once again to be found.[3] This economic importance of the City of London inevitably raises the question of the place of financial interests in British overseas expansion, a major theme of controversy in the debate on British imperialism.[4]

These various aspects of the relationships between the City and the Empire have all been the subject of recent historical works, even though there are still many gaps in our knowledge and an enormous field open both for further investigation and for questioning received ideas. This article tries to approach the links between the City and the Empire from a new angle, by paying attention to the people who were at the core of the financial operations of the City, and who used to call themselves the 'banking community' of London. However, the activities and interests of the banking community as a whole were numerous and varied, and went far beyond those directly connected with the Empire. The development of banking in England was among the first preoccupations of the financial community in London;[5] the overwhelming importance of international business transacted solely in London also tended to divert their attention from the outside world. However, the various components of the English banking system were highly complementary and it would be erroneous, in talking of the City and the Empire, only to consider the City interests directly involved in expanding colonial enterprise.

The study of the banking community of London between 1890 and 1914 goes far beyond the framework of any one article. Here, after a brief survey of the various financial institutions of the City of London, two main aspects of this community will be considered: the general structure of its economic and financial interests, as indicated chiefly in the composition of the boards of the English joint-stock banks and the Anglo-foreign banks; and the defence of these interests in the political arena, as evidenced in the direct links between the City and politics rather than through the multiple examples of the influence of the City on imperial policy in various parts of the world. It argues that the City was dominated until the First World War by private family firms which were the direct agents of the international trade based on London; and it suggests that the Empire as such did not play a major part in the political activities of the banking community. The connotations of 'empire' and 'banking community' can usefully be specified at this point. The notion of empire will not only include colonies, but also the regions of the world exposed to a high degree of informal British influence. The banking community will be understood as including the partners of the private banking firms, both private deposit banks and merchant banks, as well as the directors of the joint-stock banks and the Anglo-foreign banks.[6] Such a definition means, of course, that some people whose principal occupation was not banking have been considered as members of the banking community.

I

The pre-eminence of the City of London rested upon a combination of institutions which facilitated the financing of international trade. Banks were at the base of the whole credit system, with the traditional distinction in the English banking system being made between the clearing banks which provided the cash credit, the merchant banks which accepted the bills of exchange, and the discount houses which discounted them. The Bank of England was the keeper of the reserves.[7] The Anglo-foreign banks were English banks in the sense that their capital and management were British and their head office was usually in London, but the greater part of their business was done in a foreign country or in the colonies.[8] Insurance companies were also in possession of enormous funds. Like the clearing banks, they were also subject to an intense amalgamation movement between 1890 and 1914, as a result of which a dozen giant firms emerged; during the same period, insurance companies also considerably extended their activities abroad and became more active on the financial market.[9] A third financial sector was made up by investment trusts. They started in Scotland and grew considerably in the late 1880s, directing a significant part of the savings towards foreign investment.[10] Finally, the pattern of City life followed the rhythm of its markets. First of all, of course, there was the London Stock Exchange, with £6,561,100,000 securities quoted in 1893, and £11,262,500,000 in 1913;[11] others included the Gold Market, a prerogative of London, the Baltic Exchange, and the London Metal Exchange.[12]

In addition to these financial organizations, all sorts of companies which multiplied from the 1880s onwards had their head office in the City. Shipping companies were especially prominent, even though Liverpool maintained its share with firms like Cunard and Frederick Leyland. The head offices of the main British railway companies were either in the City itself or in the stations located at the border of the square mile. Most of the companies engaged in business abroad had their head office in the City, as did, for instance, the South American railway companies; registration overseas was, however, not uncommon, and a number of South African mining companies were registered in Johannesburg or Kimberley. Finally, such diverse undertakings as the big breweries – Whitbread and Arthur Guinness – and oil companies – such as Shell Transport and Trading Company, or the Baku Russia Petroleum Company – established their headquarters there. Alongside these companies but strongly linked to them, the City was crowded with small private firms: private bankers and merchant bankers as already mentioned, merchants, stockbrokers and stockjobbers, chartered accountants, solicitors, insurance brokers, arbitrators, brokers and agents of all kinds, not to mention independent financiers and company directors.[13]

At the level of the boards of the large companies, particularly of the financial organizations, the City was dominated by two professional groups: bankers and merchants. They were in control of the joint-stock banks, the Anglo-foreign banks, the insurance companies and the various financial companies, especially the investment trusts. Professional specialization only existed at the level of the salaried managers, the training, career and actual work of a bank manager being different from those of, for example, the manager of an insurance office.

The use of the designation 'banker' changed between 1870 and 1914. Originally it applied only to private bankers, but with the growth of the joint-stock banks they gradually disappeared. At the same time more and more managers and senior officials described themselves as bankers;[14] however, they have not been included in this study as they belonged both professionally and socially to a different world.[15] In London, the private deposit banks really began to be taken over by the large joint-stock banks after 1890. However, the former private bankers who became directors of their new bank can be considered as bankers proper, as can merchant bankers, given the growing importance of accepting houses in the London money market. Unlike the private deposit banks, merchant banks held on until well after the First World War. Merchant bankers were to be found at the head of all the financial institutions of the City, including the Bank of England, traditionally closed to clearing bankers. A third group within the banking community was made up by the directors who played an active part in the management of their institution, such as Edward Holden (1842–1919), chairman and managing directors of the London City and Midland Bank, Felix Schuster (1854–1936), governor of the Union of London and Smiths Bank, and a few others.

Merchants were a key group in the City but very little is known about them. The boundaries of the group are not always easy to fix. The designation 'merchant' was rather vague: a City businessman who did not belong to any professional corps would call himself a merchant and could range from a small trader to a powerful financier. The functions of those more specifically involved in commerce were also diverse. Messrs. R.J. Henderson, East India merchants, owned the entire capital of the Borneo Company, a mining company to which they also acted as managers.[16] In 1894, Blyth, Greene, Jourdain & Co. registered as 'bankers, general merchants and commission agents'.[17] The business of J. Hubbard & Co. was almost entirely centred in the Anglo-Russian cotton factories: they supervised and financed these concerns on commission, accepted bills on Russian houses, and conducted some investment business.[18] It is imposs-ible to enter here into the details of the activities of the big City merchants in the late nineteenth century, and very few historical studies have been devoted to them.[19] Their functions and ways of operating certainly evolved during this period as the organization of the physical exchange of goods was increasingly replaced by paper transactions, and as they them-selves became involved in the financing and supervision of commercial and industrial companies.[20]

II

The importance of bankers and merchants in the banking community can be measured by their number on the boards of the joint-stock banks and the Anglo-foreign banks. Table 1 gives the composition of the boards of the 12 largest London-based joint-stock banks and 16 Anglo-foreign banks selected by geographical areas between 1890 and 1914.[21] In the two types of banks, bankers, merchants and shipowners, with the addition of the 'company directors', made up more than two-thirds of the total, respectively 76 per cent and 69 per cent. These percentages are high, but they are nevertheless underestimated: they include only those directors for whom there is enough information to justify including them in the sample. In fact the majority of directors not included in the sample can be reasonably assumed to be merchants. Merchants were in a majority at the Court of Directors of the Bank of England during the same period:

TABLE I

THE PRINCIPAL OCCUPATION OF THE DIRECTORS OF 12 LONDON-BASED
JOINT-STOCK BANKS AND 16 ANGLO-FOREIGN BANKS, 1890–1914

	Joint-Stock Banks		Anglo-Foreign Banks	
	No.	%	No.	%
Bankers	100	50	42	41
Merchants, shipowners	42	21	27	26
Company directors	6	3	2	2
Industrialists	13	6.5	3	3
Professionals	7	3.5	7	7
Politicians, senior civil servants	17	8.5	16	16
Aristocrats, landowners	9	4.5	3	3
Unknown	6	3	3	3
	200	100	102	100

among 35 directors there were representatives of 17 merchant houses (49 per cent), 13 merchant banks (37 per cent), and five miscellaneous (14 per cent).

There was a difference, among the directors of the joint-stock banks, between the former private bankers on the one hand, and merchants and merchant bankers on the other hand. The former were no longer partners in a private firm, for their concern had been taken over by the joint-stock bank of which they were directors. However, they retained various interests in the City, in particular at the head of the other financial institutions:[22] insurance companies and investment trusts, as well as on the board of the Anglo-foreign banks, of which they often were among the promoters in the 1860s.[23] The former private bankers were above all to be found on the board of Barclays Bank (of which 95 per cent of the directors had once been private bankers),[24] as well as on the boards of both Lloyds Bank and the Union of London and Smiths Bank. Only two private deposit banks (Glyn, Mills, Currie & Co. and Robarts, Lubbock & Co.) remained independent until 1914. For their part, merchants and merchant bankers were at the same time, and probably primarily, partners in a private firm, from which they drew their fortune and their reputation in the City. They were in a majority among the directors of the old London joint-stock banks: the London and Westminster Bank, the London and County Banking Company (which merged in 1909 under the name London County and Westminster Bank), the National Provincial Bank, and the London Joint Stock Bank. The same men, or other partners in the same firms, were also on the board of the Anglo-foreign banks and, in the case of the most prestigious firms, on the Court of Directors of the Bank of England. Table 2 gives a list of the merchant banks and merchant houses represented on the boards of the joint-stock banks, with mention of representation on the Court of Directors of the Bank of England and on the board of the Anglo-foreign banks.[25] The former private bankers could have been added to the table; however, as they did not represent the joint-stock bank of which they were directors on the board of an Anglo-foreign bank, it would have been difficult to regroup them, even though the persistence of family interests after the disappearance of the private bank is not to be doubted.

The fundamental unity of the English banking system therefore appears at the level of the boards of the joint-stock banks and the Anglo-foreign banks. These boards were not very different in their composition. Forty-two per cent of directors of the Anglo-foreign banks were also partners in a private bank or a merchant bank and/or directors of a joint-stock bank. Many of them were also partners in the same firm or even members of the same family. Moreover, joint-stock banks and Anglo-foreign banks fulfilled similar functions in London. The latter took part in the various financial operations on the London money market, especially bill-discounting and short-term loans, and made a not insignificant part of their profits in London.[26] As for the joint-stock banks, they played an essential part in the finance of British commerce through the

TABLE 2

THE REPRESENTATION OF MERCHANT BANKS AND MERCHANT HOUSES
ON THE BOARDS OF LONDON-BASED JOINT-STOCK BANKS,
OF THE ANGLO-FOREIGN BANKS AND ON THE COURT OF
THE BANK OF ENGLAND, 1890–1914

Merchant Banks	Bank of England Joint-stock banks	Anglo-Foreign banks
Arbuthnot, Latham & Co.	Bank of England London County and Westminster Bank	Standard Bank of South Africa
Brown, Shipley & Co.	Bank of England London County and Westminster Bank	Standard Bank of South Africa
Frühling & Goschen	Bank of England London County and Westminster Bank National Provincial Bank London Joint Stock Bank	Chartered Bank of India, Australia and China
C.J. Hambro & Son	Bank of England London County and Westminster Bank	
Fredk. Huth & Co.	Bank of England London and Westminster Bank London Joint Stock Bank	Anglo-Egyptian Bank
H.S. Lefevre & Co.	National Provincial Bank	
Neumann, Luebeck & Co.	London Joint Stock Bank	
Speyer Brothers	Union Bank of London	
Stern Brothers	London Joint Stock Bank	
Wallace Brothers	Bank of England London County and Westminster Bank	Chartered Bank of India, Australia and China

Merchant houses

Blyth, Greene, Jourdain & Co.	Bank of England London Joint Stock Bank	London Bank of Mexico and South America Mercantile Bank of India Standard Bank of South Africa
Cater, John N. & Co.	London County and Westminster Bank	Colonial Bank
Chalmers, Guthrie & Co.	London Joint Stock Bank	
Cotesworth & Powell	Bank of England National Provincial Bank	Colonial Bank
Curtis, Campbell & Co.	Bank of England London County and Westminster Bank	Colonial Bank
Dobree, Samuel & Sons	London and Westminster Bank National Provincial Bank	
Dent Brothers	London County and Westminster Bank	Chartered Bank of India, Australia and China
Dunn, William & Co.	Parr's Bank	
Faudel Phillips & Sons	London City and Midland Bank	
Forbes, Forbes, Campbell & Co.	National Provincial Bank	Bank of Australasia
Gibb, T.A. & Co.	London & County Bank	Hongkong & Shanghai Bank
Gilliat, J.K. & Co.	Bank of England London Joint Stock Bank	
Grenfell, P. & Sons	Bank of England London County and Westminster Bank	London and Brazilian Bank
Harvey, Brand & Co.	London Joint Stock Bank	London and River Plate Bank
Hay's Wharf	Bank of England London County and Westminster Bank	
Johnston, Edward, Son & Co.	Bank of England London and Westminster Bank London Joint Stock Bank	London and Brazilian Bank
Lampson, C.M. & Co.	London and County Bank	
Lusk, A. & Co.	London Joint Stock Bank	

TABLE 2 (continued)

Nevill, Druce & Co.	Union Bank of London	
Rathbone Brothers	Bank of England London County and	Hongkong and Shanghaï Bank
	Westminster Bank	
Ritchie, W. & Son	Union Bank of London	
Rodocanachi, Sons & Co.	London Joint Stock Bank	
Trotter, John & Co.	Union Bank of London	
Wernher, Beit & Co.	Union Bank of London	

discount of bills of exchange; they also lent money to colonial governments and to the Anglo-foreign banks themselves.[27]

There is no need to enter into the details of the other professional groups represented on the boards of the joint-stock banks and the Anglo-foreign banks, except to mention the very low percentage of industrialists, and a comparatively high percentage of politicians and former civil servants on the boards of the Anglo-foreign banks. While allowing that the estimate is probably on the high side, this last group accounted for 16 per cent of directors. They were particularly numerous on the board of the Standard Bank of South Africa, where eight out of 23 directors between 1890 and 1914 were former civil servants. There were four former governors of the Cape colony: Sir Henry Barkly (1815–1898), Sir Hercules Robinson (1824–1897), Lord Loch (1827–1900), and Sir Walter Hely–Hutchinson (1832–1915). Specialists in monetary questions also sat on the board: Lord Welby (1832–1914), former permanent secretary to the Treasury; Sir Charles Fremantle (1834–1914), former Deputy Master of the Mint; Sir David Barbour (1841–1928), former financial secretary to the Government of India, as well as a bimetallist and a member since 1900 of a special commission to inquire into the finances of the Orange River Colony and the Transvaal; and Sir Spencer Walpole (1837–1907), former secretary to the Post Office. Although this is an indication of the growing importance of South Africa to the sterling-exchange standard, the particular role of the Standard Bank and its links with the government could profitably be investigated further.[28]

Bankers and bank directors were also to be found in great number on the boards of insurance companies and investment trusts, the two main types of financial institutions apart from the banks during that period. Forty-nine per cent of bankers and bank directors were directors of an insurance company, and 31 per cent of an investment trust. Although ultimately both insurance companies and investment trusts collect funds and invest them, the interest that a seat on their board represented for a member of the banking community has to be considered separately.

The role of insurance companies in the financial market grew considerably between 1870 and 1914. The investment of those insurance companies which transacted life business increased from £110 million to £500 million, whereas in the same period British capital at home and overseas was only slightly more than doubled. The pattern of insurance company investments also changed during the same period, with a fall in loans on mortgages and a spectacular growth of foreign investments from seven to 40 per cent and possibly more, according to Professor Supple. At the same time, insurance companies, in particular those concerned with fire business, extended their activities abroad, especially in the United States and the empire.[29] A merchant or a banker with a seat on the board of an insurance company was in a position to exert control over the investments of the company, not to mention personal loans and directors' fees. Most of the firms represented on the boards of joint-stock banks and/or Anglo-foreign banks were also represented on the boards of one or more insurance companies. We shall not enter into the same details as for the banks but will take only the example of three quite representative merchant banks: Frühling & Goschen, Antony Gibbs & Sons, and Frederick Huth & Co. They had one of their partners on the boards of the following companies:

Frühling & Goschen	Atlas Assurance Company
	Indemnity Mutual Marine Insurance Company
	London Assurance Corporation
	Northern Assurance Company
	Ocean Marine Insurance Company
	Royal Exchange Assurance Corporation
	Sun Life Assurance Society
A. Gibbs & Sons	British and Foreign Marine Insurance Company
	Guardian Assurance Company
	Indemnity Mutual Marine Insurance Company
	London Assurance Corporation
	National Provident Institution
Frederick Huth	Imperial Insurance Company
& Co.	Indemnity Mutual Marine Insurance Company
	London Assurance Corporation
	Northern Assurance Company
	Royal Exchange Assurance Corporation.[30]

At the same time some insurance companies, particularly the old London companies such as the Atlas Assurance Company, the London Assurance Corporation, and the Royal Exchange Assurance Corporation, had an impressive number of bankers and bank directors on their boards. At the Royal Exchange for example, in 1906, 15 out of 27 directors were partners or directors of one of the banks selected in our sample.

The situation was slightly different in the investment trusts, the function of which, unlike that of the insurance companies, was only investment. They were often linked to a geographical area and/or a particular type of security, such as the Foreign and Colonial Debenture Corporation,[31] the London and South American Investment Trust or the

Railway Investment Company.[32] This was more particularly the case with the land and mortgage companies, such as the National Mortgage and Agency Company of New Zealand, or the Trust and Agency Company of Australia, which fulfilled much the same functions as the investment trusts. Unlike joint-stock banks and insurance companies, there was no amalgamation movement in investment trusts. On the contrary, their number grew considerably between 1891 and 1914, from 464 to 725 according to the *Stock Exchange Year Book* (or from 433 to 692 according to *Burdett's Official Intelligence*). Investment trusts were also smaller than banks or insurance companies, and had fewer directors, which often meant that their directors were more involved in the management of their company and could hold considerable interests in them.[33] In such flexible conditions, the directors of investment trusts linked with South America, for example, would often also be directors of an Anglo-South American Bank and partners of a commercial firm doing business in that part of the world, and if not acting themselves, they would be represented by a partner or a member of an allied family, for these latter interests could still be strong in investment trusts.[34]

Bankers and merchants also held interests in other types of companies: 29 per cent were directors of a railway company and 14 per cent of a shipping company. However, in these concerns they rarely held such a dominating position as in banks and insurance companies, except in the case of a small railway or shipping company directly linked to the activities of a merchant bank or a merchant house. At the level of the whole banking community it is impossible to consider each separate business in which bankers and merchants had interests, even though some were of considerable importance during the period under review, such as mining, oil, rubber, electricity and telegraphs, as usually only a minority of firms and members of the community were concerned. Indeed, it is always necessary to bear in mind the essentially disparate character of these private interests.

A paradoxical conclusion can be drawn from this rapid survey of the structure of interests within the banking community of London. On the one hand there was an undeniable concentration in the financial sector of the British economy, owing both to the giant banks and insurance companies produced by the amalgamation movement, and to the fact that a comparatively small group of people was to be found on the board of all the major financial institutions. It should be added that the members of this group, the banking community of London, were also linked by a network of family relationships,[35] which further reinforced the concentration of inside knowledge, influence, and expertise. On the other hand the private family firms still dominated the scene. Overlapping directorships are meaningless if not understood through the subtle merging of banking, commercial, and family business. These intimate personal interests and connections were at the hub of London's world-wide financial operations. Theirs was an economic position which can be expected to have had some political impact.

III

The defence of the interests of the banking community and the assertion
of its political point of view were exercised at three levels: in Parliament,
through pressure groups, and through the multiple contacts between
banking and political circles.

The banking community had its representatives in Parliament. Eighty-
seven bankers and bank directors were Members between 1890 and 1914,
which represents ten per cent of all the partners and directors of the banks
selected for this study. The percentage decreased with regard to the total
number of MPs, from a maximum of seven per cent in 1895 to a minimum
of two per cent in 1910, whereas in general business interests grew in
Parliament during the same period.[37] Bankers' activity in Parliament is
more significant. One way to consider the general level of such activity,
without entering into the details of particular debates, is to consider the
number of their interventions in Parliament. It is well known, of course,
that a lot could happen unofficially in the lobby of the House; however,
interventions provide at least an indication of bankers' participation in
the official activity of Parliament. For this purpose, we have selected at
random the third session of the five Parliaments elected between 1890
and 1914. It can be seen from Table 3 that the majority of bankers and

TABLE 3

INTERVENTIONS BY BANKERS IN PARLIAMENTARY DEBATES

3rd session of Parliaments elected in

	1892	1895	1900	1906	1910
No intervention	2 (12%)	3 (14%)	7 (44%)	4 (33%)	1 (10%)
1 to 4 interventions	9 (52%)	10 (48%)	3 (20%)	1 (8%)	6 (60%)
5 to 10 "	2 (12%)	3 (14%)	2 (12%)	2 (17%)	2 (20%)
11 to 20 "	2 (12%)	4 (19%)	2 (12%)	2 (17%)	1 (10%)
More than 20 "	2 (12%)	1 (5%)	2 (12%)	3 (25%)	0 (0%)
	17 (100%)	21 (100%)	16 (100%)	12 (100%)	10 (100%)

Source: Hansard (House of Commons)

merchants with a seat on the board of a joint-stock bank or an Anglo-
foreign bank – more than 60 per cent – intervened in the parliamentary
debates less than five times a year. Eric Hambro (1872–1947), MP for
Surrey from 1900 to 1906, never spoke during the whole Parliament
elected in 1900. Only a few bankers and bank directors regularly intervened in the debates, and even then not necessarily about matters related
to banking interests. The best known was Sir John Lubbock, later the first
Baron Avebury (1834–1913), who was regularly entrusted by the City's
professional groups to introduce bills of concern to them; but he also was
the initiator of the Bank Holiday Act in 1871.[38] More talkative banker

members included Sir Henry Seymour King (1852–1933),[39] Sir Edward
Sassoon (1856–1912),[40] John Annan Bryce (1841–1923),[41] James Tomkin-
son (1840–1910),[42] and the two spokesmen of the Parliamentary Committee of Bankers, Edward Brodie Hoare (1841–1911),[43] and Frederick
D. Dixon-Hartland (1832–1909).[44] Unfortunately, very little seems to
have survived from this committee, founded to co-ordinate the activity of
the members representing banking interests in Parliament.[45] It was, in
fact, the mouthpiece of the Central Association of Bankers.

Bankers were therefore discreet in Parliament, and do not appear to
have considered it the best place for the defence of their interests.
Pressure groups were more active, but did not represent the whole
banking community. The joint-stock banks were the only ones to dispose
of organized pressure groups. The oldest and the most prestigious was the
Committee of the London Clearing Bankers, with a representative of
each bank member of the London Clearing House.[46] The Central Association of Bankers was founded in 1895 to regroup in the same association
representatives of the Committee of the London Clearing Bankers, of the
English Country Bankers' Association, of Fleet Street and West End
banks as well as of the Irish and Scottish bankers.[47] However, neither the
merchant banks, nor the discount houses, nor the Anglo-foreign banks
were represented. These three categories of banks had no professional
association between 1890 and 1914. The merchant banks formed their
association, the Accepting Houses Committee, at the outbreak of the
First World War to meet together the crisis of illiquidity which hit some of
them as a result of the non-payment of debts owing from Germany and its
allies.[48] The Institute of Bankers, founded in 1879, tended to act as a
pressure group until the late 1880s when its function as a centre of
information for bank clerks was more clearly established.[49] However, it
remained a place where the point of view of the banking community was
clearly expressed, as in the debates on bimetallism in 1895 or on free trade
and protectionism in 1903. But once again it was patronised mainly by the
joint-stock banks, even though it was open to, and had members from, all
sections of the banking community. Two other associations should also be
mentioned, which were more closely linked to foreign investments and
empire: the Corporation of Foreign Bondholders, and the London
Chamber of Commerce, founded in 1880 to unite the financial and
commercial interests of the City into a single representative organ.[50]

What were the activities of these pressure groups? Generally, it can be
said that they were limited both in their object and in their impact. Let us
consider the daily activity of the Central Association of Bankers from its
foundation in 1895 to 1911. The Association judged it important to take
action on the following problems: the company law of 1895; competition
from the Bank of England; stamp duties on cheques in 1902; borrowing
by Municipal Corporations in 1903 and 1904; the Bills of Exchange Act
Amendment Bill in 1904; the Public Trustee Bill in 1905; and the Limited
Partnership Bill in 1906. The Central Association of Bankers did not take
any particular action during the Budget crisis of 1909, and between 1899

and 1908 it appointed a special committee to enquire into the question of the Gold Reserves, without, however, any general discussion on the subject taking place. Imperial questions were totally absent from their debates. The Boer War was discussed only once, in December 1899, in the form of 'the regulations the principal banks proposed to adopt with regard to such of their clerks who should be called upon to serve'.[51]

As an educational institute, the Institute of Bankers presents but little interest for the analysis of the political influence of the banking community. But the Institute of Bankers was also a place where the members of the banking community used to meet and discuss various problems connected more or less directly with the banking profession: three times a year the members were invited to listen to and comment on a paper by one of their colleagues. The interest of the members of the Institute in foreign questions, including imperial questions, was both limited and generally linked directly to professional matters. To quote a few examples: in March 1894, Nathaniel Cork (1835–1902), managing director of the Commercial Banking Company of Sydney, discussed 'The Late Australian Banking Crisis'[52] and a year later, L.L. Mitchell talked to his colleagues about 'South African Banking – A Retrospect'.[53] India was only approached from the angle of currency questions, in two conferences: in December 1893, Sir R. Temple commented on 'The Report of the India Currency Committee',[54] and in March 1900, J.F. Darling gave a paper on 'The Currency of India'.[55] Only three conferences were more far-reaching. After Cornelis Rozenraad spoke in February 1898 on 'The Commercial Struggle of the Nations', the discussion which followed was concerned with the German threat to British commercial and financial supremacy.[56] But in January 1900 the banking community, without showing much concern, debated 'Our Commercial Supremacy', following a paper by Henry Tipper;[57] and in January 1912, Norman Angell, in a paper entitled 'The Influence of War upon International Relations', presented his thesis on the impossibility of war owing to the financial interdependence between the developed nations.[58]

The Corporation of Foreign Bondholders was entrusted with the defence of its constituents' interests, by putting pressure on the British government or by directly using its influence with the foreign govern ents. Without entering into the details of its activities or trying too hastily to evaluate its impact, the opinion of one of the leading merchant banks, C.J. Hambro & Son, is worth quoting:

> (...)the Corporation ought to be a very useful one, but unfortunately those who know best how to treat with foreign governments are all too busy to join the board and tendency naturally is that men join it who like to see their names in print. It is sometimes said, we know not with how much truth, that the Corporation is sometimes more anxious to earn its own commission than stand out for the good of the Bondholders. The Chairman is a most capable man, but a very busy one and can hardly have time to follow the negociations.

Issuing houses generally find it is best to negotiate themselves with defaulting governments.[59]

The London Chamber of Commerce was more concerned with imperial matters, and its tone could be aggressive. Demands were constantly put to the government by the geographical trade sections of the London Chamber of Commerce. Taken as a whole these called for a wide range of state action, from occasional visits by British warships to the annexation of territory. Between these extremes were requests for the appointments of consuls or vice-consuls, British residents (permanent or temporary), the policing of territory, the defining of spheres of influence, the formation of protectorates and annexation of territories, institution of currency, building of railways in existing possessions, and the negotiation of treaties.[60] However, in this case, it was not the banking community as a whole which was expressing its point of view, but merchants with particular interests in a given overseas region. Their mouthpiece, the Chamber of Commerce *Journal,* was also much more concerned with questions of imperial policy than the *Bankers' Magazine,* which can be considered as the unofficial organ of the banking community.

Finally, the political influence of the banking community was mediated through the personal and consultative contacts which its leading figures enjoyed with the politicians. Bankers, and sometimes the City as a corporate institution, frequently used two means of action: the sending of a delegation to the authorities, usually the Chancellor of the Exchequer, sometimes the Prime Minister; and the sending of a petition signed 'the merchants and bankers of the City of London' to the same authorities. Without entering here into an exhaustive list, it may be recalled that on 1 December 1891 a delegation of bankers met the Chancellor, George J. Goschen, who explained to them his scheme to increase the reserves of the banks and to give more elasticity to the Bank Act.[61] On 16 October 1897, the merchants and bankers sent a petition, carrying many signatures, to the Chancellor of the Exchequer stating their opposition to any concession to bimetallism which might be made following the visit to London of an American delegation anxious to reach a bimetallic agreement.[62] The opposition of the City to the financial dispositions of the Lloyd George budget in 1909 is better known. Not only did an almost unanimous City send a petition to Prime Minister Asquith, but on this occasion, the sending of the petition was complemented by a meeting in the City presided over, most unusually, by Lord Rothschild himself.[63]

For their part, the government and the Treasury regularly consulted the most eminent members of the banking community. At the time of the visit of the American delegation on bimetallism in 1897, the Chancellor of the Exchequer, Sir Michael Hicks Beach, consulted the Governor of the Bank of England, Lord Rothschild and Alfred de Rothschild, and Lord Aldenham, the president of the Bimetallic League.[64] During the Boer War, between 1900 and 1902, Hicks Beach and Edward Hamilton, the permanent secretary to the Treasury, consulted Lord Rothschild, Lord

Revelstoke, Sir Ernest Cassel and a few others about forms that the various war loans should take.[65] There also were many links between financiers and foreign policy-makers; something of this is revealed in recent work on the role of the Imperial Bank of Persia[66] and the National Bank of Turkey as instruments of British diplomacy,[67] or financial imperialism as it impinged on China in the 1890s.[68] At the private and individual level, it is well known that Chancellors of the Exchequer used to seek the advice of the most influential bankers. When Sir William Harcourt again became Chancellor of the Exchequer in 1892, he immediately wrote to Samuel Montagu, later the first Baron Swaythling (1832–1911), to obtain information and financial advice.[69] Until his death in 1896, Bertram Currie (1827–1896) was probably the City personality enjoying the highest prestige at the Treasury.[70] Following the Liberal victory in 1906, a new generation, characterized not only by age but by professional type, seems to have come to the fore politically: such men as Edward Holden, Felix Schuster, and Edgar Speyer were very well connected at the Treasury and with H.H. Asquith, Chancellor and later Prime Minister. In this context, the shared social world of bankers and politicians should not be underestimated; they went to the same public schools, frequented the same circles, married in the same group of families: this closeness must be considered as a characteristic contributing to the political influence of the City.

In order to understand the limits of bankers' political influence and activity, not least on imperial questions, one must make a distinction between what might be called the 'technical' and the 'political' levels. The technical level refers to political interventions mainly of a professional nature, whereas the political level refers to politics in general, internal and external, including economic policy. The activity of the Central Association of Bankers centred exclusively on professional questions, as did most of the conferences and debates of the Institute of Bankers. Whenever a banker was consulted by politicians, it was invariably on questions within the technical scope of banking, such as government borrowing, questions of money and currency, and legislation on commercial and financial matters. But it is significant that on a question such as a Budget, which is not purely technical but entails questions of general politics, Chancellors never consulted bankers. The same applies to foreign and imperial policy. Financial and commercial circles pressed claims about geographical areas in which they had their business interests; the government might work in concert with a finance house for a well-defined political purpose, but in no way did the banking community develop a global vision of British foreign policy nor did it take part in the elaboration of this policy. Vested financial interests attempted to influence decisions on specific issues in the realms of domestic, foreign and imperial policy, but the discernible pattern is not one in which national strategy had become profoundly penetrated by identifiable business lobbies. The major options of economic policy, such as gold monometallism, free trade or sound public finance were in accordance with the City's interests, owing to the independent recognition by policy-makers of the importance of the City in the British economy as well as to the social and personal links between banking and political circles. Preoccupied mainly with the routine of their daily operations in London, City bankers were therefore only very rarely driven by circumstances into taking overtly political actions.

IV

In an age of imperialism and financial concentration, the English banker remained an independent businessman, distinct from the type of senior executive more often to be found on the Continent. He was usually a partner in a private firm and a director of one or more major financial institutions, and therefore maintained a semi-professional status which made him seem more of a gentleman rather than the 'great capitalist' of the imperialist era concentrating in his hands banking and industrial capital. The joint-stock companies of which he was a director provided the financial facilities for his private enterprises. In a period of general prosperity after 1895, and at a time when the British Empire dominated much of the world, the English banker was in a position to see that legislation by the authorities hampered his business activities as little as possible, and if necessary lobby the government on specific issues related to his business interests. The more prominent of them would give their expert advice when consulted by the government on economic and financial matters. Close to the politicians on whom it could entirely rely for the elaboration of an economic policy in accordance with its interests, the banking community of London could be satisfied with sharing the general imperialist mood of the period.

University of Geneva

NOTES

1. See P. Bairoch, *Commerce extérieur et développement économique de l'Europe au XIXème siècle* (Paris-La Haye, 1976); F.E. Hyde, *Far Eastern Trade 1860–1914* (London, 1973); D.C.M. Platt, *Latin America and British Trade 1806–1914* (London, 1972); S.B. Saul, *Studies in British Overseas Trade 1870–1914* (Liverpool, 1960).
2. Cf. F. Schuster, 'Foreign Trade and the Money Market', *Journal of the Institute of Bankers* 25 (1904); M. de Cecco, *Money and Empire: The International Gold Standard 1890–1914* (Oxford, 1974).
3. See for example P.L. Cottrell, *British Overseas Investments in the Nineteenth Century* (London, 1975); M. Edelstein, *Overseas Investment in the Age of High Imperialism; The United Kingdom, 1850–1914,* (London, 1982); D.C.M. Platt, 'British Portfolio Investment Overseas Before 1870: some doubts' *Economic History Review* 2nd ser. 33 (1980) and a forthcoming article for the period 1870–1914.
4. See for example P.J. Cain, *Economic Foundations of British Overseas Expansion 1815–1914* (London, 1980), which is the most recent synthesis on the question.
5. See the series of articles published the first three months of each year by the *Bankers'*

Magazine and entitled 'The Progress of Banking in Great Britain and Ireland', which were one of its most valuable contributions.

6. This analysis is based upon a sample of 413 partners or directors of the leading London based private banks, merchant banks, discount houses, joint-stock banks, Anglo-foreign banks and the Bank of England between 1890 and 1914. Lists of partners and directors have been established for the years 1891, 1898, 1906 and 1913 from the *Banking Almanac, Year Book and Directory* and the *London Banks and Kindred Companies*. It has been possible to find sufficient information and therefore to include in the sample 55 per cent of all the bankers and bank directors of the period, ranging from more than 70 per cent for the private banks, merchant banks and the Bank of England to 44 per cent for the Anglo-foreign banks.

7. See for example W. Bagehot, *Lombard Street: A Description of the Money Market* (London, 1873); H. Withers, *The Meaning of Money* (London, 1909).

8. On the Anglo-foreign banks, see A.S.J. Baster, *The Imperial Banks* (London, 1929) and *The International Banks* (London, 1935).

9. See B. Supple, *The Royal Exchange Assurance: A History of British Insurance 1720–1970* (Cambridge, 1970).

10. On investment trusts see T.J. Grayson, *Investment Trusts. Their Origin, Development and Operation* (New York, 1928); A. Bullock, *The Story of Investment Companies* (New York, 1959).

11. E.V. Morgan and W.A. Thomas, *The Stock Exchange. Its History and Functions* (London, 1962), pp.280–81.

12. On the Baltic Exchange see H.B. King, *The Baltic Exchange: The History of a Unique Market* (London, 1977).

13. There exist only general accounts of some of these professions. On merchant banks, see S.D. Chapman, *Rise of Merchant Banking* (London, 1984); on stockbrokers and stockjobbers, see D. Kynaston, 'The London Stock Exchange 1870–1914: An Institutional History' (unpub. Ph.D. thesis, University of London, 1983); on accountants, see E. Jones, *Accountancy and the British Economy, 1840–1980: The Evolution of Ernst & Whinney* (London, 1981). For company histories see Guildhall Library, London, *London Business Houses Histories, A. Handlist.*

14. E. Green, *Debtors to their Profession. A History of the Institute of Bankers, 1879–1979* (London, 1979).

15. The social origins of the general managers, mainly from the lower middle classes, differed sharply from the upper class backgrounds of the directors. In addition, as a reflection of their devotion to the business of the bank, they did not sit on the board of any other company. General managers therefore cannot be considered as having been fully integrated into the world of the great capitalists of the City of London in the late nineteenth century, their professional status ultimately remaining that of subordinates *vis à vis* the board of directors. See. Y. Cassis, *Les banquiers de la City à l'époque edouardienne, 1890–1914* (Geneva, 1984), pp.146–161, and 'Management and Strategy in the English Joint Stock Banks, 1890–1914', forthcoming in *Business History.*

16. Papers of Antony Gibbs & Sons, merchant bankers, Confidential Information Book on Merchant Firms, 1883–1905, Ms.11,038C, Guildhall Library, London.

17. A. Muir, *Blyth, Greene, Jourdain & Co., Limited, 1810–1960,* (London, 1961), p.26.

18. Papers of J. Hubbard & Co., Ms.10,364, Guildhall Library, London.

19. Although for an earlier period, S. Marriner, *Rathbones of Liverpool, 1845–1873* (Liverpool, 1961) is an excellent case study.

20. See for example A.C. Pointon, *Wallace Brothers* (Oxford, 1974).

21. The following banks have been selected: joint-stock banks: Barclay & Co., Limited, Lloyds Bank, London and County Banking Company, London and Provincial Bank, London and South Western Bank, London and Westminster Bank, London City and Midland Bank, London County and Westminster Bank, London Joint Stock Bank, National Provincial Bank of England, Parr's Bank, Union of London and Smiths Bank. Anglo-foreign banks: Anglo-Egyptian Bank, Anglo-South American Bank, Bank of Australasia, Bank of New South Wales, Chartered Bank of India, Australia and China, Hongkong and Shangaï Banking Corporation, London and Brazilian Bank, London

and River Plate Bank, London Bank of Australia, Mercantile Bank of India, National Bank of Egypt, National Bank of India, National Bank of Turkey, Standard Bank of South Africa, Union Bank of Australia.

22. For example, Martin Ridley Smith (1833–1908), partner in Smith, Payne & Smiths, of Lombard Street and a director of the Union of London and Smiths Bank after the absorption of his bank in 1902, was chairman of the Sao Paolo (Brazilian) Railway Company and a director of the Bank of Australasia and of the Imperial Insurance Company. His cousin and colleague Lindsay Eric Smith (1852–1930) was a director of the National Bank of New Zealand, the National Mortgage and Agency Company of New Zealand, of the Industrial and General Trust and of the Ottoman Railway from Smyrna to Aidin, as well as of the Union of London and Smiths Bank.

23. See for example the part taken by the Glyns in the foundation of the London and Brazilian Bank in 1862 in D. Joslin, *A Century of Banking in Latin America* (London, 1963), pp.64–5, and in the foundation of the Anglo-Austrian Bank in 1863 in P.L. Cottrell, 'London Financiers and Austria 1863–1875: The Anglo-Austrian Bank', *Business History*, 11 (1969).

24. The foundation of Barclays Bank in 1896 was the result of an amalgamation of 20 private banks. See P.W. Matthews and A.W. Tuke, *History of Barclays Bank, Limited* (London, 1926).

25. On the meaning of a seat on the board of a joint stock bank and the real power that directors enjoyed, see Cassis *Les Banquiers de la City*, (1984).

26. See 'Colonial and Foreign Banks with offices in London', *Bankers' Magazine* 87 (1909), pp.359–68. According to Ms S. Tscherebilo's estimates, more than half of the profits of the London and Brazilian Bank were made in London. I should like to thank Ms Tscherebilo for this information.

27. C.A.E. Goodhart, *The Business of Banking 1890–1914* (London, 1972), pp.154–55.

28. On the Standard Bank of South Africa, see J.A. Henry, *The First Hundred Years of the Standard Bank*, (London, 1963).

29. Supple, *The Royal Exchange Assurance*, pp.218–24 and 330–48.

30. *Directory of Directors*, 1890–1914.

31. Established in 1889 'For the purpose of making advances upon debentures of foreign and colonial undertakings, guaranteeing principal and interests of debentures etc.' *Stock Exchange Year Book*, 1892.

32. Established in 1881, 'to make investments in certain British railway ordinary stock . . . ', *Stock Exchange Year Book*, 1892.

33. Thomas Charles Baring (1831–91) held £80,000, nominal value, and John Lubbock, later Lord Avebury, £30,000 in the stock of the London Trust Company; Company File 28,525, London Trust Company, 1890. The Bevans held £30,000 in the Merchants' Trust Company and Lord Kinnaird (1847–1923), also from Barclays and a director of the company £20,000; Company File 28,276, Merchants' Trust, 1901.

34. To quote only one example, Robert Harvey, director of the London and South American Investment Trust from its foundation in 1913, was also a partner with Col. North, the 'Nitrate king' in North & Harvey, chairman of the Anglo-South American Bank and chairman of several nitrate companies.

35. On this question see Y. Cassis, 'Bankers in English Society in the late Nineteenth Century', *Economic History Review* (forthcoming).

36. J.A. Thomas, *The House of Commons, 1832–1901. A Study of its economic and functional character* (Cardiff, 1939), pp.18–19.

38. A partner in Robarts, Lubbock & Co. He was, among several other appointments the first President of the Institute of Bankers in 1879, the Central Association of Bankers, and the Committee of the London Clearing Bankers.

39. A partner in King & Co. of Bombay, Delhi, Calcutta and London, and a director of Lloyds Bank from 1910.

40. A partner in D. Sassoon & Co. and a director of the Imperial Bank of Persia and the Daira Sanieh Company.

41. A partner in Wallace Brothers, East India Merchants, and a director of the London County and Westminster Bank and of several companies, particularly oil companies.

42. A director of Lloyds Bank since 1898 and a former partner of Williams & Co. at Chester.
43. A director of Lloyds Bank and a former partner of Banetts, Hoare & Co., in Lombard Street.
44. A director of the London City and Midland Bank and a former partner of Lacy, Hartland and Woodbridge, London.
45. *Bankers' Magazine* 81 (1906), 704, and *Midland Bank Archives*, North and South Wales Bank M153/67(2) 9–11 May 1900.
46. The building of the Clearing House at 10 Lombard Street was erected in 1833, but the clearing system had already been working for many years; it is generally accepted as beginning *circa* 1770. Committee of the London Clearing Bankers, *London Bankers' Clearing House* (London, 1966).
47. Central Association of Bankers, Minutes from the first Meeting to November 1911.
48. C.J.J. Clay and B.S. Wheble (eds.), *Modern Merchant Banking* (Cambridge, 1976), p.23.
49. Green, (1979), *Debtors to their Profession*, pp.49–73.
50. See S.R.B. Smith, 'The Centenary of the London Chamber of Commerce: Its Origins and Early Policy', *The London Journal* 8 (1982).
51. Central Association of Bankers, Minutes from the first Meeting to Novermber 1911, *passim*.
52. *Journal of the Institute of Bankers* (hereafter *JIB*) 15 (1894), 175–212.
53. *JIB* 16 (1895), 287–97.
54. *JIB* 15 (1894).
55. *JIB* 21 (1900), 177–94.
56. *JIB* 19 (1898), 103–38; discussion 139–44.
57. *JIB* 20 (1900), 107–30; discussion, 131–36.
58. *JIB* 34 (1912), 50–75.
59. Hambros Bank Archives, Private Letters, Vol. 31, 1891, C.J. Hambro & Son to R. Warschauer & Co., Berlin, 27 Nov. 1891, Ms 19,063, Guildhall Library, London.
60. Examples quoted in Steven R.B. Smith, 'British power, imperialism & the City, 1880–1900', a paper delivered at the Imperial History Seminar, Institute of Historical Research, London 7 March 1983.
61. Welby Papers, London School of Economics, Welby Collection on Banking and Currency, Vol. VII, 113/114.
62. *JIB* 18 (1897), 492–3.
63. Asquith Papers, Bodleian Library, Oxford, Vol. 12, fol. 32.
64. See St Aldwyn Papers, Gloucestershire Record Office, PC/PP 68, Correspondence with and concerning the American delegation on Bimetallism. There is another copy of this correspondence at the PRO, Treasury Papers, T 168/85.
65. See Edward Hamilton's Diary, Vols. XLVII – L, Add.MSS.48,676–48,679, British Library, London.
66. Baster, *The International Banks*.
67. M. Kent, 'Agent of Empire? The National Bank of Turkey and British Foreign Policy', *Historical Journal*, 18 (1975).
68. See D. MacLean, 'The Foreign Office and the First Chinese Indemnity Loan', *Historical Journal* 16 (1973), and 'Finance and "Informal Empire" before the First World War', *Economic History Review* 2nd. ser. 29 (1976).
69. Harcourt Papers, Vol. 221/1–3, Samuel Montagu to W. Harcourt, 16 Sept. 1892, Bodleian Library, Oxford.
70. R. Fulford, *Glyn's 1753–1953: Six Generations in Lombard Street* (London, 1953), 202; Edward Hamilton's Diary, Vol. 26, Add.MS.48,655, 11 Feb. 1891.

The Phases of French Colonial Imperialism: Towards a New Periodization*

by

Jacques Marseille

If I had to sum up as briefly as possible my research on the economic history of French colonization since the end of the nineteenth century,[1] I would say that its principal contribution has been to challenge the periodization of that history which has been accepted up till now. Based on the analysis of only limited data, previous studies proposed a chronological classification which ended up by conflating the positions of historians and economists who, however, regarded themselves as belonging to different schools. From this, the classic chronological divisions since the 1880s have been as follows:

(1) Until 1914, colonial affairs were only a matter of secondary importance, satisfying the ambitions of military men and nationalists and the appetites of certain profiteers. The low percentage which the empire represented in French foreign trade (10–12 per cent of total trade in 1913) and capital investments (less than a tenth of world capital exports) was sufficient to show that colonial conquests owed nothing to the actions of financial groups.

(2) From the beginning of the First World War, the contribution of the colonies to the defence budget of France itself revealed the interest in the colonial reserve of a French capitalism weakened both by recession in its fields of expansion, and by the instability of the franc. The economic opportunities offered by the empire consequently softened the effects of the crisis of the 1930s.

(3) Finally, from 1945 on, the empire became the pillar of French economic strength: hence the fears displayed by certain parties faced with the process of decolonization. In 1957, the Director of Economic Affairs at the Ministry of French Overseas Territories, Pierre Moussa, was thus able to say:

> One can reckon that about 500,000 French people resident in France (300,000 of whom are in industry) draw their income directly or more or less directly from commerce between the metropole and the overseas territories: thus, in France itself, one household in 28 is dependent for its basic support on the imperial connection (it is estimated that there are about 14 million households). The importance of this mutual trade is thus considerable. Each of the partners,

France on the one hand, the overseas territories on the other, owes an important part of its livelihood to the control of the other partner.[2]

In fact, this sombre prediction of disaster if decolonization went ahead was not fulfilled. In the decade which followed independence, the growth of French capitalism was particularly vigorous, and its structural changes rapid. Deprived of its colonies, France progressively made up some of the backwardness which marked it off from the industrialized powers. It is this fact which needs to be explained. How did France bear, without ill effects, the loss of a preferential zone which during the 1950s took between 35 and 42 per cent of its total exports and supplied between 25 and 30 per cent of its imports?

I

The empire: an early and preferential field of French expansion

To answer this question, we need to look at colonialism in the long term, to evaluate the place that the colonial market held during successive phases of economic growth, and to break down overall percentages in order to understand sector-based data, thus allowing us to define those sectors of activity most directly affected by colonial trade.

Statistically, this research has followed several paths. On the commercial level, we attempted to single out the areas for which the empire was a supplementary market, those for which it represented practically nothing, and finally those for which it proved to be a preferential market. We can thus understand more clearly the relationship between the foreign market and the structural evolution of French capitalism. On the financial level, we attempted to fill a gap by putting together a homogeneous and continuous imperial series on private loans, capable of demonstrating more clearly the different phases of capital exports to the empire.

To do this, we compiled a register of all the colonial companies registered in the *Annuaire Desfossés* from 1907 to 1960, in order to draw up a list of private investment limited to the issue of shares and bonds of those firms operating in the colonies. The use of foreign capital cannot, of course, be considered as the sole source of investment, but within the framework of the colonial empire this may be considered the series nearest to it,[3] with the risk of encouraging firms to tie up savers' funds, rather than their own reserves, in fixed assets. This is all the more so since colonial shares had enjoyed a lively success on world stock markets. Exploring these statistical avenues leads to a searching reappraisal of the accepted classification of the stages of French colonization.

Before 1914, far from being a minor concern, the formal empire was already occupying a leading place in France's expansion overseas. Right from 1896, that is to say 15 years after the acquisition of colonies began, the empire, taken as a geographic whole, was vying with Germany and the economic union of Belgium and Luxemburg for the position of France's second trading partner, after Great Britain (Table 1). Yet at this date (1896) the empire's share in France's foreign trade covered only 10 per cent of total French exports and 9.4 per cent of total French imports.

TABLE 1

VALUE OF TRADE (IMPORTS AND EXPORTS COMBINED)

(in millions of francs)

	G.B.	U.E.B.L.	Germany	Colonial Empire
1896	1541.2	783.4	647.5	704.3
1897	1617.7	801.1	698.3	757.5
1898	1526.5	863.6	817.1	804.8
1899	1874.8	937.9	817.1	946.4
1900	1902.2	1020.2	892.2	841.3
1901	1800.1	920.0	845.4	910.7
1902	1846.9	963.6	905.6	995.8
1903	1747.9	955.6	957.0	1010.5
1904	1734.4	984.1	984.1	1045.0
1905	1848.7	990.6	1116.0	1038.6
1906	2044.7	1180.6	1223.8	1126.9
1907	2252.0	1287.5	1287.9	1295.6
1908	1972.5	1158.7	1224.6	1301.3
1909	2147.8	1342.1	1387.0	1381.1
1910	2205.4	1473.5	1664.5	1663.7
1911	2209.8	1566.8	1774.3	1697.7
1912	2410.1	1684.6	1820.9	1797.3
1913	2569.0	1664.8	1935.6	1692.0

Source: Tableau général du Commerce et de la Navigation.

If these overall percentages mask the *early* significance of the colonial market, what they hide above all is the importance it represented for certain branches of French capitalism. In the event, the overall figures conceal variations which rob the averages of all significance. At the beginning of the twentieth century, the empire already guaranteed preferential outlets for sectors as essential as the cotton and metallurgical industries, the sugar industry, and the mechanical engineering industry (Table 2). The figures for foreign trade lead, then, to a reassessment of a period which had been discounted up till then – the time leading up to the First World War. But it is those data concerning the export of private capital which are the most significant. Of the 469 colonial companies registered in the *Annuaire Desfossés,* 200 were established before 1914, 156 of these between 1898 and 1914. In volume (in 1914 francs) the capital issued by these firms (in the form of shares and bonds), represented 1,970.1 million francs. To appreciate the importance of this figure, we need only compare it with other fields of expansion in French capitalism at this period.

René Girault has assessed the direct investment of private French companies in Russia at 2.2 milliard francs.[4] Jacques Thobie has reckoned

TABLE 2
FRENCH EXPORTS IN 1906
(in millions of francs)

Commodities	Total	Empire	% of Exports to the Empire
Candles	3.88	3.43	88.4
Bleached cotton fabric	35.37	30.52	86.2
Raw cotton fabric	23.57	19.97	84.7
Constructions in metal – iron or steel	14.43	11.60	80.3
Beer	4.27	3.23	75.6
Locomotives and steam rollers	3.00	2.21	73.6
Bearings, cylindrical pipes	3.87	2.72	70.2
Rope or thread, double twisted	5.51	3.59	65.1
Iron or steel rails	8.14	4.61	56.6
Shoes	11.00	5.89	53.5
Pure cotton fabric, plain cotton fabric, twill, dyed twill	78.84	38.81	49.2
Lard	3.45	1.36	39.4
Refined loaf sugar or lump sugar	56.06	21.92	39.1
Toilet soap	5.72	2.13	37.0
Agricultural machinery	8.83	3.19	36.1
Sesame seed oil	14.72	5.19	35.2
Brandies	6.44	2.21	34.3
Straw hats	13.24	3.66	27.6
Iron and steel, laminated or forged	24.67	5.47	22.1

Source: As Table 1

direct French investments in the Ottoman Empire at 509 million francs.[5] For Germany, Raymond Poidevin reckons 'the entire property assets of industrial and commercial enterprises in French hands at the start of the war' at 1.5 milliard francs.[6] In Austro-Hungary, 1.1 milliard were invested in shares and bonds in transport enterprises.[7] In Spain, where the contribution of French capital played a particularly important role, Albert Broder reckons direct investments at 2 milliard.[8] Latin America alone stands out distinctly: in the whole of the South American continent, the total of direct investments rose in 1913 to 4.8 milliard francs.[9] Thus, on the eve of the First World War, the empire ranked high in the fields of expansion of foreign private investment, on a footing with Spain, and with Russia hot on its heels for second place.

Furthermore, if one breaks down private investments by types of activity, one can say that behind the transport firms which are clearly dominant, financial concerns and mining companies rank above plantations and business firms – both of which had all too rapidly become the symbol of a development that was archaic and parasitical (Table 3).

TABLE 3
CAPITAL ISSUED IN 1914
(in millions of francs)

	Shares	Bonds	Total
Banking firms, real estate and property companies	283.6	14.9	298.5
Mining companies	277.6	29.6	307.2
Transport companies	180.3	906.0	1086.3
Plantations and agricultural companies	108.5	4.0	112.5
Industrial companies	57.5	29.4	86.9
Commercial companies	76.8	2.5	79.3
Total	984.3	986.4	1970.7

Source: Annuaire Desfossés

Other signs confirm the privileged position that the empire occupied at a time when the range of choices offered to investors was still largely open. The profitability of colonial firms seems even greater than that of companies operating outside the colonies. In the years before the First World War, the *Compagnie des phosphates et chemins de fer de Gafsa* (Phosphate and Railway Company of Gafsa) paid to its shareholders a dividend equal, on average, to 30 per cent of the nominal share price. As for the *Charbonnages du Tonkin* (Tonkin Coal Mines), they assured a return of 30–35 per cent. By comparison, dividends paid by Russian firms operating in the Ottoman Empire seem very paltry. *Les Mines de Balia-Karaïdin*, which were among those that handed out the most substantial profits, assured an average annual dividend of 13 per cent between 1893 and 1913.[10] In 1912, the *Mines d'Héraclée* made an exceptional profit of 1.6 million francs with a capital of 15 million.[11] At the same time the *Compagnie des minérais de fer magnétique de Mokta-el-Hadid* (Magnetic Iron Mineral Company of Mokta-el-Hadid) was making a profit of 4.5 million francs with a capital of 20 million. As for the *Compagnie des phosphates et chemins de fer de Gafsa*, it realised a profit of 11.9 million with a capital of 18 million! These commercial and financial avenues lead us to uncover in the years before the First World War a landscape which has up till now has been well hidden.

By 1914, the empire was no longer the poor relation, abandoned by a bourgeoisie avid for Russian or Ottoman loans. As the third most important commercial partner of France, the empire vied with Germany for second place, a rank it attained on several occasions between 1900 and 1914. A regular and reliable market, it absorbed, in an 'ordinary' year, 40 per cent of refined sugar exports, 56 per cent of rail exports, 85 per cent of cotton fabric exports, 73 per cent of exports of locomotives, and 80 per cent of metal construction exports. As second or third most important supplier to France, the empire made a significant contribution to agricultural raw material imports, which at this period represent more than 20 per cent of total French imports (Table 4). The empire, ranking third as a destination for investment abroad at a time when the range of choices was wide open, assured particularly high profits to the enterprises which had had the good fortune or flair to interest themselves in it. That should dispel once and for all the idea – endlessly repeated, particularly by Anglo-Saxon writers[12] – that the economic motivation behind the taking over of colonies only amounted to the speculations of a few profiteers.

TABLE 4

FRENCH IMPORTS IN 1906

(in millions of francs)

Commodities	Total	Empire	% of imports coming from the Empire
Whole rice	40.61	38.65	95.1
Powdered sugar	54.75	49.13	89.7
Non-vintage wine in barrels	273.53	240.00	87.7
Olive oil	39.82	32.35	81.2
Natural phosphates	22.28	17.61	79.0
Whole groundnuts	72.36	52.24	72.1
India rubber and gutta-percha – raw or melted down again in bulk	320.13	68.49	21.3

Source: As Table 1.

In Black Africa that may be so, but Black Africa is not the empire. Raymond Aron might well write that 'capital surpluses have not been the direct cause of either colonial conquests or of the 1914 war. Why should France have conquered North Africa or Black Africa for capital surpluses, since it did not put them there?'[13] The point, however, is that the favoured fields of expansion, the areas of high profit, the preferential markets, were in Indochina and Algeria. The majority of studies on imperialism, focused as they are on Black Africa, have too easily concluded that political motivation was stronger than economic incentives. The study of franco-colonial trade, like that of capital issues, has, rather, shown us the opposite. On the eve of the First World War, the empire was already a favoured field of expansion.

In the 1930s, during the Depression, the economic importance of the empire seems to have become reinforced. From 1928, it became the most important trading partner of France, ahead of Great Britain, a position that it held until the end of the colonial period. From 1930 on, faced with shrinking world markets, the empire offered a guaranteed outlet to all branches of the French economy (Table 5). From 1930, indeed, it provided almost all France's agricultural imports (Table 6).

As France's leading trading partner, the empire also became its leading asset, thus continuing the trend set on the eve of the First World War. Whereas 46 companies were created between 1920 and 1929 to operate

TABLE 5

THE EMPIRE'S SHARE IN FRENCH EXPORTS (%)

Commodities	1890	1900	1913	1929	1938	1949	1958
Wine	8.4	10.3	10.8	12.2	15.0	27.4	24.4
Groundnut oil	—	5.2	7.9	68.2	89.6	95.7	95.0
Refined sugar	12.7	18.0	67.6	83.5	98.5	94.1	85.5
Woollen cloth	3.0	5.2	4.7	4.7	15.7	38.1	29.7
Silk cloth	0.8	0.9	1.4	3.4	17.9	55.8	56.1
Cotton cloth	34.8	46.1	33.1	49.9	84.6	89.2	83.6
Clothes and underwear	13.7	22.7	11.2	10.4	34.5	63.3	78.8
Skin or leather work	16.6	35.4	14.6	29.8	56.6	19.4	21.4
Paper and its by-products	10.1	20.1	17.9	21.6	21.5	42.8	41.8
Soap	56.2	72.4	65.1	24.2	44.3	91.0	92.2
Cement	—	30.1	35.9	59.1	84.1	91.0	69.1
Chemical products	3.1	5.4	7.0	8.3	12.2	30.1	37.8
Metalwork and metal tools	13.3	27.4	41.4	32.3	47.0	67.9	56.4
Machinery	8.1	20.6	29.9	30.7	41.2	55.5	39.0
Iron and steel	10.0	31.0	21.6	11.9	17.6	24.8	22.8
Cars	—	—	15.7	33.4	45.5	53.9	36.8

Source: As Table 1.

TABLE 6

THE EMPIRE'S SHARE IN FRENCH IMPORTS (%)

Articles	1890	1913	1929	1938	1949	1958
Total of agricultural raw materials	18.7	28.6	37.5	71.2	63.4	71.1
Wines	16.8	56.7	83.8	96.8	91.2	83.5
Cereals	10.2	12.1	29.4	80.5	43.1	78.0
Rice	11.1	85.3	80.1	93.7	50.6	95.4
Fresh fruit	4.7	17.3	13.6	48.7	72.5	72.1
Coffee	0.4	1.9	3.7	42.7	69.8	75.9
Cocoa	3.8	2.2	56.1	88.4	98.9	85.5
Oil-seed and groundnuts	17.8	25.1	25.0	54.4	73.0	77.8
Sugar	71.8	100.0	16.5	77.8	23.9	94.0
Mineral ores	1.8	3.2	8.6	5.6	21.4	11.1
Phosphates	—	54.8	42.6	42.0	80.5	97.2
Skins and furs	4.0	10.9	17.0	16.6	26.2	14.6
Cotton	—	0.1	2.2	3.6	8.2	18.0
Wool	3.8	3.2	2.7	5.4	0.7	0.8
Silk and floss-silk	0.4	0.2	3.0	1.6	—	—
Timber	1.1	4.5	11.1	28.0	28.9	40.5
Rubber	—	14.1	9.3	25.1	45.1	30.9

Source: As Table 1.

abroad, 187 new ones were set up to work in the colonies. From 1920–29, whereas the total sum of capital issues rose to 6,746.3 million francs for firms in the colonies, it reached a ceiling of 3,254.3 million for firms operating abroad. In the 1920s, colonial firms thus represent nearly 70 per cent of the total of capital issues outside France, against 25 per cent in 1913. In 1939, by combining public and private investments, the empire absorbed between 40 and 50 per cent of the total value of French long-term investments abroad. It is, however, from the 1930s that criticism of, or reservations about, imperial policy began to proliferate, a policy accused of hampering the modernization of French industry. It was during this period that a judicious development of the riches of the colonies was repeatedly called for. In 1954 the employers of the Union française spoke out clearly against all policies inspired by ideas of self-sufficiency for 'aiming to make the Union into a sort of bloc within which internal trade would be developed by erecting high tariff walls against the outside world. Too many facts indicate that such a policy would be harmful to the economy of the franc currency zone, apart from the reasons which make trade isolation invariably dangerous, because it leads a country to accept weakness in the economy as a normal state'.[14]

These are the discrepancies between 'actual' and 'perceived' statistics which we must attempt to understand. In reassessing the importance of the colonial market, the periodization we have proposed highlights our original questions. The 'loss' of this preferential market should have caused more serious troubles than the figures alone would lead us to believe. Yet we have seen that this was not the case. Maybe it is that there simply do not exist tight links between the growth of foreign markets and competitiveness. As regards the nineteenth century, Paul Bairoch has shown that a high rate of exporting (that is to say, a high rate in relation to GNP) does not imply, as is often imagined, that commerce leads to growth.[15] Moreover, what seems to have been shown for the nineteenth century holds good for the twentieth century. Contrary to a commonly-held notion, a high degree of integration in world commerce is not a strict indicator of the level of competitiveness. The United Kingdom and Italy, early in the 1970s, were reputed to be rather uncompetitive countries. Yet they succeeded in exporting a higher percentage of their GNP than either Japan or the United States of America.

One should not, therefore, prematurely confuse the expansion of the colonial market with the mainspring of economic growth. It is conceivable that the difficulties of French industry in maintaining a high rate of internal investment may have resulted from the existence of the country's colonial outlets, for they have not helped to stimulate the development in France itself of industries with a high 'value added' component. This, certain English historians have suggested, is the case in their country, when they maintain that the sway that England held over its imperial markets had unfavourable consequences, inasmuch as the ease of access to these outlets lulled many exporters into complacency, and turned them away from competitive markets.[16]

II

The colonial market and competitiveness

If one is to provide an answer, one needs first to assess the position of those sectors most 'interested' in the colonial dimension of the structural evolution of French capitalism. It is here that the role of colonial markets from the 1930s onwards became clear. In fact, the enhanced place that the empire occupied in the global figures marked important structural changes. During the period 1930–60, the colonial market was monopolized by sectors whose importance in total industrial added value and total exports was declining.

Here, the example of the cotton industry is particularly enlightening. From the period between the wars onwards, it began an irreversible decline. Between 1924 and 1938, the percentage of cotton within total French exports dropped from 7 per cent to 4.6 per cent. After the Second World War, if one leaves aside the price explosion of 1947, the retreat turned into a rout. The share of cotton fabric fell from 5 per cent of total French exports in 1949 to 1.6 per cent in 1958. Now, it is from the period when signs started to appear of a decline in the cotton industry that sales of this industry, destined for the empire, increased in a spectacular manner (Figure 1). One may wonder if, by stemming the decline of one branch of industry already losing ground, the empire did not hinder the redeployment of the structure of French exports in relation to that of other European countries, and help to maintain the status quo of a non-competitive industrial structure. The case of the cotton industry is, moreover, not an isolated one. From the time of the 1930s crisis on, the colonial outlet has been basically monopolized by declining industries: the silk industry, the sugar industry, the candle manufacturing industry.

One can carry out the same analysis for imports coming from the empire. In the long term, we can see that the growth of colonial wealth depends on the import of agricultural raw materials, whose overall importance is diminishing, not only for France but also for the industrialized countries as a whole (Table 7). Therefore, we can say that the colonial reservoir provided, essentially, products whose world importance was diminishing, a fact which accordingly reduced their relative influence in foreign trade. In this respect, in the long term, the need for the colonial reservoir was becoming less and less important. This was all the more so since, among the imports of agricultural raw materials coming from the empire, the proportion of products in direct competition with those which France itself could produce was growing, notably cereals and wine.

This is what a businessman, Paul Bernard, a director of Indo-Chinese companies, condemned in 1938. In order to pay for cotton products expensively imported, he wrote, the colonies had been induced to offer agricultural raw materials in competition with products from home. Rice and maize from Indo-China competed with wheat; bananas from Guinea or the West Indies harmed French orchards; groundnuts from Senegal

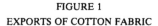

FIGURE 1
EXPORTS OF COTTON FABRIC

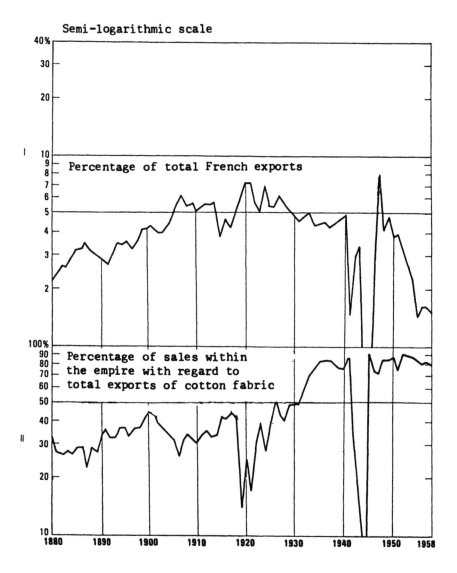

and palm products from the Ivory Coast threatened olive oil from Provence; matting and basketwork from Tonkin did away with similar articles produced in the French countryside; sugar cane from Réunion came up against sugar beet from Picardy; West Indian rum had a bad effect on marc from Burgundy.[17]

This is what the Jeanneney Report denounced (with hindsight) when it

TABLE 7

	% of agricultural raw materials in total colonial imports	% of agricultural raw materials in total French imports
1890	70.7	36
1918	66.8	23
1931	80.1	31
1958	77.2	20(1960)

argued that the changes made following decolonisation were far from having deleterious effects on France:

Trade between France and other franc currency areas is indirectly costly, the purchases made by these countries being partly brought about by aid and grants which we provide; and they are not able to grow significantly unless this aid is increased. If we deducted from French receipts the aid made via exports to these countries, it would seem that even when export prices appear to benefit the exporter, the terms of exchange after adjustment are frequently unfavourable to the French people. The conquest of normal markets would demand an effort in marketing, but this would probably be less costly than the aid granted at present.

The terms of trade could only stay advantageous, given agreed aid, if imports from countries in the franc currency zone could sell at prices lower than world prices or if, in the absence of this, France were to experience difficulties in acquiring the raw materials or basic products that it imported from these territories. Neither of these hypotheses has been borne out. In fact, in many cases France buys above the world price. Even if we did not help them, the franc currency zones would quite probably be induced to offer us their output. In the other case, similar products could usually be imported by us from other countries; and some of these, because of their being less poor, would be better markets for *our* exports. Exports could, as a secondary use, give us a comparison of techniques and of cost prices. But traditional industrial activities which are involved in franc currency zone exports are not generally liable to adopt the most advanced techniques. Besides, so far as the protection of certain markets is concerned, assuring an easy dispersal allows mediocre products to be sold at prices higher than those that potential competitors could manage. This makes the sectors that benefit from protection weaker, rendering them less able to stand up to competition in other markets. A similar fear was expressed in Great Britain by those who supported its entry into the Common Market, and who accepted the accompanying weakening of its links with the Commonwealth.

The change that has come about in the relative volume and composition of our trade with the franc currency zone is not disadvantageous to France. Little by little, anomalies which resulted both from the colonial heritage and the importance of private interests are disappearing. The independence of the franc currency states is the occasion to abandon practices which have become pointless.[18]

This is where the anomaly between 'perceived' and 'actual' statistics takes on its full meaning. The role of the colonial market cannot be measured by the yardstick of tonnages traded, but rather by the types of economic activity whose survival it permitted. In this way, we can also understand better that certain business interests have been able both to envisage with equanimity the loss of a market which was hindering the modernisation of productive equipment, and to move easily into other fields of expansion. It seems, moreover, that preparations for such redeployment were made early, as the development of assets since the 1930s shows (Table 8).

TABLE 8
DEVELOPMENT OF ASSETS
(in millions of francs 1914)

	1929	1936	1938	1954	1958
Mining companies	251.3	298.9	318.7	345.1	384.7
Plantations	248.3	303.4	239.6	240.9	230.6
Industrial companies	221.6	396.9	297.6	888.1	830.2
Transport companies	425.9	919.4	672.4	386.4	213.7
Commercial companies	265.5	227.5	196.7	400:6	361.0
Financial companies	4076.8	5006.2	4486.2	5186.7	4907.0
TOTAL	5489.4	7152.3	6211.2	7417.8	6927.2

Source: As Table 3.

For the 132 firms whose assets we have been able to study from 1929 to 1958, what is particularly significant is the growing withdrawal of private investment at a time when, according to the traditional periodization, the empire was taking on a decisive role in French economic growth. From 1936, the strong growth of previous years began to be checked. During 1958, the 132 colonial firms had not regained their assets of 1936, the decline having been particularly noticeable since 1954. All the same, we must take note of the resistance to this trend of industrial firms, who seem scarcely to have been affected by the timid withdrawal of other colonial companies. It seems as if industrialization was the only way forward for the maintenance of French interests in the empire, as though, during this final phase of colonization, the sacrifice of certain firms was being prepared, in particular that of commercial firms, which symbolized the most archaic aspects of colonial imperialism.

This withdrawal of private investment following the Second World War may be monitored by a second yardstick: profit. In volume, aggregate

benefits deriving from the development of the colonies decrease con-
tinuously from 1938 to 1958 (Table 9). This time the contrast is striking
between the surge of growth at home – a spurt that can be measured by
the growth of productive fixed capital, by that of national revenue and the
gross national product – and the timid withdrawal of colonial businesses,
sounding the retreat ahead of time. Finally, judging by yield (profits/
assets), the colonial venture cuts a sorry figure during the final stages of its
story (Table 10). Low profits and low productivity are the reasons which
account for the withdrawal of private investment from the middle of the
1950s. Prudent administrators that they were, the managers of colonial
firms trimmed their sails before the wind.

TABLE 9

DEVELOPMENT OF PROFITS FROM 1929–1958

(in millions of francs 1914)

	1929	1936	1938	1954	1958
Mining companies	31.5	24.9	56.3	24.3	15.7
Plantations	9.2	20.9	37.8	15.0	18.5
Industrial companies	20.8	17.7	16.0	33.9	25.9
Transport companies	9.3	9.9	8.9	1.2	4.3
Commercial companies	11.7	10.0	18.1	13.5	9.1
Financial companies	42.0	32.9	30.0	31.1	31.8
TOTAL	124.5	116.3	167.1	119.0	105.3

Source: As Table 3.

TABLE 10

PRODUCTIVITY OF COLONIAL ENTERPRISES

(net profits/assets in %)

	1929	1936	1938	1954	1958
Mining companies	12.0	8.0	17.0	7.0	4.0
Industrial companies	9.0	4.0	5.0	3.0	3.0
Commercial companies	4.0	4.0	9.0	3.0	2.0
Plantations	3.0	6.0	15.0	6.0 ·	8.0
Financial companies	1.0	0.6	0.6	0.5	0.6
Transport	2.1	1.0	1.3	0.3	2.0

III

Conclusion

The new periodization we have proposed enables us to formulate the
hypothesis that it is unlikely that business interests could have been the
pressure group behind those politicians hostile to every form of independence. In the 1950s, colonial business concerns had already anticipated
decolonization. This is what the experts of the *Comité monétaire de la*

zone franc (Franc currency zone Monetary Committee) were assessing when they detailed the ways in which private savings were withdrawn from the empire:

> transfers of liquid savings which have resulted from the non-repatriation, in the countries studied, of a portion of the returns from exports, or from withdrawals from different deposit accounts in local currency (banks, giro accounts, private funds, savings banks) ... finally, actual movements of capital which have directly affected the volume of investments: the slowing down, even the disappearance of the supply of new foreign goods; non-reinvestment in the field, and transfer to foreign parts of non-redistributed profits or of profits and dividends already distributed; reduction or liquidation of stocks following upon decreased activity in certain branches; certain businesses being closed down, or the transfer of operations to other countries; in a word, actual disinvestment, with the transfer of basic assests, and the sending abroad of the capital thus freed.[19]

While pulling out at the beginning of the 1950s, private investors left the responsibility for the development of the empire to the public authorities. The latter were faced with this choice: either to intervene in an attempt to reshape the economic framework of colonialism while edging out those metropolitan interests which had so far still benefited from a protected market; or to do nothing and run the risk of increasing poverty and disorder among large numbers of colonial subjects. Too much clear-sightedness and courage were required for the matter to be satisfactorily resolved.

Université de Paris VIII
Vincennes-Saint Denis

NOTES

*Translated from the original French by Juliet Hurst.

1. Jacques Marseille, *Empire colonial et capitalisme français. Histoire d'un divorce* (Albin Michel, Paris 1984).
2. Pierre Moussa, *Les chances économiques de la communauté franco-africaine* (A. Colin, Paris, 1957), p.62.
3. In 1958, for all the companies whose issues we have followed from their inception to 1958, the total amount of capital called up rose to 6,384.4 million francs in 1914. At the same time, total assets rose to 6,927.2 million. When one knows that fixed assets are considerably lower than liquid capital, one has some indication of the extent to which firms only risked in investment a portion of the capital available to them, a clear sign of their reluctance to get established on the spot.
4. René Girault, *Emprunts russes et investissements français en Russie, 1887–1914*, (A. Colin, Paris, 1973), p.85. One milliard = one thousand million (English) or one billion

(US).

5. Jacques Thobie, *Intérêts et impérialisme français dans l'Empire ottoman [1895-1914]*, (Publications de la Sorbonne, Paris, 1977), p.480.

6. Raymond Poidevin, 'Placements et investissements français en Allemagne, 1898-1914', *La Position internationale de la France. Aspects économiques et financiers. XIXᵉ-XXᵉ siècles* (Editions de l'E.H.E.S.S., Paris, 1977), p.224.

7. Bernard Michel, 'Les capitaux français en Autriche au début du XXᵉ siècle', ibid., p.228.

8. Albert Broder, 'Les investissements français en Espagne au XXᵉ siècle', ibid., p.166.

9. Frédéric Mauro, 'Les investissements français en Amérique latine, XIXᵉ-XXᵉ siècle', ibid., p.196.

10. Thobie, op.cit., p.406.

11. Ibid., p.414.

12. In particular, David K. Fieldhouse who writes: 'What advantages has Europe gained from her colonies that she would not otherwise have gained at the expense of other countries similar in every respect? ... In other words, was there a difference between the profitability of businesses nominally in the colonies and that of independent non-European states? The answer is almost certainly that formally established imperialism mattered little', *Les empires coloniaux à partir du XVIIIᵉ siècle* (Bordas, Paris, 1973), p.322. We have just seen, in the case of France, however, that the profitability of colonial businesses was clearly superior to that of companies set up in independent states.

13. Raymond Aron, *Paix et guerre entre les nations* (Calmann-Lévy, Paris, 1962), p.279.

14. Conférence plénière du comité d'études et de liaison du patronat de l'Union française, *L'équilibre économique de la Zone franc*, (1954), 145.

15. Paul Bairoch, *Commerce extérieur et développement économique de l'Europe au XIXᵉ siecle* (Mouton, Paris, E.H.E.S.S., 1976).

16. In particular, S.B. Saul, *Studies in British Overseas Trade-1870-1914* (Liverpool, 1960).

17. Paul Bernard, *Les problèmes posés par le développement industriel de l'Indochine* (Paris, 1938).

18. *La Politique de coopération avec les pays en voie de développement*, Rapport J.M. Jeanneney, Paris, Documentation française, (Paris, 1963), pp.37-8.

19. 'La Zone franc en 1958', *Statistiques et Etudes financières*, Supplément, n° 134, (February 1960), 207.

Indo-British Relations in the Post-Colonial Era: The Sterling Balances Negotiations, 1947–49 *

by
B. R. Tomlinson

The transfer of power in South Asia was an event of major importance in the recent history of the British Empire/Commonwealth. Inspired by the steady progress of Professor Mansergh's *Transfer of Power* volumes, historians are hard at work dissecting the minutiae of the constitutional and political processes that led to the establishment of the independent republics of India and Pakistan in August 1947. This detailed consideration of decolonization has also led to contemplation of the basis of British relations with its erstwhile dependencies after the ending of formal rule.[1] In one sense the study of the post-independence years is vital even to the exegesis of the decolonization process, because until we know exactly what changed on 15 August 1947 we cannot accurately assess what the motives of those involved in that process were, or what significance their actions, foreseen or unintended, actually had. The granting of independence in a Commonwealth context became the standard British decolonization strategy in the years that followed. An investigation of the links that remained between India and Britain after independence can help us assess what role the Commonwealth tie played in maintaining, or transforming, the close association between London and New Delhi that had been the essence of the colonial relationship.

The financial relations between Britain and India before and after independence is not a subject that has grabbed many of the academic headlines. The undoubted complexities and obscurity of the subject make it tempting to ignore. Political, constitutional and strategic matters are all much more approachable, and so have received far greater attention. But financial questions make a rewarding case-study of the transition from colonial to post-colonial relations for two reasons. Firstly, the most complex and exhaustive of the post-colonial negotiations between Britain and India were about this subject. Between 1947 and 1949 national negotiating teams met five times to discuss the subject, and in so doing raised issues that were much larger than were apparent from the technical complexities of the formal agreements reached. Secondly, the course and basis of these negotiations provide an excellent comparison with events before 1947, for in the inter-war period also the financial liabilities and opportunities represented by India's sterling obligations had been major concerns for British policy-makers. One important distinction between the 1930s and the late 1940s was that in the colonial period India was a debtor to Britain, while after 1945 it was Britain's largest single sterling creditor. But the transformation of the sterling debt into the sterling balances did not make the problem of Indo-British financial relations any easier to resolve, nor did it determine exactly where the balance of power in the forthcoming negotiations would lie.

By examining the financial negotiations of 1947 to 1949 in some detail, then, we can assess the importance of one of Britain's major post-imperial concerns in South Asia, and also test the atmosphere in which negotiations took place between the ex-imperial power and its newly-independent successor. By so doing, it is hoped, we may be able to define more precisely the basis of the supposed Commonwealth partnership that replaced formal British political control in South Asia.

In 1939 India had external sterling obligations of about £350 millions; by 1945 it had built up sterling assets, in the form of its sterling balances, of almost four times that amount. The sterling balances which India accumulated during the war were larger in size than those of any other country, but no different in type. Once sterling had been declared non-convertible on the outbreak of war in 1939, many countries which exported goods to Britain took payment in the form of sterling credits, usually Treasury Bills, which were lodged with their national central banks in London. In this way the British economy was able to secure unrequited imports of food, raw materials and military equipment for the war effort. With the exception of North America, most parts of the world participated in this system without protest. In the case of India, as with other strategically important bases in the Middle East, war materials for local theatres were paid for in the same way. In addition, under the Defence Expenditure Agreement of 1940, Britain met the bulk of the cost of Indian troops used in the Allied cause for campaigns beyond the borders of the subcontinent. It was this last arrangement that was responsible for the accumulation of most of India's balances.[2]

From the early days of the war it was noted in London that Britain's liability for the costs of Indian defence was potentially disturbing. But little effective action could be taken to stem the accumulation of the sterling balances. The problem was masked until 1942 by the use of India's sterling receipts to repatriate the Indian sterling debt bonds and railway annuities outstanding in the London market. By the summer of 1942 almost all of this debt had been liquidated and officials in London now became worried by the rapidity with which India's balances were accumulating and the significance of this for post-war policy. There was no simple solution to the problem, however; a series of meetings in Whitehall in July 1942 could only suggest either that the Defence Expenditure Agreement should be renegotiated on less generous terms, or that it should be made clear that India's balances would be blocked once the war was over.[3] Unfortunately, July 1942 was not a good time for taking drastic action. With the Indian National Congress gearing itself up for one last mass campaign to force the British to quit India, officials in New Delhi were adamant that the existing arrangements would have to stand. In this they were strongly supported by the Secretary of State for India, Leopold Amery, who argued that for political and moral reasons India's peace-time recovery from the war should not be put in jeopardy by any limitation on the availability of its sterling balances.[4]

Despite London's concern nothing was done to alter Indo-British financial arrangements during the war. The nearest that the British Cabinet got to suggesting a reduction in India's balances was a telegram to the Viceroy in November 1942 requiring the Indian Finance Member to state that His Majesty's Government would not re-open the question of India's contribution to the war at present. When Sir Jeremy Raisman followed these instructions by making the required announcement in his budget speech in February 1943, however, he emasculated it by omitting the words 'at present'. In London the Cabinet noted this but, with more pressing problems to attend to, did nothing about this mild act of mutiny.[5] For the rest of the war the sterling balances question was tacitly shelved, and concern over India's financial problems switched to the issue of how best to mop up surplus purchasing power to restrain inflation.

So long as the war continued the British authorities were able to follow a 'policy of drift' over the question of the future of the sterling balances.[6] The disincentives to taking firm action were strong: political realities made it hard to re-open the question with India, while some opinion in London, notably within the Bank of England, wished to maintain the status of freely available and fully convertible sterling balances as long as possible to aid the restoration of sterling's status as an international reserve and vehicle currency once the war was over. Feeling in India on the balances question certainly ran high, and by 1945 leaders of Indian opinion had suggested withdrawing from both the sterling area dollar pool and from the International Monetary Fund if India's case on this issue were ignored.[7] The policy of drift had few immediate costs. While in theory India and the other holders of sterling balances were able to use them freely, subject only to exchange controls imposed by central banks and the import licencing restrictions of national governments, in practice there was little that sterling could buy from Britain so long as the shipping shortage continued and war-time requisitioning systems were in force.

Once the war was over, however, it was clear that something would have to be done. Any loosening of controls would expose Britain's limited productive capacity to the threat of a drain of unrequited exports if the sterling balances remained freely available. In addition, the terms of the dollar loan which the British negotiated in Washington in the autumn of 1945 had considerable implications for the future of the balances.[8] Under the terms of the loan the British government undertook to make sterling freely convertible for current transactions within one year of its ratification (which, due to delays at the American end, meant that the date of sterling convertibility was pushed back to 15 July 1947). The loan conditions also included a clause calling for Britain to attempt to scale down the size of the balances themselves. Both the American and British negotiating teams at Washington envisaged that part of the wartime balances would be written off, part funded immediately in convertible sterling and part blocked and released slowly in small instalments. The British mission, developing a number of Keynes's wartime ideas on the problem, hoped that roughly eight per cent of the balances would be released in convertible currency, 31 per cent cancelled and 61 per cent funded at no interest as a war debt over 50 years. But in London there was less enthusiasm for so rigid a scheme. When the Chancellor of the Exchequer made the case for accepting the loan in parliament he deliberately played down the American insistence on the need to cancel part of the balances to make Britain's position viable, saying merely that part of the balances would be freed, part funded and part 'adju ted, perhaps in some cases adjusted downwards, as a contribution by the sterling area countries to a reasonable settlement of the war debt problem'.[9]

By 1946, however, a crisis point in Britain's relations with its sterling creditors had been reached. The metropolitan economy was now faced with a severe balance of payments crisis, and in particular a shortage of the dollars needed to purchase consumer and capital goods vital for recovery at an acceptable standard of living. The potential costs of continuing to do nothing about the sterling balances were extremely high. If holders of the balances were allowed unlimited access to them then they could be used to purchase British goods, especially capital equipment, that were vital for domestic recovery or to earn dollars; if the current earnings of sterling bloc countries became convertible then such countries could use their balances to pay for imports from Britain and convert the sterling earned from current exports into dollars. The implications of Britain's sterling debtor status, which had worried some experts (notably Keynes) since 1942, now appeared to be a major stumbling block on the road to domestic recovery.

The first months of peace were not, however, an appropriate time for detailed negotiations on financial matters with India. At the time of the Cabinet Mission to India, Attlee declared that the balances issue should be kept separate from that of arriving at a political settlement for the transfer of power,[10] and so the policy of drift was allowed to continue. Sterling was not yet convertible, but India was allowed to buy freely in Britain using current earnings or accumulated sterling, limited only by shipping and supply problems and by the continued operation of exchange controls by the rump of the colonial bureaucracy in New Delhi. India was also allowed free access to the dollar pool in the case of essential hard currency expenditure, and the Indian authorities were the sole judges of essentiality.[11] During 1946, however, a number of agreements with other holders of sterling balances were arranged and from these a pattern emerged. The principle was established that the total amount of each country's balance would no longer be freely available: instead the balances were to be blocked with agreed regular releases for current needs each year. Provision was made in these agreements for the eventual convertibility of current earnings and no fixed hard currency rations were imposed for the interim period.

In February 1947 the first set of formal talks on the Indian case were held in New Delhi between representatives of the interim government and a British mission headed by Lord Cobbold and Sir Wilfred Eady.[12] These talks were designed to be merely exploratory, with the aim of enabling both sides to set out their case and to reach some agreement about what aspects of inter-government finance any settlement might cover. The latest available figures for Indian balances were those of September 1946, a total of £1200 million, almost all of it held by the Reserve Bank of India in London and most of it (nearly £1000 million) held in British Treasury Bills. The only formal limitation on the extent to which the balances could be drawn down was the statutory requirement on the Reserve Bank to hold about £350 million in reserve as backing for its rupee note issue. The British delegation to the Delhi talks admitted that both India and Britain had made the maximum sacrifices possible for the sake of the war-efforts, and that the Defence Expenditure Agreement of 1940 had been fair to both sides. They also accepted that the Indian balances had not been swollen by profiteering at Britain's expense in the supply of raw materials and military equipment.[13] Nor did the British talk of cancellation or of scaling-down the balances directly; they did, however, propose ways in which the total debt could be reduced. It had always been clear that certain obligations and assets would remain with the successor states in South Asia after independence which could be paid for by using the sterling balances. The most important of these were the defence stores and fixed installations that the Raj would leave behind for its successors, plus the cost of the pensions of retired or retiring civil and military personnel payable in sterling. The rights and entitlements of the rusty remains of the steel frame of the colonial administration was always a potentially emotive subject in London and some form of guarantee that their pensions would be paid by their erstwhile subjects was necessary. This could best be done by a capitalization scheme, using the sterling balances to buy an annuity out of which tapering annual payments could be met. The British were extremely anxious to ensure that estimates of the size of this annuity, and of the value of stores and fixed installations, should be as high as possible to enable some hidden writing-off of the balances to take place. In addition the British sought to establish that the balances should be seen as a war debt which should, in justice, attract no interest and which should only be repaid over a generation. To this end the British proposed to block the bulk of the accumulated balances, allowing only a limited amount to be made available each year for current transactions. The figure they had in mind was £150 million over each quinquennium, plus sums to meet agreed capital transactions providing that these were policed by an effective system of exchange control.[14]

The initial Indian negotiating position was based on some of the same principles as the British, but with rather different details. The Indians were prepared to accept the need to pay for stores, installations and a capitalization scheme for sterling pensions, but they rejected the notion of scaling down or of regarding the balances as a war debt. While they were prepared to forgo any fixed funding arrangement for the debt, the Indians insisted that the balances should attract the rate of interest normal for central bank assets (around one per cent) and that any annuity for pensions should also receive a market interest rate. Again, the Indians were prepared to accept the principle of blocking, but wanted much larger agreed releases of £500 million over the first five years (although private conversations indicated that they were prepared to settle for about half this amount if other arrangements were satisfactory).[15]

By mutual agreement the Delhi talks skirted round the fundamental issues at stake, both sides contenting themselves with pleading extreme poverty and pointing to the massive dislocations of their respective economies caused by the war. Facing the questions of the size of the balances, of Britain's ability to repay them and of India's capacity to absorb them would have meant dealing with the emotional subject of past sacrifices in the Allied cause and also with the intangibles of Britain's and India's future trading position. While the British accepted that India would require to run a balance of payments deficit for some time, to meet vital consumption and reconstruction needs, it was impossible to guess at how large this permissible deficit should be. As the Indians were anxious to make clear, for them the size of the deficit was partly a matter of will; government action would fix import needs and imposing external limits on the size of the deficit would mean pre-determining domestic reconstruction policies. Instead, the negotiations revolved around the 'technical' questions concerning stores, pensions and releases. Whitehall estimates of the value of stores and installations was around £225 million, and London reckoned that £150 million for them would be a good bargain, although in the hope of some disguised cancellation the British delegation put in a figure of £200 million for this item.[16] The Indian figure, for private consumption, was £150 million, and so agreement on this issue should not have been hard to achieve. On pensions, too, the two sides were not very far apart – both teams had in mind a figure of £250 million (£6 million a year for 22 years, then tapering over the next 50 years) at an interest rate of half per cent. Over releases there was less agreement, the British not being prepared to go higher than £150 million per quinquennium, with the possibility of £200 million for the first five-year period if import and exchange controls were effective, while the Indian delegation never came below £100 million a year in public and £50 million a year in private.[17] Before any formal agreements could be reached on any of these questions, however, the complexities of the political situation caught up with the delegates and the talks had to be suspended.

In the spring and summer of 1947, with Mountbatten's 'count-down calendar' inexorably ticking off the days to partition, the issue of the sterling balances was shelved once more. India retained free access to its accumulated sterling, and to the dollar pool, although its administration was on its honour to cope with balance of payments difficulties without drawing too heavily on the funds in London. By June 1947 it was clear that no solution to the balances problem could be arrived at before the date of sterling convertibility on 15 July, and so arrangements were hastily made for an interim agreement on releases to run for six months. Discussion on this began in July and an agreement was signed to coincide with the transfer of power in August. India and Pakistan were treated as a single entity for the purposes of these negotiations. Under the terms of the agreement outstanding balances were declared to be £1160 million (although on the British side the possibility of later scaling-down was still kept open); arrangements for current releases were made under the by now standard practice of a No. 1 (transferable) Account and a No. 2 (blocked) Account. While pension payments were to be allowed out of the No. 2 Account, all current payments had to be made from the transferable account.[18] The negotiations over the size of the sum of assets to which India was to be allowed immediate access was based on estimates of India's likely balance of payments deficit, especially her need to import food from the dollar currency area to prevent major hardship. It was agreed that £35 million would be transferred to the No. 1 Account for the next six months, with a further £30 million to be placed in the account as a working balance (which was needed to back part of the note issue). The transferred sum of £35 million represented something of a victory for the British negotiators since the Indians, who wished to fund their entire projected balance of payments deficit from their London balances, initially asked for £80 million, and the British themselves had been prepared to offer as much as £45 million if necessary. There were no formal restrictions on India's ability to convert its current sterling into dollars, but it was expected that no more than £15 million worth of hard currency would be required. The British, at least, seemed quite happy with the outcome of these negotiations; the Chancellor of the Exchequer told Cabinet that 'in the exceptional political circumstances in India he did not regard the proposed settlement as too generous',[19] while Sir Wilfred Eady, the chief British negotiator, noted that

> we expect that the Agreement will creak quite frequently, but it has been made in a spirit of co-operation and we need not expect any bellicose attitudes on the part of the Reserve Bank or the Government of India.[20]

Significantly, before the talks had started in July the Indian authorities had imposed new restrictions on the export of sterling to deter an anticipated capital flight.[21]

Since the 1947 agreement lasted for only six months, negotiations had to begin in January 1948. For the first time these were now held with the two successor states, as in December 1947 India and Pakistan had decided to divide the sterling balances between themselves in the same proportion as their currency note circulation. The other new feature of these negotiations was the need to decide on a fixed dollar ration to determine the amount of current sterling releases that could be used to draw on the bloc's common dollar pool. Since sterling was now no longer convertible, and since both South Asian Dominions were net dollar spenders, it was thought essential to put some fixed limit on the availability of hard currency. This desire may have been increased by the suspicion, shared by contemporary journalists and some later commentators, that the Indian authorities had taken advantage of the convertibility crisis to buy dollars for all the sterling in their No. 1 Account.[22] All parties to the January 1948 negotiations again wished to dodge the fundamental issues at stake, and so all that was sought was another interim agreement for the next six months. This was duly reached in February, on rather less generous terms than before. India was now to retain the £30 million working balance in its No. 1 Account, and to be allowed a further £18 million from the blocked balances for current expenditure, £10 million of which could be converted into dollars. It was estimated that India would require a further £40–50 million worth of hard currency expenditure over the period and this was to be raised by borrowing. Pakistan was allowed a current account of £10 million (£4 million from the old joint No. 1 Account, plus £6 million from blocked balances) and an additional £10 million as a working balance. Its dollar ration was fixed at £3.3 million worth.[23]

These new arrangements worked smoothly enough and by the summer of 1948 the time was thought to be ripe to hold new negotiations which, it was hoped, would provide a final settlement of the balances question. In the run-up to these talks both sides took fairly clear bargaining positions. The Government of India's brief to its delegation proposed a settlement of the stores and installations and pensions questions providing that a 'reasonable' figure could be agreed upon. On releases the Indians wanted a three-year settlement of £200 million, half of it in convertible currency. It was also proposed that the agreement include a clause declaring it to be a final settlement of all claims and counter-claims between the two governments.[24]

For the British the position was more complicated. Officials in Whitehall saw two possible outcomes for the negotiations. Ideally, they wanted a long-term settlement provided that this included a considerable disguised cancellation of the balances. If this were impracticable then London wanted a short-term settlement for one year, the basis of which would be nil releases of either convertible or non-convertible sterling. Negotiating a long-term settlement required delicate calculations. The perfect solution was one in which most of the balances were written-off and the rest effectively frozen. The British hoped to persuade the Indians to agree to set aside £500–£600 million of the balances for stores, installations and a pensions annuity, and to lock up a further amount (£250 million was one sum mentioned) as a currency reserve. The remainder of the balances, about £350 million for India, were to be funded over a 60-year period, with no hard currency allowance except perhaps in the first and second years.[25]

Long-term funding of the balances was to be handled through a Capital Development Scheme. This proposal had first surfaced in discussions between Treasury and colonial Government of India officials in the winter of 1946, and was later pushed hard by old India hands in the Commonwealth Relations Office (which took over from the India Office in 1947).[26] The disadvantage of any plan for long-term funding was that it would impose definite commitments on Britain to supply capital goods to India; the advantage of a Capital Development Scheme was that such supply could be regulated by a planning process in which the British would have a right to participate, and would also allow a greater percentage of India's current earnings to be spent on consumer goods. It might be thought that this scheme represented an attempt by the British to bind India's future industrial growth firmly to the metropolitan economy, but the reality was more prosaic than this. The Capital Development Scheme was regarded with deep suspicion by the British policy-makers most concerned with domestic recovery, notably the Ministries of Supply and Food and the Central Economic Planning Staff, who were opposed to any formal commitment to supply India with any goods at all; even for its supporters the scheme was intended to be little more than cosmetic. As the Indian Working Party of the British Government's Overseas Negotiating Committee pointed out in advocating the scheme,

> Our object, therefore, was to put the scheme forward in such a way that the Indian leaders could assure their public that the releases were being devoted to capital development, while making sure that they did not, in fact, get anything *more,* in the next few years at least, than they are getting now .... Our object, after all, is not to finance Indian capital development but to secure an acceptable agreement on long-term releases (assuming that we get a generous capital settlement, which is the pre-requisite of any agreement at all).[27]

One external complication that had to be faced in considering the Capital Development Scheme was that of the possible American reaction. Concluding a long-term agreement with India without any formal scaling-down of the balances and with no release of convertible funds ran counter to the terms of the Anglo-American Loan agreement of 1946. Although the obligation to make sterling convertible had been waived after the disaster of August 1947, there were some fears in London that American opinion might object to arrangements with India that appeared to shut US exports out of the South Asian market. In practice, however, this was not thought to be a major problem since Washington was anxious to prevent dollars supplied to Britain leaking away to the Overseas Sterling Area where their spending would be difficult to monitor and where they would cease to act as a foundation for the revival of the British domestic economy. As one official put it, 'the Americans are the last people to want to facilitate any drain of dollars by India'.[28] Nor did London fear significant American penetration of the Indian market for British goods should hard currency become available. Firstly, the policy of American companies over control of direct investments would raise the hackles of Indian nationalist sentiment;[29] secondly, American and Indian business methods were thought to be so different that few close ties were likely. As Sir Wilfred Eady noted, with some satisfaction, Americans 'would find the free and easy system of advances which has regulated trade between the United Kingdom and India for the best part of a century quite unintelligible'.[30]

The British were only prepared to consider a Capital Development Scheme as part of a long-term settlement that included a substantial element of scaling-down of India's balances. Since the Indians refused to accept any such reduction the idea had to be shelved for a time, although it was to reappear later in the form of the Colombo Plan. Once negotiations began in the summer of 1948 it quickly became clear that neither the British ideal long-term or short-term solution was practicable; instead discussions concentrated on a three-year interim settlement on releases, with a decision on the stores and pensions questions as well. No formal mention of cancellation was made, and the sums arrived at for stores and pensions were too low to allow the British the luxury of pretending that they had achieved 'hidden' cancellation by this means. India and Pakistan now agreed to pay £100 million for all stores and installations left behind by the Raj, and to commit another £170 million of the balances to purchase a tapering annuity for pensions at half per cent interest. All remaining balances were to earn half per cent interest also, except for those amounts which currently attracted a higher rate. The size of the balances, after these deductions, was estimated at £960 million for India and £170 million for Pakistan.

Negotiations over the amount of releases for current expenditure again gave rise to animated discussions about projected balance of payments figures, Britain's capacity to export and the potential inflationary effect of increased Indian imports. The year from July 1947 to June 1948 had seen a substantial correction of payments imbalance in the subcontinent and, taking current earnings into account as well as permitted releases from blocked to transferable balances, India had drawn only £3 million net of the £83 million made available from its No. 2 Account over the year. Since India therefore had £80 million 'in hand' the releases allowed under the July 1948 agreement were not large, and were planned for over a three-year period. No new transfers from the blocked account were to take place in the first year, but £40 million were to be made available in each of the second and third years of the agreement as the balance of the No. 1 Account fell below £60 million. It was also agreed that India would be allowed anticipatory drawings on the second year's allowance if the balance of the No. 1 Account in the first year fell below £30 million. A dollar ration of £15 million worth was fixed for 1948–49 with the amount of subsequent hard currency allocations being left for negotiation on an annual basis. In addition India was entitled to spend the receipts of its own dollar earnings in hard currency areas, although in the unlikely event of there being any surplus dollars at the end of the trading year these would be put in the general dollar pool. For Pakistan the terms were similar, but only the releases for 1948–49 were fixed – £5 million from blocked balances for current expenditure, plus another £5 million for refugee relief, with a dollar ration of £5 million worth. Fresh releases for subsequent years were to be negotiated on an annual basis, with the proviso that such releases would not be less than £5 million a year.[31] After 1948 the Pakistani balances were dealt with separately from the Indian ones and, to avoid unnecessary complications, we will omit them from further consideration.

Although the 1948 settlement had envisaged a three-year programme of releases, events quickly conspired to undo the assumptions of the policy-makers. By the spring of 1949 it was clear that India was running into an acute balance of payments crisis and was rapidly drawing down the balance of its No. 1 Account. By May even the working balance in this account had been heavily depleted and severe restrictions on imports from the sterling area had been imposed. Despite these, India drew £81 million in all from its No. 1 Account in the year July 1948 to June 1949, and overspent its dollar ration by nearly 50 per cent (a total of £21 million worth).[32] India's heavy sterling drawings in this period were partly the result of a new government policy designed to increase hard currency earnings at the expense of current sterling receipts. In 1948–49 the Government of India concluded a number of bilateral trading agreements with non-sterling countries, which absorbed a good deal of India's export capacity and left the accumulated balances in London to carry the resulting strain in the bilateral trade position with Britain. This policy also removed the traditional profits that British firms had made out of the entrepôt trade in India goods and transferred them nearer home.[33]

As a result of these events a new set of negotiations, to conclude yet another short-term interim agreement, had to be held in the summer of 1949. This agreement had two main features. Firstly, extra non-convertible funds were made available to India from its blocked balances. As India had already spent most of the sterling allocated for 1949–51 it was allowed to draw an extra £50 million a year from the No. 2 Account for each of these years, with provision for a further £50 million of drawings in 1949–50 if necessary. Secondly, the system of a fixed hard currency ration was abandoned and India was readmitted to full membership of the sterling area dollar pool.[34] The problem of sterling countries' hard currency expenditure was exercising minds in London throughout 1949, and a meeting of the Commonwealth Finance Ministers held in London at the same time as the Indian negotiations arrived at a new strategy to cope with this. Each country now made a firm resolve to limit dollar expenditure to three-quarters of the 1948 level, and new administrative machinery was set up to monitor hard currency payments.[35] It was to this system that India was readmitted in 1949, a 'Commonwealth solution' being substituted for a straightforward hard currency ration.

The 1949 arrangements had again, however, been based on a misreading of the future, but this time the experts had erred on the side of pessimism. The devaluation of sterling in September, coupled with effective voluntary restrictions on dollar expenditure, increased dollar availability and a commodities boom resulting from rearmament all eased the payments problems of India and of the sterling areas as a whole. Thanks to this favourable climate India was able to meet its import bill from current sales and did not need to draw on any of the transferable sterling in the No. 1 Account. The sterling area as a whole prospered also, and in September 1950 the Commonwealth Finance Ministers were able to agree that there should no longer be any fixed limit on their dollar expenditure, a simple exhortation to economy being thought enough.[36] Finally, in February 1952 a last agreement on Indian balances was signed (back-dated to July 1951), covering the period down to 1957. Under the terms of this agreement the Government of India consented to hold £310 million of its remaining balances as a currency reserve in London and promised not to draw on this without consulting the British authorities. The dollar position was left as stated by the 1950 Commonwealth Finance Ministers' Conference and the release of non-convertible sterling was arranged on the basis of £35 million to be available each year from 1951-52 to 1956-57 from the blocked balances so as to maintain a minimum balance of £40 million in the No. 1 Account, with various detailed provisions for amendment. These releases were linked to an agreed strategy for Indian economic development set out in the Colombo Plan, thus reviving in part the earlier Capital Development Scheme.[37] This agreement ran for its full five-year term and, at its end, the Indian balances had been so greatly reduced as to enable both governments to forgo any further formal arrangements. By the late 1950s the wartime balances had been largely exhausted and India's public external capital needs now had to be met from other sources of inter-government finance.

Having set out the details of the protracted and complex negotiations on the sterling balances issues, it is now possible to make some evaluation of the significance of these events. The resolution of the balances problem was a major issue in Indo-British relations, and it links the last years of the colonial period with the first years of the new relationship that was set in the context of the Commonwealth tie. An analysis of the negotiations about this problem can help us to assess the importance of this tie, and also how far economic imperatives influenced, or were influenced by, other considerations based on politics, military strategy and the shaping of new patterns of diplomacy.

The underlying constraints on the British position over post-colonial financial arrangements can best be illustrated by asking why London never seriously attempted to take an extreme position on the balances problem by unilaterally freezing India's assets and expelling India from the sterling area. This course had certain superficial attractions: if India's balances were frozen it would be unable to use them to drain capital goods from Britain; if India were outside the sterling area it would have no call on Britain's scarce and precious hard currency reserves. Such a solution to the balances problem was not unprecedented; Egypt was expelled from the sterling area and had its balances blocked in mid-1947 (although it was allowed a lump sum of hard currency as compensation and continued to receive negotiated releases) because the British authorities had no confidence in its ability to impose effective exchange controls.[38] Such drastic action in the case of India was often talked about in London, especially at times when the Indians were resisting scaling-down most vehemently, but action along these lines was never taken. When British policy-makers considered this alternative seriously it became clear that such actions would be damaging and inappropriate. The reasons for this evaluation are interesting.

The first problem was that the Indian balances issue was not simply about economics. Although London attempted to keep inter-government financial relations separate from contemporaneous constitutional and political discussions, this compartmentalization could not always be sustained. Before Indian independence, as we have seen, policy-makers were anxious not to do anything that might impede the flow of constitutional negotiations. After August 1947, also, the political dimension of future Indo-British relations loomed large. Between 1947 and 1949 India was deciding what the basis of its future links with Britain should be, specifically whether it should remain in the Commonwealth. Key members of the British government, especially the Prime Minister, had hopes of using closer Commonwealth links as a means of enabling Britain to maintain its great power status. Defence ties were thought to be especially important. In the late 1940s the wartime fantasies of the Commonwealth acting as a strategic 'third force' in world affairs were revived; in addition Commonwealth links were seen as crucial in providing the buttress of regional security agreements to protect British interests in the Middle East, South-East Asia and the Pacific from both external attack and internal insurrection.[39] In London it was widely recognized that Commonwealth membership for India was not feasible without membership of the sterling area, and that Indian perceptions of injustice in economic relations would poison the atmosphere for accepting Dominion Status. To some officials, both in the Commonwealth Relations Office and outside, this was seen as the vital limiting factor on Britain's position.[40] However, although such considerations were clearly in the air when officials discussed the sterling balances problem, there is no evidence that an assessment of the importance of the Commonwealth tie, either on the basis of interest or sentiment, ever completely dominated economic decision-making.

On the economic front there were a number of other fundamental issues that affected the decision about whether or not to retain India in the sterling area. An inter-departmental committee drawn from the Treasury, the Commonwealth Relations Office and the Board of Trade met in April 1948 to consider these, and argued that drastic action on the balances might affect the strength of sterling as an international currency and might damage the interests of British businessmen in India by exposing them to the dangers of retaliatory expropriation.[41]

In practice, however, these considerations received less weight than one might expect. Firstly, India was not seen as a major asset to the sterling area since it was not a net contributor to the common hard currency pool.[42] Secondly, the traditional Bank of England argument that the aim of maintaining the sterling area should be to build up sterling's attractiveness as an international reserve and vehicle currency to prepare for the anticipated benefits of a future multilateral system dropped out of the reckoning in the late 1940s. The issue of future business links was also largely ignored. Whitehall was not very perturbed by the threat of expropriation because it was believed that India desperately needed the management skills represented by the British expatriate and multinational business sectors. Cripps was the only influential figure in London who was prepared to consider the possibility of selling off the old staple expatriate investments by compulsory purchase to set against the sterling balances.[43] But although the Treasury held to a strong position over the need to protect the interests of British investment in public, Eady assuring British business representatives in January 1947 that the government would 'react strongly' to any Indian discrimination against them,[44] opinion in private was much less clear-cut. An inter-departmental committee meeting late in 1946 had concluded, for example, that while on balance the United Kingdom would suffer if British expatriate firms were expropriated should the balances be blocked, the matter was none-the-less a 'debatable point'.[45]

The most important economic arguments for retaining India in the sterling area were based on calculations of the short-term effects of its departure on Britain's hard currency position. In the late 1940s, as in the years immediately before the war, India was usually running a current trade surplus with Britain but a current deficit with the rest of the Overseas Sterling Area. It was estimated in 1948 that in the coming year India's balance of payments with these countries would be in deficit by about £35 million (made up of a visible surplus with Britain of £8 million, a visible deficit with the OSA of £25.5 million and an overall deficit on invisibles of £17 million). But this state of affairs would hold only so long as India was willing to take payments for its exports in sterling. If India were to cut its links with the sterling area it would require dollars for its exports and cut its sterling imports to a minimum. Unfortunately the bulk of India's exports to Britain and the OSA consisted of essentials – tea, vital raw materials and semi manufactures – which could not be reduced by the importing countries. The result would be that India would convert its projected £35 million current deficit with sterling countries to a £1 million surplus; most damagingly, while Britain could reduce its purchases from India by only 6 per cent (from £103 million to £97 million), India could, by eschewing British consumer goods, reduce its purchases from Britain by almost 40 per cent (from £91 million to £56 million). If Britain's trade with India were converted to a dollar basis, therefore, the heavier burden would fall on the metropolitan economy.[46]

Thus while India remained an important market for British manufactures in the post-war years this caused little joy in Whitehall. There India's ability to purchase British capital goods was seen as a source of weakness for the metropolitan economy. In 1945 Indian industrialists had been encouraged to place extensive orders for reconstruction goods with British manufacturers and the consequences of this policy were now coming home to roost. By 1947–48 it was feared that India was obtaining more than its fair share of British capital goods, its purchases being swollen by the release of blocked balances. It was estimated that in 1947, for example, between 43 and 50 per cent of all UK exports to India had consisted of capital goods, whereas the average for all countries was only between 27 and 30 per cent. India was now the largest single market for British capital goods exports, taking 12 per cent of the total, and especially for exports of machinery, taking 17 per cent of the total.[47] There was little that could be done about this apart from exhortations to the Indian government to buy more consumer goods, and to British manufacturers to sell more to hard currency markets; Whitehall did not have the power to prevent domestic manufacturers from selling to India should they wish to.[48] Those who wished to show generosity to India argued that sales of capital goods to India were not a loss since many of these goods, such as textile machinery and railway equipment, could not find alternative markets, but the hard-liners, notably within the Board of Trade, consistently denied this.[49] The overall view in London by 1948 was that

> India and Pakistan have been receiving such a high proportion of our total exports of capital and goods as to affect adversely the increase of our exports to hard currency areas and the achievement of viability.[50]

British officials were certain that the bulk of exports sent to India would have been better employed elsewhere. Even if they were not directly sold for dollars they could have been used for domestic reconstruction or to develop the resources of those parts of the colonial empire which were net dollar earners. Thus the Board of Trade argued strongly, in May 1948, that the Indian market should be given 'low priority' because its requirements of capital goods were 'of much less importance to us, in terms of our general economic policy, than those of colonial and other Commonwealth countries'.[51]

There was only one circumstance in which British policy-makers were prepared to welcome large sales to India – if a future recession in world trade and uncompetitive prices in Britain made exports hard to sell elsewhere. Even the Board of Trade was prepared to admit in 1948 that a Capital Development Scheme which provided for regular Indian purchases of machinery would be an advantage if it were 'projected well into the period when a buyer's market for capital goods prevailed'.[52] It is tempting to assume that just these considerations influenced Whitehall in mid-1949, when at a time of trade slackness India was awarded generous supplementary release of sterling for current expenditure. Although the Treasury argued that the 1949 agreement 'involved us in as steep a tapering off of our exports [to India] as was thought to be prudent', and insisted that disengagement from the Indian market should continue so as to release goods that could earn hard currency in other markets,[53] non-official opinion was less impressed with the consistency of the government's position. As the *Economist* suggested in August, the terms of the new agreement with India made it

> hard to avoid the conclusion that the British Government, in its determination to keep Britain's crisis firmly muzzled until after the election, has been inspired mainly by a desire to do nothing which might disturb employment in the export industries which supply the India market.[54]

The existence of large Indian claims on British export capacity in the late 1940s certainly helped to smooth its transition from colonial to Dominion status. Close involvement with British firms and advisers in the first phase of post-independence planning for industrial growth was probably inevitable, but such involvement was made doubly certain by India's dependence on British capital and goods in the crucial years after 1947. The problems associated with India's sterling balances certainly ensured a good deal of superficial continuity between the colonial and post-colonial phases of Indo-British economic relations, but what is equally striking is how superficial this apparent continuity largely was. The context and conduct of the negotiations over the balances question reveal clearly how much the substance of the economic relationship had altered, especially if we contrast the events of 1947–49 with those of the previous major 'negotiations' over India's place in the imperial economic system – those of 1930–32. In the clash over the currency question in the early 1930s London had firmly overruled the colonial government's appeals for special treatment and had pushed through the transfer of the rupee from a gold-bullion to a sterling exchange standard at the old sterling rate. Although opinions differ about the nature of the interests that Whitehall was defending by these actions,[55] all who have studied this episode agree that issues important to the future of the British imperial network were at stake, and that an awareness of these issues was central to the British bargaining position. By contrast, in 1947–49 the fundamental issues were often deliberately fudged. The major problems that underlay the balances question were too often seen as insoluble by negotiation and as determined by considerations far outside the minutiae of inter-governmental financial relations. In consequence, they were usually ignored so that some agreement on something could be reached, however limited that something turned out to be. In the process, inevitably, the larger issues became resolved by default.

In the years after 1945 the Labour government in Britain developed what was probably the most positive and demanding imperial policy of any metropolitan administration in the twentieth century. Empire and its surrogate, Commonwealth, was expected to play a large part in Britain's post-war recovery. Colonial and Dominion economies were seen as vital sources of supply and demand for the domestic manufacturing sector. While full-blown models of imperial autarchy were regarded with tradi- tional disdain, a close relationship was sought between metropolitan and overseas producers and consumers, both bilaterally and to build up a dollar-surplus imperial sub-economy that would enable Britain to take its place in a multilateral trading world.[56] In strategic matters, too, Britain now had a much stronger overseas defence policy than hitherto, and in most of the world this policy revolved around imperial aims and imperial means.[57] But what is striking is how small a role was now given to India, once the star of the British imperial parade. Strategically, the Indian army was expected to do no more than defend India's borders; the economic role of the Indian consumer, with his new-found taste for British capital goods, was seen as a liability. The British expected to receive little positive gain from close economic links to India in the post-war recovery period, for India was no longer an important source of vital supplies nor a major earner of hard currencies. Thus when Whitehall totted up the imperial assets that could help keep Britain great, India occupied a lowly place on the list. If the post-war years witnessed a resurgence of British interest in the colonial estates this was an empire that did not include the South Asian sub-continent. The British now saw India as a potential or actual source of weakness, a barrier that might stand between the metro- politan base and the recapture of its former power.

This attitude permeated the negotiations over India's sterling balances. What comes out of these is a strong flavour of uninterestedness on London's part, masked by a continuation of the inspired petulance that had distinguished debate on Indo-British economic relations in both New Delhi and London over previous decades. The new flavour was part of a pervasive post-imperial atmosphere in which Indo-British relations as a whole were now conducted, one that provides scant evidence of the Commonwealth spirit or neo-colonial continuities that we might expect to find in Britain's relations with such important former colonies after imperialism. So far as British officials were concerned the sterling balance negotiations with India were not bilateral discussions about matters of vital importance. The existence of Britain's indebtedness to India caused problems for Whitehall, but these problems were seen as peripheral to London's main concerns and even the timing of attempts to solve them was largely dictated by events elsewhere. The desire to retain India in the Commonwealth, and the linked consideration of India's place in a new imperial defence network, played some part in defining British attitudes to the sterling balances, but even these bilateral goals had only a small influence on the course of negotiations. No longer were economic prospects in India seen as being vitally important to Britain, or as events that British action could do much to influence. The new spirit in Indo- British relations was perhaps revealed most starkly in August 1949 when the Treasury, surveying ways of relieving the payments crisis that was to lead to sterling's devaluation later that year, came up with the idea that the United States might consider taking over some of Britain's sterling balances and funding them at a reduced level in convertible currency. This scheme was intended to help Britain break away from its debilitating bilateral relationship with the holders of wartime balances and one advantage of it, so it seemed to London, would be that 'it might well prove that the Americans would be easier to deal with than the Indians'.[58] What judgement can we make of the maternal or sisterly relations in a family that so eagerly seeks the intervention of the social workers?

University of Birmingham

NOTES

*The research on which this article is based was made possible by a grant from the Houblon-Norman Fund of the Bank of England.

1. Evidence of this interest was provided at a conference on 'Decolonisation in South Asia' held at Oxford in June 1982, at which a first draft of this paper was read. I am grateful to this audience for their comments, and also to Dr Scott Newton of Birmingham University from whose advice I have profited greatly.
2. For a concise statement of wartime financial arrangements see H.A. Shannon, 'The Sterling Balances of the Sterling Area, 1939–49', *Economic Journal* 60 (1950), 540–3. Between 1940 and 1947 £1343 million of India's total war expenditure of £2830 million was met by Britain (ibid., 541, fn. 3).
3. See N. Mansergh *et al* (eds.), *India: The Transfer of Power 1942–7 Volume II*, Ch. 8; *Volume III*, Ch. 9. Churchill and his Chancellor, Kingsley Wood, were especially anxious to establish that HMG had the right to reopen the question of a readjustment of the financial burden at the end of the war.
4. Amery argued the case on economic grounds as well, suggesting that the spending of the sterling balances would not damage the British economy so long as they were spent on British goods. This assertion drew from Keynes the comment that Amery's analysis 'indicates that he is a dangerous lunatic', and the official Treasury reply to the India Office commented that such an idea reflected 'a very dangerous misapprehension about the prospective balance of payments with the rest of the world' that Britain would face once the war was over (see D.E. Moggridge, 'From War to Peace – the sterling balances', *Banker* 122 (1972), 1033).
5. This issue surfaced again after the war when Churchill, now in opposition, submitted a parliamentary question in March 1947 implying that HMG had foregone the right to raise the issue of readjusting the wartime settlement. Treasury officials reviewed the case and noted that the Chancellor had already declared himself ready to submit a counter-claim for Britain's expenses in defending India (in a parliamentary answer on 18 February 1947); in any case, according to Raisman, the Indians had not noticed the implications of his budget speech. In view of this Churchill was asked not to submit his question (see notes by A.W. France, 19 March 1947; H.W. Gann, 3 March 1947; N.E. Y[oung], 6 March 1947 and undated letter Rowan to Churchill in Treasury Papers (henceforth T) 236/1114.
6. See Moggridge, 'From War to Peace', 1034.
7. At a meeting of the central board of the Reserve Bank the directors had even expressed the informal view that India should only join the IMF on condition that 'she obtained an assurance from HMG that a substantial portion of the dollar loan [the] USA had agreed to give her [Britain] was placed at India's disposal' (see C.D. Desmukh to Purshottamdas Thakurdas, 12 Dec. 1945, Thakurdas Papers file 244). The British were not especially concerned by this threat. As Keynes pointed out, 'our withers would be quite unwrung' since, if the Indians 'refrain from entering Bretton Woods, that means so

many votes less likely to be cast against us' (note by Keynes, 21 Feb. 1946, T 236/1113).

8. For details of the Washington negotiations see R.N. Gardner, *Sterling–Dollar Diplomacy: The Origins and the Prospects of Our International Economic Order* (new edn., London, 1969), Part III and D.E. Moggridge (ed), *The Collected Writings of J.M. Keynes*, Vol XXIV (London, 1979).

9. See Gardner, *Sterling–Dollar Diplomacy*, pp.204–6, 234; Moggridge, 'From War to Peace', 1035.

10. See *Transfer of Power Vol VI* no.509. The members of the Cabinet Mission were instructed to say nothing that might prejudice future negotiations on any aspect of the balances issue (see note by S.D. W[aley] and N. Y[oung], 7 March 1946, T 236/1113).

11. The Indian authorities followed the policy of allowing dollar expenditure in cases where UK goods were priced more than 10 per cent above American ones or were subject to unreasonable delays in delivery. The British were aware of this policy and regarded it as standard practice within the sterling area (see F. Cohen to D.E. Evans, 16 Oct. 1946, T 236/1114).

12. Minutes of these negotiations are contained in T 236/1125. A useful summary of the course of the negotiations will be found in Eady's note 'Negotiations on the sterling balances of India, Egypt, Iraq and Iran' for the Chancellor of the Exchequer, 1 April 1947, T 236/1118.

13. But at the end of the negotiations the British withdrew all offers and concessions made during the talks.

14. Eady, 'Negotiations on the sterling balances'.

15. Ibid. For a resumé of Indian impressions of these talks see also Government of India Finance Department, 'Brief for delegation on Indian sterling balances negotiations [1948]', Thakurdas Papers, 269.

16. The Indians estimated the cost of these stores had been around £380 million (Government of India Finance Department, 'Brief').

17. Ibid.

18. For details of this and later agreements see P.W. Bell, *The Sterling Area in the Post-war World* (Oxford, 1956), pp.39–40; and B. Dhar, *The Sterling Balances of India* (Calcutta, 1956), Ch. X. Minutes of the negotiations are in T 236/1126.

19. Cabinet Minutes 70(47)7 of 7.8.47 in Cabinet Papers (henceforth CAB) 128/9.

20. Note by Eady, 4 Aug. 1947, T 236/1118.

21. *Economist* 12 July 1947, 77.

22. See *Economist* 3 Jan. 1948, 29 and David Wightman, 'The Sterling Area', *Banca Nazionale del Lavoro Quarterly Review* 4 (1951), 152, which suggests that India was able to convert all the £65 million released in August 1947 into dollars. Such suspicions seem to be ill-founded. The sterling in India's No. 1 Account remained convertible after the suspension of general convertibility in August by a special arrangement, but even so Indian non-official estimates suggest that up to January 1948 only £28 million of the Reserve Bank's sterling holdings had been spent (see *Eastern Economist* 29 Aug. 1947, p.283, and 27 Feb. 1948, p.427). Accurate figures for actual Indian purchases of dollars are hard to come by. One contemporary estimate by the Bank of England was that between 1 April 1946 and 23 Aug. 1947 India drew £42 million worth of dollars from Britain's reserves out of a total of £156.3 million worth taken by the sterling area as a whole, taking £18.4 million worth during the period of convertibility out of a total sterling area drawing then of £72.6 million worth (approx. $290 million); another set of figures gives a higher total – $395 million – for sterling area dollar drawings in the convertibility period from July to September 1947, but with no breakdown by countries. Other major sources of dollar expenditure are given here as $875 million for UK deficits with the USA and the Western Hemisphere and $165 million for Britain's dealings with Europe. See Sir Richard Clarke (edited by Sir Alex Cairncross), *Anglo-American Economic Collaboration in War and Peace, 1942–1949* (Oxford, 1982), pp.180–9; the original of the first document reproduced here is in T 236/1667. Even allowing for the fact that the Bank of England had great difficulty in keeping track of sterling conversions during July and August 1947, there seems little evidence that India's drawings represented a major drain on Britain's hard currency reserves during the convertibility

crisis.
23. *Economist* 28 Feb. 1948, 352. London admitted that a dollar ration for India and Pakistan was essential partly to import food and partly to buy raw materials the sterling area supplies of which had already been earmarked for Britain by pre-emptive purchasing arrangements. One irony of this agreement was that the balance of £33 million in India's No. 1 Account which had been convertible up until January 1948 was now made inconvertible again (*Eastern Economist* 27 Feb. 1948, 427).
24. Government of India Finance Ministry, 'Brief for delegation on Indian sterling balances negotiations [1948]', Thakurdas Papers, 269.
25. For British preparations for the 1948 negotiations see T 236/1142–3.
26. See note by S.D. W[aley], 18 July 1946, T 236/1113; 'Memorandum on India's Industrialization and Sterling Balances' by R.W.B. Clarke, 29 Nov. 1946, T 236/1117; P.J. Noel-Baker [Secretary of State for Commonwealth Relations] to Chancellor of Exchequer, 24 June 1948, T 236/1144.
27. 'Report by India Working Party', ONC (48) 209, 15 May 1948, T 236/1142. The chief architect of the C.D.S. in 1948 was G.H. Baxter, once of the India Office and now in the C.R.O. This department was most concerned to make the presentation of any offer to India appear as generous as possible to keep India in the Commonwealth and strengthen the hands of those in India favourable to continued links with Britain (see P.J. Noel-Baker to Chancellor of Exchequer, 24 June 1948, T 236/1144). Even for Baxter, however, the advantages of the C.D.S. were largely propaganda ones; as he stated:

> The capital development scheme, by giving formal shape to a flow of trade that was largely inevitable, would provide India with a secure source of capital goods and a document which the Indian Government would find of political value and it should, therefore, help us to persuade India to accept a slower rate of releases and cease to draw on the sterling area's gold and dollar reserves. (Minutes of O.N.(4) 57, 18 May 1948, T 236/1143).

28. Note for Chancellor of Exchequer by H.W.-S. [Sir Henry Wilson-Smith], 19 June 1948, T 236/1144.
29. 'Memorandum of India's Industrialization and Sterling Balances' by R.W.B. Clarke, 29 Nov. 1946, T 237/117.
30. Note by W. Eady, 31 March 1948, T 236/1142.
31. *Economist* 17 April 1948, 116–8; 24 July 1948, 157.
32. Ibid. 21 May 1949, 953; 6 Aug. 1949, 315; 13 Aug. 1949, 368.
33. Ibid. 21 May 1949, 953.
34. Ibid. 6 Aug. 1949, 315; 13 Aug. 1949, 368.
35. Ibid. 23 July 1949, 204–5; see also P.E.P., *Planning* 18 (332), 90–1.
36. Dhar, *Sterling Balances of India*, p.113.
37. The only public capital that Britain committed to South Asia under the Colombo Plan was the residue of the accumulated London balances and, as the White Paper setting out the Plan pointed out, the effect of the scheme would be 'to eliminate the problem created by the accumulated sterling balances' of India, Pakistan and Ceylon (see *The Colombo Plan*, Cmd.8080 of 1950–1, p.61). It was claimed at Colombo that Stafford Cripps's parting words to the British delegation had been 'remember now; no commitments' (J.R.E. Carr-Gregg, *The Colombo Plan – A Commonwealth Programme for South-East Asia* (London, 1951), p.262).
38. See Shannon, 'The Sterling Balances of the Sterling Area', 543–4.
39. On the rise and fall of 'third force' ideas see N. Mansergh, *Survey of Commonwealth Affairs: Problems of Wartime Co-operation and Post-war Change, 1939–1952* (London, 1958), pp.166ff. There is a useful introduction to post-war defence policy in J. Frankel, *British Foreign Policy, 1945–1973* (London, 1975) Ch. 12.
40. See, for example, P.J. Noel-Baker to Chancellor of Exchequer, 24 June 1948, T 236/1144; F.E. Turnbull [C.R.O.] to J. Mark, 12 May 1948, T 236/1142.
41. Draft memorandum, 'India and the sterling area, prepared April 1948', India and Pakistan Negotiations papers, IPN/14, T 236/1145.
42. As Eady pointed out in March 1948, the arrangement of giving India a fixed hard

currency ration was 'for all practical purposes . . . equivalent to having India outside the sterling area, without the political and strategic consequences of a formal expulsion or an indignant departure' (Note by W. Eady, 31 Mar. 1948, T 236/1142) – provided, of course, that the dollar ration could be made to stick.

43. See 'Stafford' [Cripps] to 'Hugh' [Dalton], 16 Jan. 1946, T 236/1145.

44. 'Note of meeting with representatives of Joint Committee on India', 15 Jan. 1947, T 236/1119.

45. 'Note of a meeting held to discuss Indian Sterling Balances Negotiations', 12 Dec. 1946, T 236/1117.

46. Draft, undated memorandum, 'India and the Sterling Area', T 236/1145.

47. See 'Report by India Working Party', ONC (48) 209, 15 May 1948, T 236/1142 and ditto, ONC (48) 223, 27 May 1948, CAB 134/560.

48. The Commonwealth Relations Office was fond of pointing this out to support its case that Indian purchases of capital goods were inevitable. See, for example, P.J. Noel-Baker to Chancellor of Exchequer, 24 June 1948, T 236/1144.

49. See, for example, 'Some notes on the Indian sterling balances', enclosed with J.E. Meade to E. Bridges, 27 Jan. 1947, T 236/1117.

50. 'Report by India Working Party', ONC (48) 223, 27 May 1948, CAB 134/560.

51. Statement by Mr McGregor at ON (48) 57, 18 May 1948, T 236/1143. The full Overseas Negotiating Committee took the same view, concluding that Britain 'did not get such a good return for our exports to her [India] as from many other parts of the Commonwealth' (ON (48) 60, 27.5.48 no.3, CAB 134/556). Thus the Chancellor reported to the Cabinet Economic Policy Committee that any increase in sales to India 'would affect our export prospects to destinations more important to our balance of payments' ('Memorandum by Chancellor of Exchequer on Financial Negotiations with India and Pakistan', EPC (48) 44, 1 June 1948, T 236/1143).

52. Statement by Mr McGregor at ON (48) 57, 18 May 1948, T 236/1143. Sir Wilfred Eady of the Treasury had made the same point in March:

> it might be quite interesting to us, when the current seller's market dies away, to have the opportunities of employment for the engineering industry which would be represented by these unrequited exports of capital equipment to India. (Note by W. Eady, 31.3.84, T 236/1142).

53. 'Sterling Balances and Sterling Area', memorandum by the Treasury, 24 Aug. 1949, CP(49) 179, CAB 129/36.

54. *Economist* 13 Aug. 1949, 368.

55. For recent analyses of the crisis in Indo-British financial relations in the early 1930s see B.R. Tomlinson, 'Britain and the Indian Currency Crisis, 1930–2', *Economic History Review* (2nd Series) 32, 1 (1979), 88–99; C. Bridge, 'Britain and the Indian Currency Crisis, 1930–2: A Comment' and B.R. Tomlinson, 'Britain and the Indian Currency Crisis, 1930–2: A Reply', ibid., 33, 2 (1981), 301–7; D. Rothermund, 'The Great Depression and British Financial Policy in India, 1929–34', *Indian Economic and Social History Review* 18, 1 (1981), 1–18.

56. On British overseas economic policy see G.D.N. Worswick and P.H. Ady, *The British Economy, 1945–1950* (Oxford, 1952), Part VI. On British economic policy as a whole see also J.C.R. Dow, *The Management of the British Economy, 1945–60* (Cambridge, 1960); T.W. Hutchinson, *Economics and Economic Policy in Britain, 1946–1966* (London, 1968); Andrew Shonfield, *British Economic Policy Since the War* (London, 1958).

57. On post-war defence policy see P. Darby, *British Defence Policy East of Suez, 1947–1968* (London, 1973); M. Fitzsimmons, *Empire by Treaty* (London, 1965); Frankel, *British Foreign Policy*, Ch. 12.

58. 'Sterling Balances and the Sterling Area', memorandum by the Treasury, 24 Aug. 1949, CP(49) 179, CAB 129/36.

Britain, the Sterling Area and European Integration, 1945–50

by

Scott Newton

Throughout the period from 1945 to 1950 the Attlee government worked for the establishment of a world economy in which full employment could be reconciled with multilateral trade. But Anglo-American attempts at the restoration of multilateral trade after 1945 were bedevilled by the dollar shortage. The first attempt broke down in the 1947 convertibility crisis, which revealed a basic connection between the health of the British economy and the viability of the sterling area. The second attempt was centred on the Marshall Plan, which aimed to construct an integrated Europe of which Britain would be the leader. Most histories of post-war European integration, and of British policy towards it, are characterized by two basic assumptions. First, the Marshall Plan not only saved Western Europe from political and economic ruin after 1947 by helping it to overcome the dollar shortage, but created the conditions for international expansion. Secondly, the British held aloof from the development of an integrated Europe out of an antiquated determination to play an imperial role in the post-war world.[1]

This article challenges those assumptions. It is true that after 1947 Britain placed the maintenance of its world role at the centre of the sterling area before any irreversible commitment to European integration. British imperialism did not perish with decolonization in South Asia: but the invocation of *folie de grandeur* does not explain its survival. Britain's experience in the convertibility crisis led it to believe that Europe's dollar problem was part of a world-wide disequilibrium with which the Marshall Plan was inadequate to cope. Further, the liberal model of European integration implicit in the Marshall Plan threatened sterling area viability. In consequence Britain worked for inter-governmental European co-operation and argued that sterling–dollar partnership to stimulate international expansion would be the most effective way of restoring multilateralism.

Britain's reluctance to become a good European frustrated the Americans, contemporary European politicians and later commentators. But in 1949 the onset of a new crisis, which suggested that the Marshall Plan would not lead to Europe's bridging of the dollar gap, justified British policy. Fearing the demise of plans to restore multilateralism, the United States accepted the international economic importance of the sterling area. Ironically, however, this support did not herald a genuine Anglo-

American financial partnership but implied British subordination to the international economic hegemony of the United States.

I

The domestic shift to the left in Britain between 1940 and 1945, along with Keynesian theory and the lessons of wartime economic management, encouraged the Labour government which came to power in July 1945 to embark on an ambitious programme of social and industrial reconstruction.[2] Leading members of the Cabinet, such as Prime Minister Clement Attlee, Chancellor Hugh Dalton and Foreign Secretary Ernest Bevin, had no desire to see this reconstruction achieved within the framework of a completely socialized economy. Rather, they opted for a liberal socialism characterised by a mixed economy, progressive taxation and high levels of government expenditure on housing and social services.[3]

The pursuit of this liberal socialism had implications for British foreign economic policy. In particular it meant the rejection of imperial and Commonwealth autarky involving the comprehensive planning of foreign trade. Instead, the commitment to a mixed economy with a large and healthy private sector implied that British costs and prices would have to compete with those prevailing in world markets. Given its domestic priorities, then, it was unsurprising that the government stood by Article VII of the Mutual Aid Agreement signed with the United States in February 1942, by which Britain had pledged itself to work for the elimination of all forms of discrimination in international commerce. Multilateralism abroad was linked to liberal socialism at home.

One major problem, however, was that, historically, open economies with balance of payments deficits had been forced to deflate. The construction of an escape-route from this trap, with all its unhappy memories of 1929–31, became the overriding objective of the Labour government's foreign economic policy. The ideal was an international environment in which creditor countries would bear the burden of adjustment to any disequilibrium through domestic reflation, extensions of foreign investment and reductions in tariffs. The existence of such a system would allow debtor countries to reconcile full employment with membership of an open world economy. Given Britain's position at the end of the war as the world's greatest debtor, owing over £3,000 million to the rest of the sterling area, and facing a prospective cumulative balance of payments deficit of £1,250 million between 1945 and 1950, both altruism and self-interest required international expansion.

II

It was clear before 1945 that the United States would be the world's greatest creditor. British attempts to make the United States realize its global economic obligations had, however, been thwarted when Keynes's Clearing Union plan was rejected in favour of the modest Bretton Woods institutions, the International Monetary Fund and the International Bank for Reconstruction and Development.[4]

The frustrating experience of wartime Anglo-American talks did not, however, lead the Labour government to conclude that it was impossible to persuade the United States to act as the world's creditor. Confronted by what Keynes called a 'financial Dunkirk'[5] on its election, the government immediately went to the Americans in search of an interest-free credit, or even a grant, of $5 billion to cover the likely 1945–50 deficit. Financial assistance from the United States was the price Britain would have to pay for its liberal socialist experiment: going it alone meant either accepting multilateralism without full employment or trying to maintain high levels of employment at the cost of adopting a 'Gosplan' style socialism, anathema to most of the Cabinet.[6]

The British attempt to negotiate post-war financial aid from the Americans was made at Washington between September and December 1945. Like the United Kingdom, the United States was committed to working for a multilateral world, but the Washington talks revealed profound Anglo-American differences about the best means to that end. Whereas the British favoured the common pursuit by nations of domestic expansion, the Americans concentrated on the need to eliminate barriers to the cirulation of goods. American politicians and officials operated within a framework of liberal–capitalist assumptions about the world which held that the best guarantee of global peace and order lay in a regime of free circulation for men, goods and capital.[7] Besides guaranteeing export markets, a non-discriminatory world would protect Washington against the emergence of international rivals with no interest in upholding the Pax Americana, something seen by senior policy-makers such as Will Clayton and Dean Acheson as the United States' duty both to itself and to the world.[8] American faith in the principles of multilateral trade was bolstered at the end of the war by the obvious fact that the United States was now the world's leading industrial and military power. America should therefore use its new international influence to create an open world economy with no place either for old-fashioned imperialism or for new-style socialism.

The story of the Washington talks has been told before and need not be repeated here.[9] What should be stressed is that the principal American negotiators, Will Clayton and Treasury Secretary Fred Vinson, saw Britain, an old imperial power with a new left-wing government, as the main threat to an open world. Accordingly Clayton and Vinson used the talks to force Britain to commit itself by deeds as well as by words to Article VII. In return for financial assistance the British would have to modify the imperial preference system, an old *bête noire* of American policy-makers. Nor was this all. Washington viewed the sterling area, with its system of rationing hard currency through the operations of the gold and dollar pool, as a major obstacle to multilateralism, and the most acrimonious part of the talks centred on the issue of whether or not Britain would accept the international convertibility of sterling as a condition of any loan. If sterling became convertible, countries would be able to use the foreign exchange they earned from Britain to import dollar goods. Sterling–dollar interconvertibility would automatically lead much of the world into an economic era based on the principles of Article VII. But if sterling remained a soft currency, Britain's trading partners would be forced to earn money which could only be spent in the United Kingdom or in the rest of the sterling area.

The upshot of the Washington talks was a Financial Agreement, concluded in December 1945 and finally approved by Congress in July 1946. Britain was to receive not $5 billion but $3.75 billion, repayable over 50 years at 2 per cent interest. The sum was smaller than the British had hoped but their real disappointment centred on the terms, the most objectionable of which concerned the issue of convertibility. Under the Bretton Woods agreements, Britain had been provided with a transitional period 'of several years' duration'[10] before it was obliged to make sterling convertible. During this period Britain would have been able to maintain exchange restrictions on current payments, but under American pressure at the Washington talks it lost this entitlement. The British resisted the early introduction of convertibility, fearing that they would accumulate inconvertible foreign currencies while their trading partners gained access to large amounts of hard currency when they sold goods to the United Kingdom.[11] In the end, however, the Cabinet bowed to American pressure and agreed that convertibility would become operative for current transactions involving sterling one year after the presidential signature of the Financial Agreement, so that the effective date for its implementation was 15 July 1947.

Far from ushering in a new order of international Keynesianism, the final terms of the American loan led Britain away from wartime hopes to a world in which international economic exchanges resulted from the operation of the free market. This ideological defeat implied economic danger. The immediate task of restoring the world to the ways of non-discrimination was to be achieved by a Financial Agreement in which the largest debtor nation was to dismantle its most effective safeguards against the deflationary effects of a growing deficit with the dollar area. In these circumstances London's disappointment was as understandable as its fears were justified. Sterling convertibility lasted only five weeks after 15 July 1947. On 20 August, following a frightening drain on the British reserves, the Labour government suspended convertibility.

The failure of the Financial Agreement to achieve its ambitious goals derived from its total inadequacy in the face of the world economic upheaval resulting from the war, which had adminstered the *coup de grâce* to the old triangular pattern of international settlements. The United States was left in 1945 as the world's greatest supplier of manufactures, capital goods and foodstuffs. After the war, Western Europe, Britain and Japan were heavily dependent on the United States for the equipment which would allow their industries to operate and for the consumer goods and food which would provide their populations with a reasonable standard of living. But since the war had reduced the immediate dollar-earning capacity of Far Eastern countries,[12] neither Britain nor the nations of continental Europe were now able to finance their dollar deficits with offsetting surpluses. The result of this process was the dollar shortage, or a vast financial disequilibrium in the world economy. The United States estimated in 1947 that it would export $16 billion in goods and services but receive only $8 billion in return. Europe's deficits with the United States in 1946 and 1947 were respectively $4.2 billion and $5.4 billion. Given the existence of this disequilibrium, the central problem facing any nation in deficit with the United States was how to finance all the essential goods it could obtain from across the Atlantic without a severe fall in living standards.

In the attempt to conserve their diminishing supplies of hard currency, West European nations in 1946 and 1947 increasingly sought to eliminate the dollar from intra-European trade through state trading and bilateral agreements, which exceeded 200 by later 1947.[13] These bilateral agreements, together with American aid under the United Nations Relief and Rehabilitation Administration (UNRRA), did for a time sustain economic expansion in Western Europe. By 1947 all European countries except Germany had either almost attained or even exceeded 1938 levels of production. But success created its own problems: had post-war growth been less pronounced the demand for food, raw materials and capital goods from the United States would not have been so great. With the termination of UNRRA at the end of 1946 and the widening of the dollar gap caused by recovery, Europe's hard currency shortage became acute by mid-1947.

Given this background of global disequilibrium, it was hardly surprising that sterling convertibility was a fiasco. After 15 July Britain's trading partners had used convertibility to accumulate dollars by stepping up exports to the United Kingdom and by adopting restrictive practices to cut down on imports. With the abolition of exchange controls on current transactions involving sterling, Britain found itself taking the strain for the world's demand for dollars. There is no need here to give a detailed account of the convertibility crisis,[14] but it should be said that the British dollar drain, running at a rate of $650 million a month after 1 August, was intensified by capital transactions out of sterling by holders of sterling balances. As bankers to the sterling area the British also had to finance these operations out of their dwindling reserves. Quite apart from the fact that the suspension of convertibility probably prevented the exhaustion of Britain's entire American credit by the end of September, it was also necessary in order to forestall the disintegration of the sterling area as a whole. Since a large part of the non-dollar world's trade was conducted in sterling, a continuation of the British dollar drain would have resulted in a very substantial reduction in the amount of liquidity at the disposal of the non-dollar world, leading to a shrinkage in the volume of global trade. Further, as if a global liquidity crisis were not a sufficiently frightening prospect for London, studies in the Treasury during July 1947 had con-

cluded that its domestic implications involved mass unemployment and
the ruin of the government's reformist social programme.[15]

III

American policy-makers in the State Department had shown alarm at the
implications of the dollar shortage even before the convertibility crisis
destroyed this first post-war attempt at the restoration of an open world
economy. They feared that if unchecked the dollar shortage would pre-
cipitate an economic collapse in Western Europe which the Soviet Union
would turn to its advantage. However, the prospect of Soviet hegemony
over Western Europe was not Washington's only concern. Even if the
USSR failed to exploit the crisis it was likely that given the general
post-war reaction against orthodox liberal economics, Western European
nations would seek to control their dollar needs by intensifying the trend
to bilateralism, exchange controls and state trading so marked since
1945. In any case both possibilities – Soviet dominance or planned capitalism – threatened the total frustration of America's post-war strategic and
international economic objectives. The prospect of such a calamity led
the United States to launch the Marshall Plan in the summer of 1947. The
Plan's immediate purpose was to secure Western Europe's commitment
both to the containment of perceived Soviet expansion and to the maintenance of liberal capitalism. Central to these objectives was Europe's
ability to balance its trade with the United States in the near future.

Despite Western Europe's post-war industrial recovery, Washington
held the view that the dollar shortage 'represented [the] failure of Europe
to produce'.[16] Searching for a way to encourage higher production, American policy-makers turned to a currently fashionable proposition of customs union theory. This proposition held that the most effective way to
maximise the efficiency with which factors of production were used in a
given area was to remove restrictions on their movement.[17] Thus it was
believed that the creation of a large single market in Western Europe,
together with American aid to ensure the continuing flow of vital imports,
would stimulate output and so correct the imbalance with the United
States. Once Western European nations could be assured of overcoming
their dollar deficits without resort to further controls, the way would be
clear for progress towards an open international economy.[18] From the
moment the Marshall Plan was launched, therefore, Washington made it
clear that American aid would be conditional on Western Europe's
gradual transformation into an integrated economic community. This
tranformation in turn depended on the willingness of participating countries to turn away from national planning in favour of encouraging mutual
aid and the free flow of men, goods and capital. The Marshall Plan, in
brief, was designed to give the United States the economic leverage to
create a new international system. In this new system a liberal–capitalist
Western Europe would become the United States' junior partner both in

the second post-war attempt to restore multilateralism and in the containment of the USSR.

The British had a key role in this ambitious American design. They were to lead the process of West European integration. The events of 1947 – the fuel crisis, the withdrawal from Greece and Turkey, and the convertibility crisis – had led Washington to conclude that Britain no longer possessed the resources to act as a global power. Yet Britain remained the most stable and powerful country participating in the Marshall Plan and should therefore substitute leadership in Europe for its world role.

The British welcomed Marshall aid because it would enable them to avoid the choice between massive austerity or massive deflation likely to result from the exhaustion of their reserves. Since they, like the Americans, were concerned about Soviet expansion, they agreed that Western European nations should co-operate to offset the power of the Soviet bloc. It became clear during the summer of 1947, however, that the British neither accepted the analysis of the dollar shortage upon which the Marshall Plan was based nor the American effort to confine them to a European role. British ministers and civil servants argued that there were two basic flaws in the 'continental' approach to European recovery adopted by Washington. First, it ignored Britain's pivotal position in the world economy, traditionally financing its deficits with the West by surpluses with the East. Secondly, London argued that the dollar shortage was a function of global disequilibrium rather than of Europe's failure to produce. With the dollar drain mounting steadily, London stated that 'unless sufficient steps can be taken to fill the world's dollar supply' Britain might be forced to abandon multilateralism, and 'eke out a painful existence on the best terms of bilateral trade which we can secure'.[19] The best way to avoid this was by increasing the world's supply of dollars through an Anglo–American financial partnership. Dollars could then be re-cycled through the sterling area to Empire and Commonwealth primary producers. By stimulating recovery in the Eastern hemisphere, dependence on the Western hemisphere would diminish and the revival of triangular trade would lead the world economy back to equilibrium.

The British argument for special treatment cut no ice with the Americans.[20] But this failure to make a direct impression did not rule out more circuitous methods. Under British influence the countries participating in the Marshall Plan had formed the Committee for European Economic Co-operation (CEEC). The CEEC meeting in Paris was given the task of setting out the dollar requirements of participating countries, allowing for mutual aid, up to 1951–52. Washington, pressed by an economy-minded Congress and keen to push ahead with the new international system implicit in the Marshall Plan, hoped for a report which showed Western Europe's dollar needs to be relatively modest and which placed a premium on firm steps to integration. Britain, however, tried through its chairmanship of the CEEC to produce a report which played down economic integration and emphasized the global nature of the dollar problem. The final CEEC report requested $22 billion and stressed the importance of triangular trade in allowing participating countries to earn dollars.[21]

The attempt to remould the Marshall Plan into a scheme which underwrote international economic expansion failed. The reality was that Washington had the final say over how much aid participating countries would receive. And the Americans were not prepared to sponsor what they regarded as inflated requirements stemming from a report whose commitment to mutual aid and integration was so weak that it merely resembled 'sixteen shopping lists'.[22] Accordingly the autumn of 1947 saw a successful American campaign both to scale down the European request and to extract firm commitments to economic co-operation from participating countries. In the end the Europeans were forced to settle for $17 billion in return for the establishment of a continuing organization which by co-ordinating recovery plans and dividing American aid would provide the framework for political and economic unity on the continent.

IV

The key to the British position lay in the sterling area. Given the domestic and international economic implications of the convertibility crisis, the Labour government made the preservation of sterling area viability the dominating factor in its economic foreign policy. The British consistently argued from 1947 until 1950 that sterling viability was essential to any initiative designed both to overcome the dollar shortage and lead the world into an era of international Keynesianism. It followed, as the Paris Conference had shown, that Britain would cling to its world economic role rather than accede to the American desire that it should become part of an integrated Europe.

Yet the commitment to the sterling area did not mean a lack of concern for European reconstruction. British concern was real and stemmed from three lines of thought. First, national security dictated the encouragement of a credible Western defensive alliance, underpinned by economic strength, to deter Soviet expansionism. The other two lines of thought were contradictory, although few in London appeared to realize this at the time. On the one hand, Britain felt that its European colleagues in the Marshall Plan were so enfeebled that its assistance was essential to full recovery. In particular the sterling area had a vital role to play because it was a valuable source of non-dollar food and raw materials. A glance at the composition of Europe's imports in 1948 shows that there was some justification for this view. Imports from the United States fell from $6.1 billion in 1947 to $4.8 billion in 1948 while supplies from other overseas areas increased from $7.8 billion to $10 billion over the same period. About half this rise was accounted for by goods from the sterling area. The most significant commodities were wool, meat and butter from Australia and New Zealand, textiles from India, rubber from Malaya, and raw cotton, copper, oil seeds and cocoa from the British African dependencies.[23] Yet on the other hand this solicitude for Western Europe was accompanied by profound fear of the consequences for British industry of European recovery. The main anxiety, which centred on what would happen when the post-war limits on German recovery were lifted, was felt in two ways. First, it led Britain to feel it could not opt out of Europe lest it be faced by the growth of a large continental market protected against its imports. At the same time it led the Board of Trade to mount an unimaginative and blatantly protectionist campaign against British membership of a European customs union.[24] This ultimately successful campaign suggested no awareness of the different models of a European customs union currently on offer. While the Belgians and Italians, with American support, favoured a union based on old-fashioned liberalism, the French desired a planned and regulated customs union precisely because they shared Britain's anxiety about the consequences of German recovery.

Since Britain could not afford to neglect its commitment to European co-operation, the question became, for what sort of European community should it work? Given Belgium's concern to earn hard currency by increasing exports to participating countries and Italy's anxiety to offload surplus agricultural produce, it was no surprise that America's determination to unite Western Europe through the dismantling of trade and exchange controls met with support. The Board of Trade's attitude to the customs union had shown that on grounds of industrial policy Britain was not going to throw its weight behind the creation of a liberal Europe. But the major factor behind Britain's determination to thwart a sweeping liberalization of European exchanges was concern for the sterling area.

After 20 August 1947 the sterling area once more became a discriminatory economic bloc. The wartime dollar pooling arrangements were reintroduced, and throughout the area import and exchange controls were intensified to prevent leakages of hard currency. These controls were strengthened in the effort to 'seek to maintain the acceptability of sterling as an international currency and to foster multilateral trade as far as we can, without damaging our gold and dollar reserves'.[25] Since these reserves were the first line of defence for the sterling area as a whole there had to be no chance that the events of July and August 1947 would be repeated. The health of the reserves now became the Labour government's central preoccupation and it was decided that every effort should be made to ensure they did not decline below £500 million.[26]

Independent sterling area members accepted the stringency of post-convertibility controls on hard currency expenditure. These countries conducted most of their trade within the area and consequently needed the exchange stability of the sterling system. Thirty-eight per cent of all Australia's exports and 90 per cent of all New Zealand's exports, for example, went to the United Kingdom in 1947–48.[27] The resources of the central pool were also beneficial since they offset the dollar deficits of independent members against the dollar surpluses of dependent members, and so provided them with more dollars than they would have been able to obtain outside the area. By running the sterling area as a discriminatory bloc, the British were therefore able to sustain multilateralism throughout the Commonwealth and Empire and insulate themselves against the deflationary pressure of the dollar shortage.

The creation of the dollar pool was complemented by the signature of a series of bilateral trade and payments agreements between Britain and countries outside the sterling area. Belgium was one such country. Throughout much of the early post-war period Belgium, and to a lesser extent Switzerland, tended to accumulate large amounts of sterling. In July and August 1947 Belgium had taken advantage of convertibility to transfer £34.4 million to the dollar area.[28] After the suspension of convertibility, however, Belgium was forced to negotiate a new agreement with Britain which ensured that in future it would be unable to transfer all sterling earned in current transactions into hard currency The Anglo–Belgian talks were long and difficult, and only in March 1948 did the two countries agree that Belgium would have to accumulate a surplus of £12 million before transferability became possible.

Britain's determination to insure itself against heavy losses of hard currency through the pursuit of anti-dollar discrimination and bilateralism was matched by that of France, itself a debtor in intra-European trade. No more than Britain did France wish to see its creditors given the opportunity to convert its currency into dollars. In consequence, neither in 1948 nor in 1949 were American and Belgian attempts to replace bilateralism in Western Europe particularly successful.[29] By the end of 1949 Western Europe was not much nearer to a single market characterized by the free movement of goods and the automatic settlement of debts than it had been two years before.

The key to the Anglo–French success in slowing Marshall Europe's progress to economic liberalism lay in the Organization for European Economic Co-operation (OEEC), established in April 1948. This body, the 'continuing organization' whose existence the United States had made a condition of Marshall aid, fell under Anglo–French control from the start. The United States hoped that the OEEC would act as a powerful interventionist body, equipped with supranational powers. Ideally it should advocate bold schemes of European trade and payments liberalization as well as allocating Marshall aid between participating countries. But such a conception stood no chance of being realized over Anglo–French opposition, and the OEEC which finally emerged was an intergovernmental body. Decisions had to be taken unanimously, so that national governments lost no real power to plan foreign trade and payments. Although the French were quite satisfied with the final shape of the OEEC, it was viewed in Whitehall as a vehicle for exerting British influence over European reconstruction. Given that the British could neither opt out of Europe nor opt in as wholeheartedly as the Americans wanted, they needed an institution which would enable them to reconcile their commitment to Europe with their world economic role.

The loose form of European co-operation implicit in the OEEC was greeted unenthusiastically in Washington. Paul Hoffman, the Administrator of the Economic Co-operation Administration (ECA), the United States Government agency which administered Marshall aid, and his special representative in Paris, Averell Harriman, were both firm supporters of the positive approach to European integration. Together with the State Department, ECA blamed Britain's preoccupation with the health of its reserves for the very limited progress participating countries were making towards integration. As a result, throughout 1948 and for much of 1949 there was a sustained American attempt to force Britain to reduce her commitment to the sterling bloc. The British Ambassador in Washington reported a State Department 'source' as calling for 'the dissolution of the sterling area', whose continued existence was described 'as a menace to ERP [the European Recovery Programme, or Marshall Plan] second only to the activities of the Communist Party.'[30] These views were supported by Averell Harriman, who felt that Britain overrated the economic value of the sterling area and should make up its mind 'to integrate at once with Europe.'[31]

With some justification the British felt that these arguments against the sterling area owed more to doctrinaire liberalism than to a dispassionate view of the problems facing the world economy. Sir Edmund Hall-Patch[32] spoke for many civil servants and ministers when he lamented the American disposition to view the sterling area 'as a menace to American economic expansion, and as a manifestation of the powers of evil.'[33] His view, orthodox in London, was that America's 'short-sighted and inadequate financial policies' had made the dollar so scarce that sterling was now the world's only major international currency. Given American reluctance to give away the proceeds of its export surplus over a period of several years, the most effective way of sustaining international trade lay in policies designed 'to nurse sterling back to health'[34] rather than to weaken it. In response to American criticisms of their fixation with the sterling area, therefore, the British argued that they would be able to take more chances in Europe if the United States supported the area's reserves. British reluctance to become integrated with Europe was therefore linked with the argument that the United States should embrace international Keynesianism by assuming its responsibilities as the world's creditor.

In 1949 events bore out the argument that Marshall aid was inadequate to counter the disequilibrium. The imbalance between the Western hemisphere and the rest of the world, instead of narrowing, widened under the impact of a recession in the United States. This recession exposed the fallacy that higher production in participating countries would automatically bring European and American trade back into balance. During the second quarter of 1949 Western European output reached 117 per cent of its 1938 level – its highest point since the war. Yet the overall deficit of participating countries rose from $1.2 billion in the last quarter of 1948 to $1.6 billion in the second quarter of 1949. Of this second quarter deficit $1.0 billion was with the United States. As the American market contracted, European, and particularly British, producers sustained domestic growth and employment by switching exports to soft currency areas. The existence of the sterling balances, totalling £3,554 million on 31 December 1948,[35] was of particular value to British industry because it stimulated a steady flow of unrequited exports from the metropolitan country.

The existence of boom conditions in the partially insulated British economy did not, however, prevent another sterling crisis. The American recession also made it difficult for sterling area raw material producers such as Malaya to earn dollars. Dollar earnings in the overseas sterling area declined by 21 per cent in the second quarter of 1949 and by 41 per cent in the third quarter.[36] The growing sterling area trade deficit with the United States, together with black market speculation against sterling, thus precipitated a serious outflow of hard currency from the central reserves. By 16 June Britain's dollar drain was running at an annual rate of £600 million and the reserves faced exhaustion by the end of the year.[37]

Renewed sterling crisis led the Labour government to consider salvaging British reconstruction by retreating into the siege economy it had briefly contemplated in 1945 and 1947.[38] It should be reiterated that this course was not an attractive one to the British because of its implications both for the future of liberal socialism and for containment. Nevertheless, it offered the Labour government more than the prospect of a re-run of 1931 which followed from full exposure to the impact of American recessions.[39] Given rising production throughout the sterling area and the continued expansion of its multilateral trade, this policy, though it involved intensified austerity at home, was more feasible than before. There was even a chance that it might attract some Western European countries whose trading links with the sterling area were particularly strong. Certainly the British were not short of supporters when they successfully frustrated the ECA's attempt to introduce convertibility into intra-European trade during the summer of 1949.

Feasible though the siege economy might appear as a theoretical alternative, it would have been very difficult to achieve in practice. Its success would have been dependent on the willingness of independent sterling area members to accept still tougher restraints on dollar purchasing because of the low level of the central reserves. Ties of sentiment, political outlook and trade between Britain and the Commonwealth could not by themselves secure this willingness. With the aid of their accumulated sterling credits, countries such as Australia, South Africa and India were keen to pursue their own paths of development, but Britain alone could not provide them with all the machine tools and capital goods they required. Increasingly, therefore, these countries looked to the United States and coveted the dollars vital to their own modernization programmes. In the aftermath of the convertibility crisis, however, it seemed that only membership of the sterling area could guarantee Commonwealth producers access to steady supplies of hard currency. Australia, South Africa and India, along with the rest of the area, reluctantly accepted voluntary restraints on imports from the dollar area in September 1947; nevertheless the price of belonging to the sterling club was too high for the South Africans, and they left the area at the end of that year. Thereafter strains within the sterling area became still more apparent. Australia failed to reach agreement with Britain on the level of its dollar expenditure in 1948.[40] At the same time India, in the grip of food supply problems, relaxed its import controls and overshot its allocation of accumulated sterling balances by £80 million.[41]

It would clearly be wrong to view the sterling area as an united monetary bloc in the post-war period. Its existence was a matter of convenience for Commonwealth nations, and membership was an attractive proposition only as long as the resources of its dollar pool were not dissipated. This was re-emphasized for the British after the Commonwealth finance ministers had met in the summer of 1949 to agree on a response to the growing dollar crisis. The ministers agreed to a 25 per cent reduction in the level of dollar imports and Harold Wilson, President of the Board of Trade, reported to the Cabinet that 'the meeting was notable for the identity of views'.[42] This superficial harmony did not, however, preclude criticisms of Britain's trade performance in the Western hemisphere, and Edgar Whitehead of Southern Rhodesia complained about the uncompetitive prices of British exports.[43] While the cuts in dollar purchasing were accepted 'without much difficulty',[44] these rumblings suggested that sterling countries might not agree to austerity if its only positive effect was to sustain full employment in Britain. Rather than risk the disruption of Commonwealth economic relations, therefore, London rejected any remaining ideas of a siege economy and, after weeks of discussion,[45] decided in August 1949 to devalue the pound[46] in order to stimulate exports to the dollar area and so replenish the central reserves. This choice was thus partly determined by Whitehall's sensitive understanding of the limits to Commonwealth solidarity even under the rather special conditions created by a common shortage of US currency.

The demands of nationalism in the developing world could not necessarily be reconciled with the international economic implications of Britain's search for social justice at home. Nevertheless, it would be as wrong to make too much of the centrifugal tendencies of the sterling area after 1947 as it would be to exaggerate its cohesiveness. Independent sterling area members needed as much cushioning against the dollar shortage as Britain after 1945, and for the period 1947–49 inclusive they made significant withdrawals, totalling $956 million,[47] from the gold and hard curency pool. Whatever the practical difficulties experienced by the British in managing the sterling area, American policy-makers were impressed in the summer of 1949 by its capacity to act with a fair degree of solidarity. Indeed, in Washington the 1949 sterling crisis provoked a real fear that the non-Soviet world might disintegrate into rival currency blocs, a dollar area and a sterling area which included part of Marshall Europe. It seemed clear after all that through its position at the centre of the sterling area Britain possessed the power, reluctant though it may sometimes have been to use it, to frustrate America's objectives in international reconstruction. In Washington recognition of this reality led to a reassessment of the sterling area's value. Led by the Secretary of State, Dean Acheson, American policy-makers at last accepted that sterling was different from other European currencies. Exhortations to Britain that it should weaken its links with the sterling area fell away, and it was agreed that the British economy could not become integrated into that of a liberal Western Europe. Franco–German rapprochement was henceforth regarded as the key to European integration while the pursuit of multi-lateralism was to be based on sterling–dollar diplomacy. In return for the devaluation which signalled Britain's long-term commitment to multi-lateralism, the United States accepted the role of international creditor, and agreed to stimulate a high level of American domestic demand, reduce tariffs, resume raw material stockpiling and encourage dollar investment in the sterling area. From the Washington talks of September 1949 the British finally achieved the American commitment to conquer the dollar shortage through the programme for international expansion that Washington had failed to espouse in 1947.[48]

As a consequence of the Washington talks, the dangers facing sterling in any liberalization of European payments were significantly reduced. Britain was able to participate in the European Payments Union, established in September 1950, in the knowledge that it would be compensated by the ECA for losses of gold and dollars incurred in the multilateral use of sterling balances within Marshall Europe. Nevertheless, Britain's triumph at Washington did not mean that it would be able to control the nature of European co-operation. The prospect of European integration founded on Franco-German rapprochement revived British fears of exclusion from a protected European market.[49] Since the die had been cast in January 1949 against any irreversible commitment to European integration,[50] Britain would be unable to prevent the Europeans from going it alone if they had the political determination to do so. However, with the revival of Franco-German antagonism early in 1950, it appeared that this determination did not exist. Britain therefore took advantage of this hiatus to propose the Atlantic Community, which was to be organised under the umbrella of NATO and replace the OEEC as the framework for an intergovernmental Europe. But the Atlantic Community was hardly a satisfactory vehicle for the achievement of the closely-knit Europe favoured by the Americans and, albeit for different reasons, by the French, Belgians and Italians. In particular, the loose form of European co-operation implicit in the concept of the Atlantic Community offered no material solution to the problem of Franco-German rivalry.

It was, therefore, hardly surprising that the French Schuman Plan initiative, designed to protect French industry from the impact of unrestricted German competition, was welcomed by the United States. The liberal economic credentials of the Schuman Plan may have been rather dubious, but it did at least herald the establishment of an integrated

Europe based on Franco-German co-operation.[51] These political advantages were so great that after May 1950 Washington lost interest in the British scheme and gave diplomatic backing to the Schuman Plan. The demise of the Atlantic Community undermined British policy on European reconstruction. Refusing to go beyond the 'limited liability' policy developed in January 1949, London declined to participate in the new scheme. For a generation to come Britain was forced to treat with a Franco-German leadership of Western Europe unenthusiastic about accommodating its interests either in the organization of international trade or in industrial and agricultural policy.

V

In retrospect, Britain's decision to concentrate on its world economic role rather than share in a rapidly expanding European market after 1950 appears to have contributed to its seemingly unending industrial decline. Yet at the time there was no indication that the Labour government's sterling policy implied de-industrialization. The achievements of post-war reconstruction were considerable. Full employment was maintained, the volume of exports rose more rapidly than suggested by even the most optimistic forecasts in 1945, and both productivity and manufacturing output increased well beyond pre-war levels, to 145 and 120 respectively (1938 = 100).[52] A real shift in the balance of industry was effected away from old staples such as coal and textiles towards machine tools, electronics, chemicals and vehicles. Up to 1950 the annual rate of inflation never exceeded three per cent, well below the levels of most participants in the Marshall Plan. Whatever the causes of this success, it is difficult to see how it could have been achieved if Britain had either prematurely liberalized the sterling area or cut its links with it. The existence of the sterling area as a discriminatory economic bloc allowed Britain to pursue a foreign trade policy which sustained the growth of the domestic economy.

In these circumstances it is necessary to ask whether Britain exploited the sterling area for its own benefit during the post-war years. The sterling area was a grouping of independent states and colonies whose economic relations with the metropolitan power were, in general, reflective of their political status. Hence the independent members of the area were net drawers on the dollar pool until 1950 and received substantial imports of capital, totalling £683 million, from Britain up to 1951.[53] But the dependent sterling countries, who earned surpluses with the dollar area throughout the period 1945–51, were forced by virtue of their colonial position to surrender hard currency to the central pool. Given that the heaviest contributions were made by British Malaya, the Gold Coast and Nigeria,[54] it is hard to deny that Asian and African peasants laboured to support both 'the conspicuous consumption of Indian maharajahs and the *nouveaux riches'*[55] and living standards throughout the white Commonwealth.

Those seeking to accuse Britain of exploiting its empire after 1945 have not, however, restricted themselves to comments on the inequitable operations of the dollar pool. They have also fastened on to Britain's colonial development policy after 1947.[56] Until the convertibility crisis the Treasury had considered expenditure on colonial development to be low on their list of priorities. But after the *annus horrendus* it was prepared to work for the integration of the British and colonial economies. What could be extracted from the colonies, such as cocoa, cotton, tobacco, groundnuts and chromium, need not be purchased from North America. The determination of ministers such as Bevin, Strachey and Shinwell to preserve British prosperity and independence by developing the material resources of Africa would have been applauded by Joseph Chamberlain.

Britain's post-war economic vulnerability therefore stimulated not a steady retreat from empire but a new spasm of imperialism. Nevertheless, it is an oversimplification to castigate the Attlee government for naked social-imperialism. The interest of the Treasury in African development after 1947 reflected more than a ruthless drive to save dollars. Hugh Dalton's neglect of the empire had stemmed not so much from anti-colonialism as from a deeply embedded racism.[57] Cripps' willingness to support the Overseas Food Corporation and the Colonial Development Corporation owed as much to Fabian paternalism as it did to a single-minded commitment to social reform in Britain whatever the consequences for the Asian and African millions. When Bevin suggested the formation of an Empire and Commonwealth Customs Union, implying that sterling area members should be little more than hewers of wood and drawers of water for Britain, he received a dusty answer from the Cabinet.[58] 'Fabianizing the empire' implied not simply exploiting it but building an infrastructure of basic services, clean water supplies and cheap housing.[59] To Cripps, and to Arthur Creech-Jones at the Colonial Office, economic development was a genuine prelude to political independence, a necessary counterpart to Sir Andrew Cohen's enthusiasm for the encouragement of local government in British Africa.

This is not to deny that Fabianism can be a fig-leaf for imperialism, nor that in Whitehall the countdown to decolonization was measured in generations rather than in terms of two decades.[60] Rather, it is to accept the familiar argument that imperial controls were often closely linked with colonial opportunities.[61] Even though the Commodity Marketing Boards prevented African producers from maximizing profits, the existence of the sterling bloc provided for an expansion of colonial exports after 1945. As long as sterling was internationally available at a time when the dollar was scarce, countries which were short of hard currency would import vital raw materials from the British Empire. The exports of the African dependencies to Marshall Europe (including the United Kingdom) increased in value from just under $700 million in 1947 to over $1.0 billion in 1948.[62] Further, as Gallagher has argued, government intervention to stimulate economic development in East and West Africa brought together hitherto isolated communities and encouraged the development of popular nationalist movements.[63] The British were to be surprised by the strength of these movements, which they themselves had unwittingly created. Up to 1945 the British African Empire had survived for 60 years because little had been done to develop it. After the war the exigencies of Britain's international economic and political position stimulated a positive imperialism which contained the seeds of its own disintegration. Britain would not be able to coerce independent states either to hand over hard currency or to sell staple commodities at prices below those obtaining on world markets.

The radicalizing of the empire helped to destroy the international foundations of the sterling bloc in the two decades following 1947. After 1951 domestic social change and economic weakness reinforced developments on the African periphery and accelerated the dissolution of the imperial economy. At home a slow but unmistakable shift to the right[64] undermined the political consensus which had allowed the government to resist external calls, mostly from Washington, and internal demands, mainly from the City and the Bank of England, for a dismantling of controls. 'Butskellism' notwithstanding, the lure of economic orthodoxy to the incoming Conservative government of 1951 was powerful. Despite the rejection of the 'Robot' plan for convertibility in 1952 the government put a higher premium on the full integration of Britain into the international economy and on encouraging the widest possible use of sterling by dismantling controls on foreign trade than on the maintenance of full employment.[65]

That full employment was maintained owed more to global expansion than to domestic policy, since with gradual liberalization Britain's commitment to sterling became a hindrance to sustained growth. The causes of the long post-war boom are a matter of debate between historians,[66] but one thing is clear. Had the dollar shortage continued to impose a straitjacket on the world economy the expansion of the 1950s would have been difficult to achieve because the liquidity necessary to sustain it would not have existed. Here again events bore out Labour's commitment to sterling. By the start of 1950, with two years left to run, the Marshall Plan had not succeeded in closing Europe's dollar gap; one third of Europe's imports from America, which now totalled $16 billion, had still to be financed by aid.[67] On the termination of this assistance the problems of 1947 threatened to reappear. Only a Marshall Plan for the sterling area would have allowed European countries, including Britain, to earn hard currency in trade with the East and thereby finance Western hemisphere imports. The events of September 1949 suggested some such scheme might be in the offing, but it was the Korean War which in practice changed priorities in Washington. In 1950 and after, as a consequence of the Korean War and the subsequent global expansion of the American military machine, dollars were pumped into the underdeveloped nations of the Far East. The United States' enthusiastic performance as world policeman finally closed the dollar gap and stimulated international economic growth.

It has therefore to be granted that there were sound economic reasons for Britain's cautious approach to European integration and for the resolute commitment to the sterling area which accompanied it. Yet ultimately the price paid by Britain for the continuing ability to run sterling as a reserve currency during the 1950s and beyond involved its subordination to the hegemony of the dollar. This outcome was clearly implied in the 1949 Washington talks despite the fact that Britain believed they foreshadowed an Anglo-American financial partnership. But how many genuine partnerships are heralded by the dependence of one partner on the other? In 1949 it became clear that Britain could not sustain the sterling area by itself without sacrificing the liberal socialism to which the Labour government was committed. For many years now historians have seen Britain's long delay in committing itself to European integration as one of the central problems of post-war foreign policy. Perhaps, in the light of events in 1949, the greater problem awaiting explanation is why Britain did not begin to consider for another 20 years curtailing its international financial obligations.

University College, Cardiff

NOTES

1. See for example Jean Monnet, *Memoirs* (London, 1979) and Richard Mayne, *The Recovery of Europe* (London, 1970), *passim;* Walter Laqueur, *Europe since Hitler* (London, 1970), pp.102–3; F.S. Northedge, *Descent from Power* (London, 1974), p.142; and Ernst van der Beugel, *From Marshall Aid to Atlantic Partnership* (New York, 1966), *passim.*
2. See Paul Addison, *The Road to 1945: British Politics and the Second World War* (London, 1975), p.183; Kenneth O. Morgan, *Labour in Power 1945–1951* (Oxford, 1984), Ch. 1.
3. Morgan, pp.94–9.
4. See Armand van Dormael, *Bretton Woods: Birth of a Monetary System* (London, 1978).
5. PRO CAB 129/1, CP (45) 112, 14 Aug. 1945.
6. See C.C.S. Newton, 'Britain, the Dollar Shortage, and European Integration, 1954–50' (unpublished Ph.D. thesis, University of Birmingham, 1982), 20.
7. The American commitment to multilateralism has been analysed by, for example, Richard N. Gardner, *Sterling–Dollar Diplomacy: Anglo–American Collaboration in the Reconstruction of Multilateral Trade* (Oxford, 1956), and by N. Gordon Levin, *Woodrow Wilson and World Politics: America's Response to War and Revolution* (Oxford, 1968).
8. Acheson, like Clayton, was then an Assistant Secretary of State.
9. See R.F. Harrod, *The Life of John Maynard Keynes* (London, 1951), Ch. 14.
10. PRO CAB 128/4, CM (45), 50th conclusions, Confidential Annex, 6 Nov. 1945.
11. This fear was articulated by Keynes at a meeting held in Washington on 19 Nov. 1945. The minutes are reproduced in PRO FO 371/45714, UE 6249/1094/53.
12. See Alan S. Milward, *War, Economy and Society 1939–1945* (London 1977), p.355.
13. William Diebold, *Trade and Payments in Western Europe: A Study in Economic Co-operation* (New York, 1952), p.65.
14. For an account see C.C.S. Newton, 'The Sterling Crisis of 1947 and the British Response to the Marshall Plan', *Economic History Review* 37, 3 (1984), 391–408.
15. PRO T 229/136, memorandum by R.W.B. Clarke, 15 July 1947.

16. *Foreign Relations of the United States* (hereafter *FRUS*), 1947, Vol. III, pp.276–83, Clayton to members of the British Cabinet in a meeting held on 25 June 1947.
17. Alan S. Milward, *The Reconstruction of Western Europe 1945–51* (London, 1984), p.58.
18. Robert Triffin, *The World Money Maze* (New Haven, 1966), p.400.
19. PRO FO 371/62399, UE 4755/168/53, Treasury memorandum for US Department of State, 16 June 1947.
20. See Clayton at the meeting with members of the Cabinet on 25 June 1947, recorded in *FRUS*, 1947, Vol. III, p.278.
21. Committee of European Co-operation, *General Report* (London, 1947), p.71.
22. *FRUS*, Vol. III, pp.372–73, Lovett to Marshall, 24 Aug. 1947.
23. United Nations, Economic Commission for Europe (hereafter UN, ECE), *Economic Survey of Europe in 1948* (Geneva, 1949), p.132.
24. Milward (1984), p.237; PRO FO 371/62773, UE 10878/10020/53, EPC (47) 11th meeting, 7 Nov. 1947.
25. CAB 129/22, CP (47) 311, 22 Nov. 1947, memorandum by the Chancellor: 'Balance of Payments: the Non-Dollar Plan for 1948'.
26. See for example, FO 371/68893A, UE 1203/28/53, R.W.B. Clarke to Lord Inverchapel, 10 Feb. 1948.
27. Commonwealth Economic Committee, *Commonwealth Trade in 1949* (London, 1950), pp.11–12.
28. Newton, 'The Sterling Crisis', 400.
29. Milward (1984), Ch. VIII.
30. PRO FO 371/71830, UR 595/417/98, Inverchapel to Bevin, 27 March 1948.
31. PRO FO 371/71863, UR 1491/948/98, Hall–Patch to Foreign Office, 12 May 1948.
32. Head of the British delegation to the OEEC.
33. PRO FO 371/71851, UR 873/873/98, memorandum by Hall–Patch, 9 March 1948.
34. Ibid.
35. *The Economist*, 3 Sept. 1949, 515–17, 'The Sterling Balances'.
36. ECA, *The Sterling Area: An American Analysis* (Washington, 1951), pp.638–39.
37. PRO FO 371/75578, UE 3830/150/53, minute by R.W.B. Clarke, 16 June 1949.
38. PRO CAB 134/222, EPC (49) 27th meeting, 7 July 1949.
39. See PRO T232/92, *passim*.
40. Elliot Zupnick, *Britain's Postwar Dollar Problem* (New York, 1957), p.125.
41. Partha S. Gupta, *Imperialism and the British Labour Movement, 1914–1964* (London, 1975), p.306.
42. PRO CAB 129/35, CP (49) 60, memorandum by the President of the Board of Trade, 'Meeting of the Commonwealth Finance Ministers', 21 July 1949.
43. Douglas Jay, *Change and Fortune* (London, 1980). p.186.
44. PRO FO 371/75582, UE 4667/150/153, minute by R.W. Jackling, 'Recommendations of the Commonwealth Finance Ministers' Conference' 18 July 1949.
45. See for example PRO CAB 134/220, EPC (49) 24th meeting, 1 July 1949; PRO CAB 134/222, EPC (49) 73, memorandum by Cripps, 'The Dollar Situation', 7 July 1949; PRO CAB 129/36, CP (49) 159, memorandum by Morrison, 'The Economic Situation', 21 July 1949; and PRO CAB 128/16, CM (49) 48th conclusions, 28 July 1949.
46. From £1 = \$4.03 to £1 = \$2.80.
47. Zupnick, p.129.
48. For the British view of the talks see PRO FO 371/75590. UE 5984/150/53, Franks to Bevin, 19 Sept. 1949.
49. For Washington's encouragement of this prospect see Newton, 'Britain, the Dollar Shortage, and European Integration', 284–86.
50. This policy was approved at a meeting of the Economic Policy Committee on 26 Jan. 1949. See PRO CAB 134/220 EPC (49) 5th meeting.
51. Milward (1984), p.400.
52. Dudley Seers, 'National Income, Production and Consumption', in G.D.N. Worswick and P.H. Ady, *The British Economy 1945–50* (Oxford, 1952), p.36.
53. Zupnick, p.151.
54. See Zupnick, p.142, Table 40.

55. Gupta, p.341.
56. See R. Palme Dutt quoted in Gupta, p.309. A more recent statement of the view that Britain was a selfish imperial power after the war can be found in N.J. Westcott, 'Sterling and Empire: The British Imperial Economy, 1939–51', Institute of Commonwealth Studies Seminar Paper, January 1983.
57. See John Gallagher, *The Decline, Revival and Fall of the British Empire* (Cambridge, 1982), p.143. Dalton's remarks about 'diseased, pullulating nigger communities' are well-known.
58. PRO CAB 128/10, CM (47) 77, 25 September 1947.
59. Gupta, p.323.
60. Gallagher, pp.142–3; and see R.F. Holland, 'The Imperial factor in British strategies from Attlee to Macmillan, 1945–63', and John Darwin, 'British Decolonisation since 1945: A Pattern or a Puzzle?', *Journal of Imperial and Commonwealth History* 12 (1984), 165–86 and 187–209, for interesting speculative discussions of British decolonization.
61. Most recently, see Bill Warren, *Imperialism: Pioneer of Capitalism* (London, 1980), for a brilliant and provocative exposition of this view.
62. UN, ECE, 131, Table 80.
63. Gallagher, p.148.
64. Morgan, pp.314–22.
65. Stephen Blank, 'Britain: The politics of foreign economic policy, the domestic economy, and the problem of pluralistic stagnation', *International Organisation* 31 (1977) 674–721.
66. For a review of this debate see Milward (1984), pp.477–91.
67. *FRUS*, 1950, Vol. I, pp.834–35, Acheson to Truman, 16 Feb. 1950.

Notes on the Contributors

Amiya K. Bagchi is the author of *Private Investment in India 1900–1939* and *The Political Economy of Underdevelopment*. He has also written several articles on banking and finance in India during the colonial period. He is Professor of Economics at the Centre for Studies in Social Sciences, Calcutta.

Peter Cain is the author of *Economic Foundations of British Overseas Expansion 1815–1914* and of several articles on imperial themes in the Edwardian period. He is collaborating with A.G. Hopkins in a wide-ranging analysis of British imperial growth and decline since the eighteenth century.

Youssef Cassis now teaches history at the University of Geneva. His research in London under Professor E.J. Hobsbawm has recently borne fruit in a study of British banking, *Les Banquiers de la City à l'époque edouardienne, 1890–1914* (Geneva, 1984). He is also a contributor to *Business History* and the *Economic History Review*.

Lance Davis is the author (with Peter Payne) of *The Savings Bank of Baltimore 1818–1860* and (with D.C. North) of *Institutional Change and American Economic Growth*. He is the Mary Stillman Harkness Professor of Social Science at the California Institute of Technology, Pasadena, and is engaged with Robert A. Huttenback on an extensive study of British overseas investment patterns from the mid-nineteenth century until the First World War.

Robert A. Huttenback is the author of *Gandhi in South Africa: British Imperialism and the Indian Question, 1860–1914* and *Racism and Empire: White Settlers and Coloured Immigrants in the British Self-governing Colonies, 1830–1910*. He is Chancellor of the University of California, Santa Barbara.

Jacques Marseille is the author of numerous articles in the *Revue Historique, Mouvement social, Relations internationales*, and the *Revue française d'histoire d'outre-mer*. He recently received his Doctorat d'Etat from the Sorbonne, and a revised version of his thesis has been published as *Empire colonial et capitalisme français. Histoire d'un divorce* (Albin Michel, Paris, 1984).

Scott Newton was a research student at the University of Birmingham, and now lectures in Modern British and International History at University College, Cardiff. He has recently contributed an article on Britain's sterling crisis of 1947 to the *Economic History Review*.

D.C.M. Platt is the author of *Finance, Trade and Politics in British Foreign Policy, 1815–1914* (Clarendon Press, Oxford, 1968) and *Foreign Finance in Continental Europe and the U.S.A., 1815–1914. Quantities, Origins, Functions and Distribution* (Allen and Unwin, London, 1984). He is Professor of the History of Latin America in Oxford University and a Fellow of St Antony's College.

B.R. Tomlinson has written extensively on India's political and economic connections with Britain in the twentieth century. His most recent book is *The Political Economy of the Raj 1914–47*. He is a lecturer at the University of Birmingham.